Jane Austen

Jane Austen

OBSTINATE HEART

A Biography by
Valerie Grosvenor Myer

Arcade Publishing • New York

Arcade Publishing books may be purchased in bulk at special discounts for sales promotion, corporate gifts, fund-raising, or educational purposes. Special editions can also be created to specifications. For details, contact the Special Sales Department, Arcade Publishing, 307 West 36th Street, 11th Floor, New York, NY 10018 or arcade@skyhorsepublishing.com.

Arcade Publishing® is a registered trademark of Skyhorse Publishing, Inc.®, a Delaware corporation.

Visit our website at www.arcadepub.com.

10 9 8 7 6 5 4 3 2 1

Library of Congress Cataloging-in-Publication Data is available on file.

ISBN: 978-1-61145-813-8

Printed in the United States of America

To Jean Gooder

I have now attained the true art of letter-writing which, we are always told, is to express on paper exactly what one would say to the same person by word of mouth; I have been talking to you as fast as I could the whole of this letter.

Jane Austen to her sister Cassandra, 5 January 1801

Contents

Preface

Jane Austen was never secure financially and was less secure socially than many readers of her novels have assumed. She belonged not to the squirearchy but to the upper end of the professional middle class and spent her entire life as a poor relation. Although socializing with richer neighbours and visits to landed relatives gave her an insight into the way wealthy people lived, it was very different from her own life of genteel poverty, especially after her father's retirement. She lived on the outside looking in. Correctly speaking, she was not even 'Miss Austen'. As a younger daughter, less admired than her sister, who took precedence of her, she was merely 'Miss Jane Austen'. Seniority counted. Her immediate family had brains, energy and titled connections, but not much money. They were constantly in difficulties. As a single woman without money, she was marginal to society. Her equivocal position moulded her outlook, and her surviving letters betray moments of bitterness. Although a rich man proposed, her obstinate heart prevented her from marrying except for love. Despite a few years of growing reputation as a writer, which she keenly enjoyed, hers was a life of disappointment and frustration. Her criticisms of other writers show she knew the value of her own work and she fretted that it was not better paid. She admitted being 'greedy' for money and grudged Walter Scott his place among the novelists when he was already rich and famous as a poet. Such recognition as she received came late in her short life and during her lifetime only four of her books were published, all of them anonymously.

Acknowledgments

For generous help and advice I have to thank Tom Carpenter, Keith Crook, Rodney Dale, Sylvia Greybourne, David Keane, Gina Keane, Jascha Kessler, Susan McCartan, Derek McCulloch, Ken May, Brian Sibley, Ken Turner, David Weeks and Margaret Wilson. Yvonne Holland's sympathetic and creative editing has been invaluable: and for his proofreading skills, inwardness with Jane Austen, and constant support, I am grateful to my husband, Michael Grosvenor Myer.

Jane Austen's

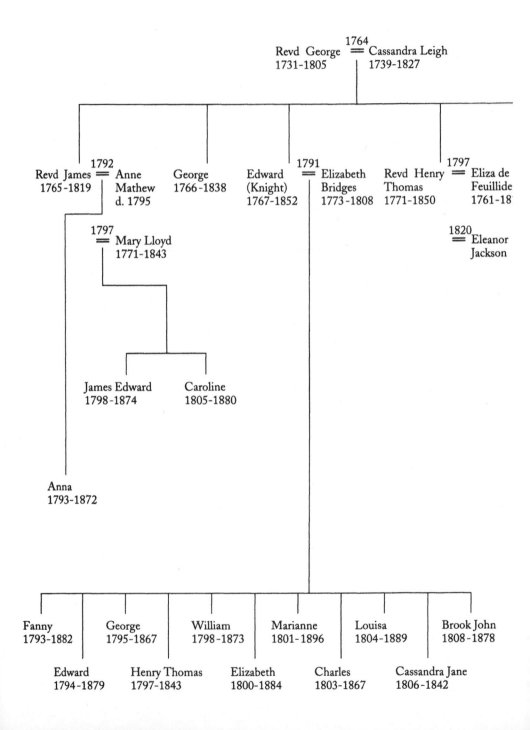

Revd George 1764 = Cassandra Leigh
1731-1805   1739-1827

Revd James 1792 = Anne
1765-1819   Mathew
     d. 1795

George
1766-1838

Edward 1791 = Elizabeth
(Knight)   Bridges
1767-1852   1773-1808

Revd Henry 1797 = Eliza de
Thomas   Feuillide
1771-1850   1761-18

1797
= Mary Lloyd
   1771-1843

1820
= Eleanor
   Jackson

James Edward
1798-1874

Caroline
1805-1880

Anna
1793-1872

Fanny
1793-1882

George
1795-1867

William
1798-1873

Marianne
1801-1896

Louisa
1804-1889

Brook John
1808-1878

Edward
1794-1879

Henry Thomas
1797-1843

Elizabeth
1800-1884

Charles
1803-1867

Cassandra Jane
1806-1842

Family Tree

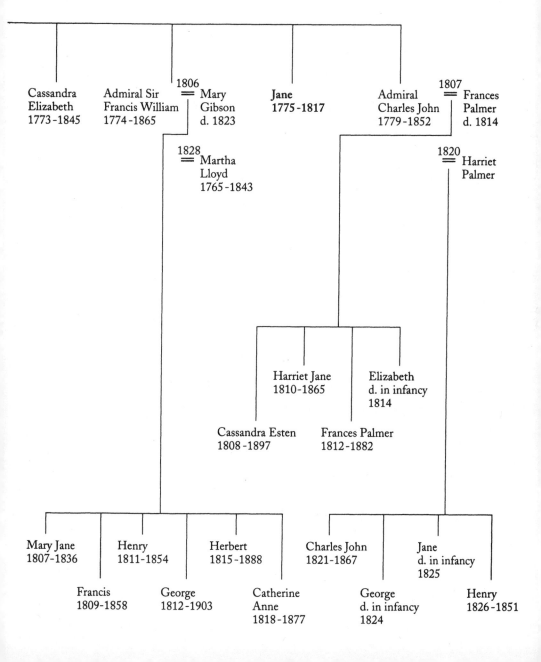

Cassandra Elizabeth 1773-1845

Admiral Sir Francis William 1774-1865

1806
= Mary Gibson d. 1823

Jane 1775-1817

Admiral Charles John 1779-1852

1807
= Frances Palmer d. 1814

1828
= Martha Lloyd 1765-1843

1820
= Harriet Palmer

Harriet Jane 1810-1865

Elizabeth d. in infancy 1814

Cassandra Esten 1808-1897

Frances Palmer 1812-1882

Mary Jane 1807-1836

Henry 1811-1854

Herbert 1815-1888

Charles John 1821-1867

Jane d. in infancy 1825

Francis 1809-1858

George 1812-1903

Catherine Anne 1818-1877

George d. in infancy 1824

Henry 1826-1851

Jane Austen

1

What Was She Like?

EOPLE WHO KNEW Jane Austen described her as pretty. She was attractive, both in appearance and in personality. The only authenticated likeness is an amateurish pencil and watercolour drawing, now in the National Portrait Gallery, London, by Jane's elder sister, Cassandra. Yet Cassandra's drawing shows a woman more sharp-featured than appealing: the eyes are large and beautiful, glancing keenly at something to the left of the picture, and the eyebrows are well marked. Her curls escape charmingly from the cap, but there are lines of disappointment running from nose to mouth, and the mouth itself looks small and mean. She looks like a peevish hamster. Her niece Anna Austen Lefroy, daughter of Jane Austen's eldest brother, dismissed the portrait as hideously unlike.

An even more mysterious picture of Jane by Cassandra is a pencil and watercolour sketch giving a back view of her in a pale blue dress, and in which most of the face is concealed by a large blue bonnet.

Although it was said by a fellow author that her cheeks were 'a little too full' when she was a young girl, she was agreed to be good-looking, with a fine complexion of a rich colour, brown rather than fair. Her reddish-brown hair curled naturally. A lock survives but time has bleached it. Her nose was narrow and possibly rather long, like those of her mother and sister.

In 1944 a bookseller found a profile silhouette pasted into a copy of the second edition of *Mansfield Park* (the 1816 edition, the first having been published in 1814). Unfortunately there was no bookplate or other evidence of ownership of this volume but underneath the silhouette an unknown hand has written '*L'aimable Jane*'. This cannot refer to a character in the novel, for though *Pride and Prejudice* has Jane Bennet and *Emma* has Jane Fairfax there is no Jane in *Mansfield Park*. So this tantalizing outline is presumed to be a portrait of Jane herself. Jane's niece Caroline Austen, Anna's half-sister, recorded that her Aunt Jane was the first person she consciously thought of as pretty. This silhouette picture shows us a young woman who could certainly be described as pretty, and probably less than thirty years old. The sitter has neat features balanced by a trim chignon worn fairly high, a graceful neck and shoulders, and a high, firm bosom. She is wearing some sort of necklace.

Another silhouette owned by the Dean and Chapter of Winchester Cathedral, and 'supposedly done by herself in 1815', shows a woman with the Austen family nose and apparently not wearing the cap she habitually wore.

At one time a full-length portrait of a young teenager, which may just be by Johann Zoffany (who died in 1810), was thought to show Jane Austen, but costume experts have confidently dated it at about 1805, when Jane was thirty. At that time, Jane's father died, and she and her widowed mother were reduced to poverty. They could not have risen to the extravagance of employing a fashionable portrait painter. It has been suggested that the artist is in fact Ozias Humphrey (or Humphreys or Humphries) and that the face is Jane's, but the bone structure looks different from that suggested by Cassandra's sketch. The painting shows a round face, unlike the pointed chin of Cassandra's picture. It may be of a younger, distant cousin also named Jane Austen.

When the *Memoir* by Jane's nephew the Revd James-Edward Austen-Leigh was published in 1869, although dated 1870, a Mrs Charlotte Maria Beckford, who as a child had known Jane in middle age, was disappointed with the portrait used as the frontispiece. Cassandra's original drawing had been softened and falsified in a miniature watercolour by a Mr Andrews of Maidenhead, the eyes enlarged, the mouth forced into a demure smile. This picture was a bland lie: it failed to tell any sort of truth about either Jane's personality or her looks. The steel-engraved version of Mr Andrews's picture was worse: it made her look smug instead of sharp, and sentimentalized her into a mimsy Victorian icon in a prettified cap with added ribbons and lace. Regrettably this travesty is still often reproduced. Only the pose and the costume bear any resemblance to Cassandra's sketch of a wary, watchful Regency lady. Mrs Beckford remembered a tall, thin, spare person with very high cheekbones, colour in her cheeks, and sparkling eyes, which were not large but joyous and intelligent. She said Jane's face was by no means as broad and plump as represented. She recalled Jane's keen sense of humour and, like Jane's own nieces, said children liked her because she entered into their games.

Perhaps some clue to what Jane looked like are two portraits of her niece Anna Austen Lefroy in middle age. Anna resembled her aunt in colouring, with the same chestnut hair and hazel eyes, and in figure. She looked, too, like Jane's brothers, of whom we have convincing like-nesses, and fits Mrs Beckford's description. We know that Jane's step was light and firm, that her speaking voice was sweet – she excelled in reading aloud – but we cannot find a real face. However, enough evidence exists to reconstruct something of the real woman, who was more interesting and less inhibited than we have been allowed to believe.

Jane's was the restricted life of a respectable spinster, though her age was violent and raffish enough. The American Revolution happened the year she was born, 1775, and the Bastille was stormed at the height of the French Revolution when she was thirteen. England was threatened with revolution, and was at war with France for a large part of her adult life. Invasion was feared. Nor were England's towns and countryside always safe and peaceful places to live. The Prince of Wales and his brother the Duke of York were robbed in broad daylight in London, near Berkeley Square. It was estimated that there were 100,000 criminals in London alone. Highwaymen lurked on Hounslow Heath. Thieves were hanged in public. On 23 February 1807 a triple hanging in London attracted a crowd of 40,000 people. In 1813 seventeen machine-breakers were publicly executed at York.

Jane's own conduct was blameless but she took a keen pleasure in gossip and the sensational. She read and enjoyed the Gothic horror novels she makes fun of in *Northanger Abbey*. She had a robust and wicked sense of humour and liked to tease her prim sister, Cassandra, by being outrageous. Her teenage writings deal flippantly with sibling rivalry, drunkenness, adultery, seduction, illegitimacy, destitution, suicide, mercenary marriage, murder, prison, the gallows, deformity, speech impediment, galloping consumption, steel mantraps, physical injury. There is allusion in *Sense and Sensibility* to duelling, in *Mansfield Park* to sodomy, in *Emma* to slavery, in *Pride and Prejudice* to prostitution.

Jane was a keen reader of newspapers. Tantalizingly, she mentions 'political correspondents' with whom she discussed the issues of the day but these unknown correspondents would have seen no reason to keep her letters. The letters that have survived, especially those to her sister, Cassandra, are full of gossip and family news, with occasional flashes of spite and anger. They can be epigrammatic: 'Lady Elizabeth Hatton and Annamaria called here this morning; yes, they called, but I do not think I can say any more about them. They came and they sat and they went.' They are also full of astringent comments on her acquaintance and constant wistful remarks about not being rich. Cassandra, fortunately for us, had the foresight to keep Jane's letters but in old age looked them over and burned most of them. More letters were destroyed than survive and those that did survive had bits chopped out.

Jane's surviving relatives, particularly those who lived into the second half of the nineteenth century, pretended the waspishness of the letters and the biting satire of the novels did not represent the real woman. They were concerned to gentrify her, to portray her as cosy and sweet, ignoring the vinegary vein which fascinates us. They censored her letters and doctored her image. She was tougher, more irritable and more sardonic than they liked to acknowledge.

Jane's letters express appreciation and envy of the ease, elegance and luxury to be found at Godmersham Park, the home of her rich brother, Edward, who had, like Fanny Price in *Mansfield Park*, been adopted by wealthy relatives, the Knights. Edward was the father of Jane Austen's eldest and favourite niece, Fanny Knight, who became Lady Knatchbull. At the age of eighty-five, Fanny wrote to her younger sister Marianne:

> Yes, my love, it is very true that Aunt Jane from various circumstances was not so *refined* as she ought to have been from her *talent*,

and if she had lived fifty years later she would have been in many respects more suitable to *our* more refined tastes. They were not rich and the people around with whom they chiefly mixed, were not at all high bred, or in short anything more than *mediocre* and they of course though superior in *mental powers* and *cultivation* were on the same level as far as *refinement* goes – but I think in later life their intercourse with Mrs Knight (who was very fond of and kind to them) improved them both and Aunt Jane was too clever not to put aside all possible signs of 'common-ness' (if such an expression is allowable) and teach herself to be more refined, at least in intercourse with people in general. Both the Aunts (Cassandra and Jane) were brought up in the most complete ignorance of the world and its ways (I mean as to fashion etc) and if it had not been for Papa's marriage which brought them into Kent, and the kindness of Mrs Knight who used often to have one or other of the sisters staying with her, they would have been, though not less clever and agreeable in themselves, very much below par as to good society and its ways.

Old Mrs Knight had adopted Fanny's father, Jane Austen's brother Edward, as her heir when Edward was sixteen. Fanny, unlike her aunts, was brought up in wealth and comfort. We can only wonder what sort of refinement the fastidious Jane Austen can have been deficient in and what sort of 'common-ness' she might have had to grow out of. She criticized a Mrs Britton in a letter written in November 1813: 'she amuses me very much with her affected refinement and elegance'. At the same time she admired the manners of Lady Honeywood for their 'ease and good humour and unaffectedness'. Who could quarrel with these comments on good manners?

Possibly Lady Knatchbull remembered Jane and Cassandra wearing pattens, wooden soles mounted on iron rings to raise shoes above the mud. Later pattens were worn only by the poor. Perhaps Jane's pronunciation was old-fashioned? Since her Oxford-educated brother Henry praised the sweetness of her speech, and both her parents would have been well-spoken, a Hampshire accent is unlikely. Purity of accent was valued in the better educated women of the gentry class in the eighteenth century. Her brother James's daughters, Anna and Caroline, both of whom loved her dearly, emphasize Jane's charm of manner. They admit she was not well dressed, as she could not afford to be, but Lady Knatchbull's discomfort seems to have deeper resonances. Embarrassed by her aunt Jane Austen, Lady Knatchbull chooses to emphasize her own glory as a member of the rich Knight family (by adoption), though her paternal grandmother, Mrs Austen, had aristocratic Leigh antecedents. Lady Knatchbull's mother was the expensively educated daughter of a baronet and may have found Jane provincial or uncomfortably sharp. Jane the spinster aunt was not fully appreciated, according to Fanny's cousin Anna, tolerated rather than loved in the wealthy, well-bred but unintellectual Godmersham household where Fanny grew up, though Fanny was appreciative enough of her aunt's talent to read *Pride and Prejudice* aloud once more to her sister Louisa fifty years after Jane's death.

Lady Knatchbull has been censured for this notorious judgment as heartless and snobbish but Jane was just too plain-spoken to suit a later generation. Fanny Knatchbull's letter reflects the change in manners between the Regency and the later Victorian age, when under the influence of the Evangelical movement the middle classes became careful to distinguish themselves from the foul-mouthed, blaspheming proletariat by fastidious avoidance of any expressions which could be stigmatized as 'coarse' or 'common'. Bad language became known in polite society as 'Billingsgate', the name of the fish market, where the swearing by the porters was notorious.

Jane and Cassandra were sometimes embarrassed by their mother's cheerful indifference to what they felt to be propriety: they were afraid she was likely to darn stockings in the parlour in front of visitors. As the great-niece of the Duke of Chandos she had perhaps married beneath her and could afford an aristocratic indifference to petty notions of correctness. In 1805 Jane Austen described one acquaintance as being, like other young ladies, considerably more genteel than her parents. The word is used without irony as a term of unqualified praise. The notion of progress in politeness was already established. By the time Fanny Knatchbull wrote the infamous letter to her younger sister Marianne, the word 'genteel' had lost any cachet it might once have had and was considered a vulgarism. Today it implies an uneasy, affected anxiety about polished manners, and nervous use of euphemisms.

The progress towards prudery had already started by the 1780s, when the term 'pregnant' was considered more polite than the traditional expression 'with child', and instead of being 'brought to bed' or 'delivered', a woman was 'confined' or even had an 'accouchement' as in French. In her letters of the early 1800s, Jane Austen unblushingly uses the older forms. But even as early as 1818, the year after she died, Dr Thomas Bowdler brought out the *Family Shakespeare*, with the bawdy cut out. The range of permissible topics for conversation dwindled as the nineteenth century became increasingly mealy-mouthed.

Another possible explanation for Lady Knatchbull's embarrassment is that Jane Austen was animated. In 1838, Fulwar-William Fowle, who was born in 1791, remembered her as 'pretty, certainly pretty – bright and a good deal of colour in her face – like a doll – no, that would not give at all the idea for she had so much expression – quite a child, very lively and full of humour – most amiable, most beloved . . .' Fulwar-William said she was attractive, animated and delightful. But expressiveness was not valued by Victorian society matrons. The fashionable manner was a haughty reserve, an icy indifference.

Nor might Lady Knatchbull have approved the topics of her aunt's letters. Writing from London in 1814, Jane hoped her little niece Cassandra, her brother Charles's eldest girl, had 'found my bed comfortable last night and has not filled it with fleas'. In her next letter, Jane writes resignedly, 'If Cassandra has filled my bed with fleas, I am sure they must bite herself.' This may have been a family joke, or perhaps the little girl, then aged eight, did have fleas. Either way, Lady Knatchbull would not have been amused and would have thought any mention of parasites in poor taste.

Jane Austen, two days after her twenty-third birthday, wrote to Cassandra: 'My mother continues hearty, her appetite and nights are very good, but her bowels are still not entirely settled, and she sometimes complains of an asthma, a dropsy, water in her chest, and a liver disorder.' When Lady Knatchbull's son, the first Lord Brabourne, edited Jane Austen's letters for publication in 1884, he excised the references to bowels and to fleas, together with ones to bad breath and pregnancy. He censored Jane's irritated references to her brother James, and softened her anger at the way married women became breeding machines. He insisted that while a vein of 'good-natured satire' might be found in the letters and conversations of many of the Austen family, no malice ever lurked beneath. No one, he emphasized, was in reality more kind-hearted and considerate of other people's feelings than Jane. This concern with a 'reality' at odds with the evidence suggests that Lord Brabourne's celebrated great-aunt needed, in his view, some apologizing for. Jane's letters were only too often demolition jobs on the neighbours.

Jane grew up in the last quarter of the plain-spoken eighteenth century among clever and interesting relatives, who expressed themselves with frankness, elegance and precision, in conversation and in letters. Her mother composed messages in verse, her father was a classical scholar, and her elder brothers published a satirical Tory journal which offered burlesques on the sentimental literature of the day. Her earliest works were comic parodies along similar lines. Her mature works are social comedies ending, after difficulties and misunderstandings have been overcome, in marriage. Her pleasant female characters are rewarded with loving husbands, her unpleasant ones remain single or are caught in bad marriages. Among possible motives for writing are wish-fulfilment and resentment. Both have been detected in the novels of 'gentle Jane', who could be scathing. After she died, her brother Henry wrote, 'Though the frailties, foibles and follies of others could not escape her immediate detection, yet even on their vices did she never trust herself to comment with unkindness.'

Henry lied, probably in defence of what he thought of as his sister's reputation, or he may not have seen the letters to Cassandra, with their touches of black humour. Jane Austen could never resist a joke, even one about an acquaintance 'brought to bed yesterday of a dead child', prematurely born because of a fright. Jane pretended to think the stillbirth was caused by the mother happening 'by chance to look at her husband'. This appalling sick joke has the power to make us wince, even today. Dead babies are not funny. Certain of her admirers dismiss these 'remarks in bad taste' as aberrations, nothing to do with 'dear Jane'. On the contrary, they express an important part of her personality. She could be savage in her comments about people, the real people she moved among; and when it comes to her invented characters, she makes them expose themselves in all their awfulness.

Jane was, though, also warm and affectionate. She and Cassandra, who were less than three years apart, loved each other deeply. With only two years' formal education, they had small chance to develop the school and college friendships which became so important for women in later generations. In their day, parents were often remote and families large. Children were likely to make themselves into tightly knit groups. Jane liked first cousins to be friends, as they were, she said, but one remove from brother and sister. Her relatives emphasized her attachment to family, but while Jane Austen cannot be understood in isolation from her relatives, the account of her they handed down to us should be taken with a large pinch of salt.

2

Origins

JANE AUSTEN was born on 16 December 1775. Her mother had had a long and difficult pregnancy, the baby arriving a month later than expected. Her delighted father, the Revd George Austen, described her as a 'present plaything for her sister Cassy and a future companion'. He wrote to his sister-in-law:

> You have doubtless been for some time in expectation of hearing from Hampshire, and perhaps wondered a little we were in old age grown such bad reckoners but so it was, for Cassy certainly expected to have been brought to bed a month ago: however last night the time came, and without a great deal of warning, everything was soon happily over. We have now another girl . . . She is to be Jenny . . .

Calculation of dates was important in those days, when there were no chemical pregnancy tests. The Austens should have been able to work out their dates, for this was Mrs Austen's seventh confinement. The little girl who would later achieve worldwide fame was called Jenny, a recognized diminutive of Jane, within the family circle. Nicknames were used: among Jane's brothers, James was 'Jemmy', Edward was 'Neddy' and Francis 'Frank'.

George Austen was 'old' only in experience of fatherhood, not in years, being only in his mid-forties when Jane arrived. He came from an old Kentish family who had manufactured woollen cloth and were picturesquely known as 'the Grey Coats of Kent'. George's ancestor

John Austen of Horsmonden, Kent, was married to Joan Berry in 1584. At his death John owned land in Kent and in Sussex. John and Joan had a large family. One of their sons, Francis Austen (1600–87), set up as a manufacturer, doing well enough to buy a pair of Tudor manor houses, Grovehurst and Broadford, which descended down the generations. Francis's son John married Jane Atkins, and fathered another John Austen, who married Elizabeth Weller. Only after his death did his widow realize that he had left nothing but debts. A resourceful woman, Elizabeth sold what she could and moved to Sevenoaks, Kent, where she set up a boarding house and sent her sons to the grammar school without fees in return for taking care of the Master and some of the boys. She knew the importance of education.

One of her sons, Francis Austen, was apprenticed to a lawyer, and set up for himself 'with £800 and a bundle of pens', according to his great-nephew Henry, and prospered. Francis's younger brother William (1701–37) was Jane Austen's grandfather. William was a surgeon, who married the widow of another surgeon, Rebecca Walter. Rebecca's father, Sir George Hampson, was a baronet. The widowed Mrs Walter had a son of her own, who became the father of Jane Austen's half-cousin Philadelphia ('Phila'), not to be confused with George Austen's sister Philadelphia Hancock.

Among the four children of William and Rebecca was Jane Austen's father, George, born in 1731. Rebecca died while George was still a toddler and the children had a stepmother, Susannah Kelk. According to family tradition Susannah was not kind to them. William died when his son George was six years old. Susannah, who had been left nothing in William's will, took no interest in the young orphans, unrelated to her. William's brother Stephen, a publisher, took in George and his two surviving sisters, Philadelphia and Leonora, but resented the children as a burden and neglected them.

Uncle Francis Austen, by now a successful solicitor and landowner, who dressed in sober grey and wore a dignified wig, took over the care of the boy George. Francis was an astute man of business, agent to the Duke of Dorset at Knole in Kent. Jane Austen's brother Henry, aged nine, met his great-uncle when he was eighty-two. A burly man with a heavy jaw and tight-lipped mouth, he exuded power. 'I think he was born in Anne's reign, and was of course a smart man of

George the First's. It is a sort of privilege to have seen and conversed with such a model of a hundred years since,' Henry recalled. Francis had married two women of wealth and persuaded his eldest son's god-mother, Viscountess Falkland, to leave him £100,000.

George was sent at Francis's expense to Tonbridge School and went on a closed scholarship, reserved for a Tonbridge pupil, to St John's College, Oxford, at sixteen, in those days not unusually young. He had a sweet temper and a sunny disposition, despite his early privations. After graduating he returned to Tonbridge School as a teacher, was ordained deacon in Oxford in 1754 and was priested a year later. He combined teaching with being Rector of Shipbourne in Kent.

Requirements for a career in the Anglican Church were not exacting. The only preparation necessary was a degree from one of the two universities. When Ben Lefroy, husband of George's granddaughter Anna, later presented himself for ordination, the bishop asked him only two questions: was he the son of Mrs Lefroy of Ashe, and had he married a Miss Austen? That George Austen was more conscientious than most is proved by his taking a bachelor's degree in divinity in 1760, again funded by his connection with Tonbridge School.

He became a part-time curate, thanks to family help. Although the Archbishop of Canterbury earned £25,000 annually, many livings brought in as little as £100 a year, which is all George's parish of Steventon was worth. Because salaries were so low, 'pluralism' (later frowned on) was common. Those who could get more than one appointment were known as 'gallopers', because they hurried about on horseback to take services at their various churches. Gallopers could not always manage to fulfil all their duties and too many churches and graveyards tumbled into decay. Adjacent parishes, such as those held by George after 1773, represented good luck indeed. Many clerics were absentees, living lives of pleasure and possibly excess, and merely drawing their stipends without doing anything to earn them though they might appoint curates on starvation wages, sometimes as little as thirty pounds a year. It was not unknown for others to do one service on Sundays and communion once a quarter.

At the age of twenty-seven clever, hard-working George returned to his college as chaplain. This appointment made him a Fellow, and his college chaplaincy was augmented by a university job as well: he was known as the 'handsome proctor'. The proctor is responsible for discipline among the undergraduates. He had a slim, erect figure and bright hazel eyes, even though they were on the small side, eyes of a colour which his daughter Jane inherited. His hair went prematurely white. Even at seventy it was curly and described by his granddaughter Anna as beautiful. As a young man he wore a wig with sausage curls above the ears.

Fellows of Oxford and Cambridge colleges were not allowed to marry but family connections again came to the rescue. Once ordained, a young clergyman had to wait for a living to become vacant. Bishops and deans were appointed by the Crown, but parish clergy were appointed some by the Crown, some by Cathedral chapters, and many by private patrons, landowners like Lady Catherine de Bourgh in *Pride and Prejudice*. As forty-eight per cent of livings were in private hands, it was important for an aspiring clergyman to know the right people. Mr Collins in *Pride and Prejudice* has every reason to be pleased with the patronage of Lady Catherine, who has given him his living, which brought with it a snug parsonage and dinner at the great house twice a week, followed by a ride home in her ladyship's carriage. A distant cousin, Thomas Knight of Godmersham Park, in 1761 made George Rector of Steventon, a village on the northern border of Hampshire. Thomas Knight owned extensive tracts of land in Hampshire and Kent, which provided livings for various relatives and friends. Such nepotism was considered right and proper, a responsible use of influence. Benefices were looked on as a fund for the provision of younger sons of gentry and nobility.

Steventon is a remote hamlet, still accessible only by narrow, winding lanes. Nowadays these lanes are surfaced and in good repair, but in the eighteenth century they were no more than rough, muddy cart tracks, full of ruts. The rectory stood near the main road into the village. The small grey Early English church of St Nicholas, with characteristic lancet windows and dating from the thirteenth century, stands higher up on the hill behind it, set apart from the village.

The stipend of £100 a year was not enough to live on, but a rectory entitled George to glebe land, which he farmed, and to tithes which he had trouble in collecting. Originally tithes represented one-tenth of the layman's produce but by a slow process of erosion, and after the Enclosure Acts which privatized the common lands on which the poor had grazed their animals, they were often changed from goods in kind to money theoretically handed over by landowners in whose hands the livings rested. The system was complicated, and the revenue unreliable. Apples were subject to tithe, but windfalls uncertain until the courts decided they should be included. A bad harvest could impoverish the priest as well as his flock. Scanty rural populations produced meagre tithings.

George also rented Cheesedown Farm from his patron and worked it with the help of a bailiff, John Bond.

Aged thirty-three, George married Cassandra Leigh, who was nine years younger. She had been reluctant to give up her freedom but needed a home for her recently widowed mother. George was remarkably handsome so the sacrifice can hardly have been great. The marriage took place in Bath, at the church of St Swithin, Walcot. The ceremony was conducted by the Revd Thomas Powys, in the presence of Cassandra's brother James Leigh-Perrot and her sister, Jane Leigh, on 26 April 1764. Quiet weddings were then the custom. Cassandra was married in a red wool riding dress, which she wore without buying any new ones for her first two years of marriage, and which was eventually cut down to make a coat and breeches probably for her son Francis to wear in the hunting field. Jane Austen's mother knew, of necessity, how to practise thrift. Their honeymoon was a one-night stop at Andover on their way to Hampshire.

Cassandra Leigh was a rector's daughter and granddaughter on her mother's side of an Oxford physician, Dr John Walker. A sincere Christian, she knew what the life of a clergyman's wife was like. There were eight clergymen in her family, and when her daughter Jane wrote *Pride and Prejudice* Jane's mother enjoyed reading about Mr Collins. Not only Jane's father but two of her brothers and four of her cousins were clergymen. As well as the landed gentry on whose periphery she moved, Jane Austen drew on her own family to write about the classes she knew best, including well-connected, but not rich, clergymen. Several of her characters marry clergymen: Mrs Grant and Mrs Norris have already done so in *Mansfield Park* when the story starts, and Fanny ends up married to the Revd Edmund Bertram. The heroes of *Northanger Abbey* and *Sense and Sensibility*, Henry Tilney and Edward

Ferrars, are both clergymen. The secondary characters Charlotte Lucas in *Pride and Prejudice*, Miss Augusta Hawkins of Bristol in *Emma*, and Henrietta Musgrove in *Persuasion* all marry parsons.

Cassandra Leigh was well connected. Not only was her uncle Master of Balliol College, Oxford, famous for his wit and mentioned in a letter from Mrs Hester Thrale to Dr Samuel Johnson, but she was the great-niece of a Duke of Chandos. Her father was the Revd Thomas Leigh, Rector of Harpsden (pronounced 'Harden'), Oxfordshire, previously a Fellow of All Souls College, Oxford. All Souls is a distinguished company of scholars which has no teaching function. Cassandra, like several of her relatives, was named after her great-aunt the Duchess. She was descended from Sir Thomas Leigh (1498–1571), knighted by Queen Elizabeth I while he was Lord Mayor of London. Among other relatives were William Pitt the Elder, first Earl of Chatham, and his son William Pitt the Younger, who was Tory Prime Minister from 1783 to 1801 and again from 1804 to 1806. She was also related to William Lamb, second Viscount Melbourne, Queen Victoria's first Prime Minister, and to the family of another Prime Minister, Sir Winston Churchill (1874–1965).

At the age of six little Cassandra Leigh impressed her uncle, the Master of Balliol, with her cleverness and her ability to write verses. Yet, because she was a girl, her intellectual gifts were not nurtured. We do not know whether this made her angry or whether she accepted this treatment as woman's lot. Her granddaughter Anna said it was regrettable that Cassandra's formal education had been neglected, but commented that her quick apprehension and retentive memory made up for lack of instruction. Anna added that she was a quick-witted woman with plenty of sparkle and spirit in her talk, who could write an excellent letter, either in prose or verse. These made no pretence to poetry, but were simply playful common sense in rhyme. She had been taught to read and the art of fine needlework by her aunt, Miss Anne Perrot. In ability, if not in intellectual culture, she was a worthy wife for George. She wrote fluent and elegant letters. She would inherit, like Elizabeth Bennet in *Pride and Prejudice*, £1,000 on her mother's death, which with other investments brought her in an annual income of £140.

She was dark-haired, retaining the colour till late in life, and more than ordinarily good-looking, though her face and lips were thin and by fifty she had lost her front teeth. She lacked confidence in her own attractions, however, because her sister Jane Leigh, who became Mrs Cooper, was an acknowledged beauty. Cassandra Leigh's eyes were large and grey, with clearly marked eyebrows, and her features were good.

The Austens were a handsome, elegant couple, both with aristocratic aquiline noses, and they produced attractive children. Steventon rectory was in bad repair so George and Cassandra settled at the neighbouring hamlet of Deane, where the rectory was conveniently empty. They paid rent of £20 a year to the absentee incumbent for a low, damp house with small inconvenient rooms, but moved to the rectory at Steventon, seven miles from Basingstoke, in 1774, the year before Jane was born. George's stepmother, Susannah, had died and the house she was living in was sold. George's share was £1,200, so he could afford to do up his house and make it habitable. The removal was wearisome and the ride on a cart along a bumpy rutted mud track was only made tolerable for Mrs Austen by the provision of a feather bed.

The landscape around Steventon seemed bland and unimpressive to Mrs Austen, the girl from Henley-on-Thames. The chalk hills where sheep grazed were smooth rather than rugged. The well-watered valleys grew cereals, turnips, sainfoin, peas and beans, the meadows produced hay and clover. Today that landscape is largely unspoiled. Austen country is still agricultural, with gently rolling hills, farm homesteads and picturesque villages with thatched houses. In contrast with the subtopian sprawl characteristic of so much of late twentieth-century England, Jane Austen's part of Hampshire surprises and delights with its neatness.

Steventon Rectory, where Jane Austen was born, was a double-fronted house at the edge of the village with a trellised porch and sash windows, and dormer windows above. The square house had been extended at the rear with double wings. On the ground floor were the best parlour and the common parlour, or as we should say living room, where the family ate their meals. There was also a kitchen. Behind them was Mr Austen's study, with a pleasant view through the bow window of the garden leading to the sundial at the end of it; above were seven bedrooms and three attics. The beams were exposed, then not a picturesque survival but considered a sign of poverty, and the walls met the ceiling without cornices, which later generations of the Austen family thought wretchedly inadequate. They were apologetic about the poor way their brilliant relative had lived.

When the sisters grew up, a bedroom next to theirs was made into a sitting room for them. It had a patterned carpet on a chocolate ground, with a cupboard and bookshelves painted brown to match, blue wallpaper and blue striped curtains. An oval mirror hung between the windows. Jane preferred it to the parlour downstairs, as being more comfortable and more elegant.

Behind the living quarters was a washhouse with a pump over a well which supplied the house with pure water. The site was levelled in the 1820s, but the pump is still there, alone in a field. There was the old-fashioned sort of garden in which flowers and vegetables were mingled, and strawberries bordered the grass walk. The east wall was of mud, topped with thatch. There was a green slope of fine turf for the children to roll down, as the young Catherine Morland did in *Northanger Abbey*. The Revd George Austen and his wife were energetic garden planters and improvers. They created a 'sweep' in the front garden and put in timber and shrubs behind. The house stood in a shallow valley, surrounded by sloping meadows well sprinkled with elm trees. There were a solitary silver fir draped in honeysuckle and a white pole surmounted by a weathercock, which made what the children called a 'scrooping' sound as it turned.

Not far from the church was the Steventon manor house, an early Tudor building, owned by George's patron, Thomas Knight, but rented by the Digweed family, with whom the Austens were friendly; Jane was concerned when James Digweed's horse 'kicked a great hole in his head'. The church and churchyard, where wild violets grow, have Digweed monuments and Digweed graves, together with a plaque inside the church saying that Jane Austen worshipped there. Inside it, too, are marble memorial tablets to her eldest brother James's first wife, Anne Mathew; to James from his second wife and their children; and to their mother from those children.

When Jane was twenty-four, she described in a letter to Cassandra:

an odd kind of crash which startled me – in a moment afterwards it was repeated; I then went to the window, which I reached just in time to see the last of our two highly valued elms descend into the sweep! The other, which had fallen, I suppose, in the first crash, and which was the nearest to the pond, taking a more easterly direction sank among our screen of chestnuts and firs, knocking down one spruce fir, beating off the head of another, and stripping the two corner chestnuts of several branches in its fall. This is not all. One large elm, out of the two on the left-hand side as you enter what I call the elm walk, was likewise blown down; the maple bearing the weathercock was broke in two, and what I regret more than all the rest is, that all three elms which grew in Hall's meadow and gave such ornament to it, are gone; two were blown down, and the other so much injured that it cannot stand.

However, she was relieved that the only damage done by the storm was to the trees. Jane wrote playfully to her sister:

The three Digweeds all came on Tuesday, and we played a pool at Commerce [a card game]. James Digweed left Hampshire today. I think he must be in love with you, from his anxiety to have you go to the Faversham balls, and likewise from his supposing that the two elms fell from grief at your absence.

Mr Austen, farming parson, used to join with Mr Digweed, James Digweed's father, in buying twenty or thirty sheep at a time. In order to manage things fairly, when the pen was opened the first half of the number to run out were Mr Austen's, the rest Mr Digweed's. One day Mr Austen noticed among his stock a particularly fine specimen. He said to his man John Bond, 'Well, John, I think we've had the best of the luck with Mr Digweed today, in getting that sheep.'

John smiled. 'Maybe not so much in luck as you think, sir. I see'd her the moment I come in and set eyes on the sheep, so when we opened the pen I just gived her a *buck* with my stick, and out a' run.' Scattered through Jane Austen's letters are references to sheep, pigs, turkeys, ducks, chickens, guinea fowl and bee-keeping. George Austen's life as practical farmer and man of literary culture is reflected in one of Jane's letters of November 1798 to her sister when Cassandra was staying at Godmersham with her brother Edward: in one sentence she tells Cassandra that sheep had cost her father twenty-five shillings each and her father wanted news of Edward's. In the next she mentions buying books.

In her next letter she reports that her father is glad to hear Edward's pigs are doing so well and wants Edward to know that Lord Bolton was deeply interested in pigs: he had built them elegantly constructed pigsties and visited them first thing every morning. Pigs had to be killed. One of her father's pigs, sold to the butcher, weighed twenty-seven and a quarter pounds per quarter. Jane's sister Cassandra, remembering a happy childhood, wrote later in life that there was so much amusement and so many comforts attaching to a farm in the country that people who had experienced such pleasures did not easily forget them.

Between the rectory and the church were hedgerows which sheltered primroses, anemones and wild hyacinths. Steventon was remarkable for its hedgerows. In Hampshire at that time a hedgerow was not a mere boundary, but an irregular border of copsewood and timber, often broad enough to have a path inside it. A few of these can be seen today. The elm walk, also called 'the wood walk', stretched from the terrace westward, skirting the glebe meadows, and led to a shrubbery on the sunny side. Another hedgerow-lane was known as 'the church walk', leading through the wood up the hill to the church. There were sycamores, thorns and lilacs, making a rich habitat for wildlife. Jane Austen writes of such a hedgerow in *Persuasion*, one whose density makes it possible for Anne Elliot to overhear a conversation about herself between Captain Wentworth and Louisa Musgrove.

George and Cassandra lived from the start with her mother and a ready-made child. Penniless orphan Philadelphia Austen, George's sister, had been sent to India at twenty-one to catch herself a husband. This expedient for matching up lonely white businessmen and administrators with British wives was cynically known as 'the fishing fleet'. The sea voyage took eight months. Philadelphia, slender and elegant, with dark upswept hair and large dark eyes, took just six months more to marry a middle-aged surgeon, Tysoe Saul Hancock. He was punctilious, and her scatterbrained ways sorely tried his great affection for her.

Saul and Philadelphia Hancock came home from India taking care of a sickly boy called George Hastings, motherless son of the famous Warren Hastings, later Governor-General of Bengal. George Hastings had been sent home, as the custom then was, for his education. The return journey cost Saul Hancock £1,500. He was disappointed to discover that he could not afford to live in Britain at the same standard as he had done in India so went back to make his fortune but got into further difficulties. In 1772 Warren Hastings gave him £5,000, later doubled. The pair traded in salt, timber, carpets, rice and opium. An attempt has been made to sensationalise Jane Austen's father as a drug-dealer, because he helped as an agent to distribute these goods; but opium, though known to be addictive, was used as an everyday painkiller, as easily available as aspirin today. Hancock, a doting father, died in Calcutta, a world away from his wife and daughter Eliza, the month before Jane Austen was born. He was sixty-four. Mrs Hancock was reduced to £600 a year, the income on Hastings's gift. This was inadequate for life in London, so she settled abroad, first in Germany and Belgium, and then in Paris, where she cut a dash and gave Eliza a polish which later dazzled her Austen cousins.

Warren Hastings was a hero to the Austen family. Jane Austen was gratified with his praise of *Pride and Prejudice*, which her brother Henry had forwarded to him. Mr Austen sought the help of Warren Hastings to get a promotion for his nautical son Frank. When Hastings was impeached before the House of Lords in 1788 for cruelty and extortion, Jane's half-cousin, Phila Walter, heard the famous orators, Sheridan, Burke and Fox, at his trial. The dramatist Richard Brinsley Sheridan spoke so low he could not be heard, Edmund Burke was so hot and hasty he could not be understood, and every word spoken by Charles James Fox (famous leader of the Whig opposition to the Tory Prime Minister William Pitt) was distinct, but offensive to Phila in being hostile to Warren Hastings. Hastings was eventually cleared after a trial lasting seven years.

Possibly George Austen offered to educate Warren Hastings's boy himself. Neither the child nor old Mrs Leigh, Cassandra's mother, survived long. Jane Austen never knew her grandparents. Cassandra grieved as much for little George Hastings, who lived with them for only six months, as if he had been her own child, though she soon became pregnant herself.

Saul Hancock had predicted accurately that George would 'find it easier to get a family than provide for them'. George and Cassandra did get a family, almost at the rate of a baby every year, and were soon in debt. His income fluctuated from year to year and was never more than £600. Later he had a small pension but was never well off. George borrowed the then substantial sum of £865 from his rich brother-in-law James Leigh-Perrot four years after his marriage, when he already had three children. George managed to pay back only £20 of the loan because he was helping his sister Philadelphia. In 1772, when there were four children, he borrowed another £300 which he did succeed in paying off, thanks to Uncle Francis.

Two years before Jane Austen was born Uncle Francis bought him the adjoining parish of Deane, a mile and a half away, worth another £110 a year. George's combined parishes held only about 300 people. Surprisingly, there were no professed Dissenters or Roman Catholics. The Ashe living, also in the gift of Uncle Francis, was taken by the Revd Dr Richard Russell. Later Uncle Francis sold the presentation of Ashe to another rich kind uncle, Benjamin Langlois, who gave the living to *his* nephew, the Revd Isaac Peter George Lefroy, whose wife, Anne, became a dear friend of Jane Austen. Mr Austen, like other hard-pressed clergymen in the period, took in boy pupils. Today the parishes of Steventon, Ashe, Deane and North Waltham are combined under one rector who earns a single stipend.

Although the parishioners were so few, George and his wife were far from being a gentleman and lady of leisure. They had to be largely self-sufficient in feeding themselves, their children and servants. Mrs Austen took charge of the poultry and the dairy, making butter and cheese. Bread was baked and beer brewed at home. When there was honey, the Austens made mead. Sometimes George received rent money from land owned by the Austen family. He was trustee of an estate in Antigua, like the one owned by Sir Thomas Bertram in *Mansfield Park*. There were to be eight children, Jane the seventh.

The Austens were a devoted couple and George missed his wife sorely when she visited her sister Jane, Mrs Edward Cooper. Mrs Austen's reaction on getting home was one of relief. She complained that she had been 'hurried' while in London. It was 'a sad place; I would not live in it on any account; one has not time to do one's duty either to God or to man,' she wrote later.

In the same letter she recorded that she was pleased with her little Alderney cow, who made more butter than they could use, and had just bought another. Mrs Austen liked country life and grew her own vegetables, wearing an old green smock frock like a labourer's, when digging up potatoes. In those days potatoes were something of a luxury in England. A tenant's wife visiting the parsonage had never seen them before. When Mrs Austen suggested that the visitor should plant them in her own garden, the woman replied, 'No, no; they are all very well for you gentry, but they must be terribly costly to rear.' Potatoes did not become a poor man's crop till the 1820s. The gap between 'gentry' and the rest was real. Clergymen of the established Church were gentlemen, though Dissenters were not, but many, including the Austens, found it a struggle to maintain anything like a gentry lifestyle.

3

Siblings and Society

THE ELDEST AUSTEN son was James, born 13 February 1765. He became a clergyman like his father, and it was James's son by his second wife, the Revd James-Edward Austen-Leigh, who published his *Memoir* of his aunt Jane Austen in 1869, when he was the oldest living person to remember her. He had been the youngest mourner at her funeral in 1817.

The second Austen son, George, was hardly ever mentioned, and the *Memoir* leaves him out. He was handicapped, and suffered from fits. His mother wrote sadly when he was four, 'My poor little George is come to see me to-day, he seems pretty well, tho' he had a fit lately, it was near a twelvemonth since he had one before, so was in hopes they had left him, but must not flatter myself so now.' It is believed he was deaf and dumb, as Jane knew how to 'talk on her fingers'. He did not live at home. His father drew comfort from the reflection that 'he cannot be a bad or wicked child'.

The third son, Edward, born 7 October 1767, was luckier. At the age of sixteen he was adopted by his father's patron, rich and childless Thomas Knight II, and inherited Godmersham Park, a fine estate in Kent. Thomas Knight's father had been born Thomas Brodnax, but changed his name to May when he inherited an estate. This was not an unusual condition at the time but changing one's name required an Act of Parliament. Thomas May found it worth his while to change once more, to Knight, when a distant cousin, Mrs Elizabeth Knight, bequeathed him her estates at Steventon and Chawton in Hampshire.

His rapid changes of name provoked one Member of Parliament to comment, 'This gentleman gives us so much trouble that the best way would be to pass an Act for him to use whatever name he pleases.' Thomas was generous to his various relatives, presenting those in Holy Orders with livings in his gift. Edward was a special favourite with the son (also Thomas Knight) and spent a lot of time at Godmersham. When Thomas Knight II proposed to adopt the boy Mrs Austen advised her husband to accept the offer. Edward and his wife and children are usually written of as 'Knight', although they were called Austen until Edward changed his name in 1812 when old Mrs Knight died.

Mrs Austen wrote after James's early death that Edward was 'quite a man of business', while James had 'classical knowledge, literary taste and the power of elegant composition'. Both, she added, were equally good, amiable and sweet-tempered. Their mother recognized and accepted that Edward was not as academically gifted as James or Henry.

A silhouette group shows Edward's father presenting the boy to his wealthy patrons. Edward, in tight-fitting coat and knee-breeches, stretches out his hands towards them, his back towards his father, while Mrs Knight looks up coolly from the game of chess she is playing with another lady. Mr Knight stands at the extreme right of the picture. The women wear stays and high coiffures with beribboned caps, while the grown men wear wigs tied behind. Edward's hair is his own, and hangs long at the back.

Edward missed out on Oxford but was more than compensated by the opportunity of the Grand Tour. He visited Switzerland, Dresden and Rome, staying in Dresden for about a year. But his family ties were strong and he was always specially close to Cassandra, while there was a strong bond of intellectual compatibility between Jane and the fourth son, Henry.

Henry, born 8 June 1771, was brilliant and charming, but seems to have been the least stable among the brothers, although, in his father's opinion, Henry was the 'most talented' of the children. He was generally considered the handsomest of the young Austens, though to modern eyes and in the opinion of their friend Mrs Lefroy the best-looking among the lot was the baby of the family, Charles. Henry was agreed to be a wonderful conversationalist. Jane delighted in his companionship. He had an optimistic outlook, which was just as well, as his career, unlike those of his brothers, was chequered. He followed his elder brother James to Oxford, where their mother's aristocratic connections entitled them to financial concessions as 'Founder's Kin'. The statutes provided for the maintenance of six scholars who could prove their relationship to Leighs, Walkers, Perrots or Whites. They became Fellows on entering the college and could remain so until they followed the usual route to Holy Orders. They were not Fellows in the modern sense, as their erudite father was, but rather privileged scholarship holders. This custom of giving preference to descendants of founders of colleges was peculiar to Oxford and was discontinued during the nineteenth century.

The immediate Austen family was warm and affectionate. George Austen was fond of his wife and children. When Mrs Austen left for a month in 1770 to take care of her sister, Jane Cooper, who had had a premature baby, he complained to his 'Dear sister Walter', 'I don't much like this lonely kind of life, you know I have not been much used to it, and yet I must bear with it about three weeks longer, at which time I expect my housekeeper's return, and to make it the more welcome she will bring my sister Hancock and Bessy along with her.' Bessy was Eliza Hancock, Philadelphia Hancock's daughter. Sisters and sisters-in-law nursed one another through childbirth. Mrs Austen, writing to Mrs Walter during her fifth pregnancy, described herself as 'heavy and bundling as usual'. 'I believe,' she wrote, 'my sister Hancock will be so good as to come and nurse me again, for which I am sure I shall be much obliged to her, as it will be a bad time of the year for her to take so long a journey.'

The baby Cassandra, born 9 January 1773, like her sister Jane later, was sent away to live with a neighbouring farmer's wife, where she was visited 'almost daily' by her parents. The motive was not wet-nursing, though that was quite usual at the time. A contemporary, William Cobbett, said, 'Nothing is so common as to rent breasts to suck.' However, Mrs Austen was proud of suckling her babies, at least for the first few months, and found them entertaining companions when they could talk. But it seems to have been the custom then to send tiny children away from home for a year or two, both in England and in France. French parents often sent a blank death certificate with the baby, in case it died. The foster parents for the little Austens were John and Elizabeth Littleworth, whose family worked for the Austen family for nearly a century.

Mrs Austen wrote proudly to her sister-in-law Mrs Walter that Cassy 'has been weaned and settled at a good woman's at Deane just eight weeks; she is very healthy and lively, and puts on her short petticoats today. Jemmy and Neddy are very happy in a new play-fellow, Lord Lymington, whom Mr Austen has lately taken charge of.'

Poor little Lord Lymington, son of Lord Portsmouth, must have found his Latin lessons a struggle, as he was considered 'backward' and showed his distress in a stammer. Eventually his mother took him away in order to have him cured by a Mr Angier in London, and a pleasant fourteen-year-old 'Master Vanderstegen', son of a neighbouring family, took his place. The 'cure' seems to have been ineffectual, as after succeeding his father, Lord Portsmouth, the third Earl, was declared a lunatic. He was twice married, the second time late in life, as Jane noted in a letter in 1814, to a young Miss Hanson, whose father was Lord Byron's solicitor. Byron gave the bride away, clumsily ramming the left hands of bride and groom together. Lady Portsmouth, aware that her husband was a sadist and necrophile, brought in her lover to live, and had three children by him. They ill-treated her husband, as he had ill-treated his servants and animals. The Earl's brother rescued him and in 1823 had the marriage annulled. While he stayed fairly sane, Lord Portsmouth showed his gratitude to the Steventon family by inviting them to his annual ball at Hurstbourne Park near Andover. This suggests he had not found the Revd George Austen's regime oppressive.

As well as her husband's pupils and her own babies, Mrs Austen was still concerned with her four-legged and feathered creatures. She wrote to Mrs Walter, 'I have got a nice dairy fitted up, and am now worth a bull and six cows, and you would laugh to see them; for they are not much bigger than Jack-asses – and here I have got jackies and ducks and chickens . . . In short, you must come, and, like Hezekiah, I will show you all my riches.'

Little Cassy was followed by Francis on 23 April 1774, and Jane arrived the following year. The baby of the family was Charles, born 23 June 1779. He was to Cassandra and Jane their 'particular little brother', a deliberate misquotation from *Camilla* by Fanny Burney, in which the heroine is referred to as 'my own particular little niece'.

The relationship between the fictional sister and brother Fanny and William Price in *Mansfield Park* reflects Jane's pride in her nautical brothers. Both Frank and Charles rose to be admirals and Frank was knighted after becoming Admiral of the Fleet. Even as a small boy he showed initiative. Aged seven, he saved up his own money, bought a chestnut pony called Squirrel for a guinea, hunted on him for a year or two, and sold him at a profit of one hundred per cent.

The Austen boys liked nothing better than to follow the hounds after a hasty breakfast in the kitchen. Fox hunting was a new and fashionable sport. William Price, in *Mansfield Park*, enjoys a hunting party when visiting his sister. To tease Frank, his brothers insisted on calling his pony 'Scug'. His own nickname was Fly.

He entered the Royal Naval Academy at Portsmouth just before his twelfth birthday, followed later by his young brother Charles. Frank, although intelligent, was not specially good at classical languages. His flair was for mathematics, and he wisely insisted on the navy as a career. This was no inconvenience to their father, for once boys were accepted there, they received free board and tuition. When Frank finished his studies, he left with a glowing report. He joined the frigate HMS *Perseverance* in order to learn practical seamanship for a year. In 1788 he sailed for the East Indies. He became a midshipman in 1789 and stayed on the *Perseverance* for nearly two years before moving to HMS *Minerva*. He was promoted lieutenant at the end of 1792, and did not return to England for another year. When Frank died at the age of ninety-one, in his pocket was a letter of fatherly advice, stained with sea water and almost worn out.

The rest of the family relied mainly on each other for companionship. Mrs Austen wrote to Mrs Walter at Tonbridge in Kent wishing they were a mere thirty miles apart instead of eighty. She assured Mrs Walter that only distance prevented her from visiting as often as she would have wished. Educated people, or even those who could read, were thin on the ground. The moral tone was low. Among the peasantry bastardy was cheerfully accepted and considered no disgrace. In 1800 one-third of the nation's brides were pregnant. Many parishioners were foul-mouthed, including the apparently wealthy but crude squire Harwood who lived at Deane House, next to Deane church, and habitually decorated his sentences 'with an oath'. Mr Harwood was so ignorant he once asked Mr Austen, 'You know all about these things. Do tell us. Is Paris in France, or France in Paris? . . . my wife has been disputing with me about it.' People who cannot spell or are ignorant of geography are laughed at in Jane Austen's novels (though her own spelling was less than perfect).

One of the Harwood ancestors has been suggested as the original of the uncouth Squire Western in Henry Fielding's novel *Tom Jones* though the identification can be only conjectural. Squire Harwood was involved in a lawsuit with a neighbour, Mr Hillman. In a phrase which might have been penned by his daughter Jane, George Austen wrote that they had commenced actions against each other and seemed 'to promise good sport for the lawyers'.

The troubled history of Squire Harwood's second son Earle runs through Jane's letters. Earle, born in 1773, set up as a coal merchant at the age of twenty-one, then joined the Royal Marines. In 1797 he married to spite his family. His wife was said to have a bad reputation, though Jane Austen suspected that she was only an innocent country girl. Earle and Sarah lived at Portsmouth 'without keeping a servant of any kind', desperate poverty indeed for the officer class. Jane Austen thought they must be very much in love to survive such conditions. In 1800 Earle managed to shoot himself in the thigh at St Marcouf, an island off Normandy, where a British garrison was stationed. Two young Scottish surgeons wanted to amputate, but he refused. He was put on board a cutter and carried to Haslar hospital in Gosport, where the bullet was extracted. The surgeon who took it out wrote to the family and his brother John left at once to see him. His parents were terrified that he might have been involved in an illegal duel, but the surgeon confirmed that the angle of the wound proved it to have been the result of an accident. However, there was damage to the bone. Earle died in 1811, a captain in the Woolwich division of Marines, two years before his father.

Earle's elder brother, John Harwood VII, a clergyman, was the heir, but he inherited nothing but debts, previously secret, and a dependent mother and aunt. He had become attached to a wealthy widow, a friend of Jane Austen, Mrs Elizabeth Heathcote, who had a small son. Mrs Heathcote had been a Miss Bigg, of Manydown Park. The Revd John Harwood felt in honour bound to end their association. The poor man loved the house and land which had passed from father to son over six generations. Had he been willing to sell, he could have paid off the loans. Eventually he did part with a small piece of land, but died a broken man. In happier times, he had danced with Jane Austen at a ball when she was twenty -three.

In 1813 Jane, hearing the news of his troubles, wrote, 'Poor John Harwood! One is really obliged to engage in pity again on his account – and where there is lack of money, one is on pretty sure grounds.' She knew from personal experience what she was talking about.

Other families with whom the Austens mixed were the Portals of Freefolk, the Holders of Ashe Park (though Jane was embarrassed, or afraid, at finding herself alone for ten minutes with Mr Holder), the Bramstons of Oakley Hall and the Biggs of Manydown Park. The squirearchy among whom the young Jane Austen moved was less stable than one might think from a superficial reading of her novels. If one reads between her lines, one finds an exploration of social tensions, social and economic change. Yet the skeletal outline of Jane Austen's world is still recognizably present in pockets of English rural life, which has something to do with her continued popularity as 'gentle Jane', though as we shall see she was tougher and more forthright than many readers have assumed. Jane Austen herself belonged to what has been called the 'pseudo-gentry', that is, well-spoken, well-brought-up people without much income. Her father as an Oxford graduate belonged to a cultivated élite, then numerically tiny, and held a position of dignity and influence.

In 1814 baronets, knights, country gentlemen and others having large incomes were reckoned as numbering nearly seven thousand families. Baronets are the highest rank of commoner, and their titles descend to their nearest male heirs. They are not 'Mr' but 'Sir' and their wives are not 'Mrs' but 'Lady'. Knights and their wives are also 'Sir' and 'Lady', but their titles are not hereditary. Jane Austen's fictional world straddles this class and the next class, to which her own immediate family belonged, the professional and business classes, estimated at some twelve thousand families.

Like most country gentlefolk who educated their sons for the professions of the law, the Church, the army and navy, the Austens were Tory in politics. The great landowning families were more likely to be Whigs, some of them even republicans. Jane Austen believed in King and Country, and the established Church of England in which her father was employed. She was a loyal supporter of King Charles I of England and of Mary, Queen of Scots, both of whom had the misfortune to be beheaded. Although herself a convinced Anglican Protestant, she admired Catholic Mary for sticking to her religion. On the whole, she liked traditions without being hidebound or reactionary. She described an acquaintance as 'as raffish in appearance as I would wish every disciple of Godwin to be'. William Godwin was author of *Political Justice*, advocating Utopian communism, a book that influenced Karl Marx.

There was tension between the Tory country gentry and the Whig aristocracy. Jane's novels rarely deal with aristocrats, and the few who turn up in her pages are handled with hostility: Lady Catherine de Bourgh in *Pride and Prejudice* is rude and overbearing, while Viscountess Dalrymple and her daughter in *Persuasion* are vapid, cold and snobbish. Jane Austen's viewpoint is very much that of the middle class of her day. Darcy in *Pride and Prejudice* is the son of Lady Anne Darcy, the daughter of an earl whose family name is Fitzwilliam. ('Fitz' as a prefix implies royal bastardy in an ancestor.) But the story shows Fitzwilliam Darcy, initially arrogant, being tamed and domesticated. In *Emma* we see the process by which Mr Weston and the rich Coles, originally in trade, infiltrate the landed society of Highbury.

Despite the stigma of being 'in trade', rich manufacturers were buying estates, and even if they were not accepted as gentlemen themselves, their sons and grandsons would be. Incomes from estates came from rents and the sale of timber. There were many landowners who ran counties and parishes, served as magistrates and administered poor relief, in conjunction with the Anglican clergy. Some of them were ten times as rich as Mr Darcy, though Darcy's £10,000 a year is the equivalent of millions today. To compare incomes with those at the end of the twentieth century, it is necessary to multiply by at least 200. Early in the nineteenth century even a modest landholding would bring in some £5,000 a year. To sustain the rank of gentleman, an income of at least £2,000 was necessary; £300 a year was genteel poverty. On that a family could barely afford two maids. A senior servant might earn £80 a year; a junior one, such as scullerymaid, as little as £5, plus food and lodging.

With no electricity and no labour-saving gadgets, household work was heavy and servants a necessity for all but the poorest. Food preparation was time-consuming: chickens, for instance, had to be killed, plucked and drawn before they could be cooked. Jams, pickles and sauces all had to be made at home. Coal fires created dust, which had to be removed every day. Furniture had to be polished with beeswax. Labour was cheap.

Although Mrs Bennet in *Pride and Prejudice* indignantly rejects Mr Collins's suggestion that one of his cousins might have cooked the dinner, Jane and Cassandra at least supervised work in the kitchen. Their nephew James-Edward Austen-Leigh recorded in his *Memoir* that ladies in their day undertook more domestic responsibilities than in his own (he was writing in the late 1860s). It was certainly customary, early in the nineteenth century, for ladies to wash valuable china themselves, for fear of breakages, and to starch their own linen after it had been washed. The Austens employed a cook, but no housekeeper. Meals had to be planned and supplies organised, servants trained. Jane, aged nearly twenty-four, wrote playfully to Cassandra, who was on one of her visits to Godmersham, 'My mother desires me to tell you that I am a very good housekeeper, which I have no reluctance in doing, because I really think it my peculiar excellence, and for this reason – I always take care to provide such things as please my own appetite, which I consider as the chief merit in housekeeping.' The recipe book collected and written out by her friend and lodger Martha Lloyd survives. Mrs Austen contributed one in rhyme.

Jane Austen did not do her own housework. In December 1798 she writes of the inconvenience of having been without a maid for a long while, and having to employ casual charwomen. Jane carried the keys of the wine and tea closets when her mother was indisposed and gave orders in the kitchen. But though a lady, she was a poor relation, socially insignificant, all her life and she resented it.

4

Upbringing

ANE'S FATHER BAPTIZED her himself when she was one
day old. Infant mortality was high and the weather was too
cold to take so young a child out of doors. Her official
christening, with godparents, took place the following spring on 5
April 1776. Her sponsors at the font were the Revd Samuel Cooke,
Rector of Cotsford, Oxfordshire, and Vicar of Bookham in Surrey, Mrs
Jane Austen, a great-aunt and wife to the rich and generous Great-
uncle Francis, and Mrs James Musgrave, wife of the Vicar of Chinnor
in Oxfordshire, whose mother was a rich great-aunt of Mrs Austen.
Samuel Cooke's wife, born another Cassandra Leigh, cousin of Jane's
mother, was a published novelist. Perhaps she smiled on Jane Austen in
her cradle.

Seventh child and second daughter among eight children, Jane
formed close bonds of affection chiefly with her sister Cassandra and
with her brothers, and later with those brothers' children. She did not
always get on so well with her sisters-in-law. In *Persuasion* friction between in-laws is made the subject of wry comedy. It is possible, though
unlikely, that Jane never learned the ability to make deep relationships
with outsiders. She dismissed an acquaintance, admittedly during an
unhappy and unsettled time in her life, as liking people rather too easily. Jane wrote in *Mansfield Park* that the link between siblings is
unique and stronger even than the marriage tie. The four youngest
Austen children, Cassandra, Francis, Jane and Charles, remained specially close emotionally, though physically scattered after the boys

joined the navy, all their lives. They may have felt crowded by George's pupils, the other children in the house, and drawn tighter together as a consequence.

When little Jane Austen was fetched home from her foster parents' house, she followed her big sister Cassandra everywhere. Jane loved Cassandra best of all her siblings. They seemed to share a life with each other within the general family life. Except when paying visits, when they were separated, they shared a bedroom all their lives and probably slept in the same bed. A bedroom to oneself, especially in large families, was a luxury except among the very rich until recently and for sisters to share a bed was not unusual even in the mid-twentieth century. As a child Cassandra spent much of her time with her maternal aunt and uncle, the Coopers, in Bath. On one occasion her father had collected her for the last stage of the journey in a hackney chaise. Some distance from home they met Jane, aged six and a half, in the roadway, holding her little brother Charles, then just three, by the hand. Impatient for her sister's return, Jane had gone to meet her.

Mr Austen educated his boys at home along with his other pupils but in 1782 Cassandra was sent to boarding school at Oxford, with a Mrs Ann Cawley, a sister of Mrs Austen's brother-in-law, the Revd Edward Cooper, and widow of a former Principal of Brasenose College, Oxford. Cassandra was nine and Jane seven. Jane pined for her sister, so was allowed to join her.

'If Cassandra's head had been going to be cut off,' declared their mother, 'Jane would have hers cut off too.'

Jane was not happy away from home even though Cassandra was with her. The seven-year-old girl hated being dragged round Oxford by her proud undergraduate brother James on sight-seeing trips through dismal chapels, dusty libraries and greasy halls. They depressed her. All her life she was more interested in people than in museums. She was too young to notice, as her cousin Eliza did on another occasion, how becoming black gowns and square caps, later known colloquially as 'mortarboards', were to young men. Oxford and Cambridge university students wore them as a distinctive uniform well into the twentieth century.

Mrs Cawley then took the girls with their cousin Jane Cooper to Southampton where she and the children caught a 'putrid fever', the name then current for both typhus fever and diphtheria. Mrs Cawley did not bother to notify the parents but Jane Cooper wrote to her mother who came to fetch her and the Austen girls. Mrs Cooper caught the illness and died. The children narrowly escaped death. Infectious diseases, before modern drugs, could easily and with shocking rapidity prove fatal, especially to children. Another killer disease at the time was 'putrid sore throat', or gangrenous pharyngitis, mentioned in Jane Austen's letters as having killed a boy at Eton. Mrs Cooper's husband did not remarry. He brought up his son Edward (whom Jane Austen did not like) and daughter Jane alone. He gave Cassandra and Jane mementoes of their dead aunt: Cassandra had an emerald and diamond ring, Jane a headband which she later wore to dances.

The ability to dance was recognized as necessary if a girl was to mix in society, and parents otherwise neglectful of their daughters' development made sure that the girls never went without dancing lessons. The elaborate routines of country dances, minuets and cotillions had to be memorized and the exercise of dancing would, it was hoped, lead to a graceful carriage. Good deportment was the mark of a lady, who was also expected to play the pianoforte or the harp, and, if she had a good voice, to sing. Accomplishment was supposed to add up to eligibility.

The Austen girls next went with the motherless Jane Cooper to the Abbey School at Reading, which may have been like Mrs Goddard's school in *Emma*, where girls might 'scramble themselves into a little education'.

Boys went to grammar or public school and then to Oxford or Cambridge, at that time the only two universities in England, with students numbering only a few hundred. The universities exercised an influence out of all proportion to their size, preparing a social élite for the professions of the Church and the law, or in some cases for a life of gentlemanly leisure. Girls did the best they could. Elizabeth Bridges, a daughter of Sir Brook Bridges, baronet, and who was to marry Jane's brother Edward, went with her sisters to a grand girls' boarding school in Queen Square, Bloomsbury, London, known as 'the ladies' Eton', where there was heavy emphasis on etiquette and they were required to practise the art of descending gracefully from a carriage. Little else was learned except French, music and dancing.

It was rare for girls to go to school of any kind, as many fathers disapproved. In the late eighteenth century governesses were employed only by the very wealthy and grand, like Lady Catherine de Bourgh in *Pride and Prejudice*, who is surprised that the Bennet girls did not have one. Neither country gentlemen like Mr Bennet nor clergymen like George Austen aspired to employing governesses, though his rich son Edward and his wife, Elizabeth, had governesses for their five daughters while their six sons went to public school. Often children were taught to read by their mothers. It was usual to start with the Psalms. In *Northanger Abbey* Mrs Morland, a clergy wife, teaches her eleven children to read, write and number.

Jane as a child owned *The History of Goody Two-Shoes* and a French textbook, *Fables Choisies*, given her on 5 December 1783, together with an anthology, *Elegant Extracts*. Her brother Edward gave her a copy of Dr Percival's *A Father's Instructions to his Children, consisting of Tales, Fables and Reflections; designed to promote the love of virtue, a taste for knowledge, and an early acquaintance with the works of Nature*. She also had a copy of Ann Murry's *Mentoria: or, The Young Ladies' Instructor,* from which she picked up general knowledge.

The headmistress of the Abbey School was a Miss Sarah Hackett who used as her professional name 'Mrs Latournelle' to give authenticity to her credentials as a French teacher, though she knew not a word of that language. She was a stout woman with a wooden leg, who never did any work in the afternoons. Her dress was always the same, with a white muslin kerchief round her neck, a muslin apron, short sleeves, cuffs and ruffles, with a breast bow to match the bow on her cap, both being flat with two notched ends. She may have been a former actress, for her conversation centred on plays and acting, gossip about the private lives of performers and even backstage anecdotes. This must have been more entertaining for schoolgirls than French irregular verbs. She acted as housekeeper, giving out clothes to be washed, ordering dinner and making tea. There was also a Miss Pitts, whose French was fluent and who played and sang well and was an excellent needlewoman. The curriculum comprised writing, spelling, French, needlework, drawing, music and dancing. Jane was happy enough there to write later, 'I could die of laughter at it, as they used to say at school.' At this time her cousin Eliza de Feuillide, née

Hancock, wrote to her cousin Phila Walter that all Uncle George Austen's children seemed to be everything their parents could wish.

The school itself was in part of the ancient Abbey building, formerly occupied by Benedictine monks. It consisted of an antique gateway with rooms above its arch and with vast staircases either side, whose balustrades had originally been gilt. Pupils were received in a wainscotted parlour, hung round with chenille representations of tombs and weeping willows. There were several miniatures over the tall mantelshelf. There was a beautiful wild garden, where the girls were allowed to wander under tall trees on hot summer evenings. They could climb the embankment and look down on the Abbey church, begun by King Henry I and consecrated by St Thomas à Becket. As Jane Austen wrote at fifteen in her facetious *History of England*, the abolition by King Henry VIII of religious houses 'and leaving them to the ruinous depredations of time has been of infinite use to the landscape of England in general'.

In 1785, Jane and Cassandra's brother Edward and Jane Cooper's brother Edward called at the school and took their sisters out for a meal at an inn, which shocked their Victorian descendants as most unseemly. Their cousin the Revd Thomas Leigh of Adlestrop called to see the girls and tipped them half a guinea each.

Mr Austen had difficulty paying the school fees and the girls left after two years in 1787. Their stay had cost their father £140, as the fees were the same as he charged for board and tuition, £35 per pupil per year.

Schools at that time offered girls little more than 'finishing school' was to do later. In *Sense and Sensibility* the brainless Charlotte Palmer's landscape in coloured silks is sarcastically described by the narrator as 'proof of her having spent seven years at a great school in town'. Moralists criticized the fashion for superficial and showy accomplishments but there was little more solid on offer anywhere. Girls' boarding schools were not widespread until later in the next century and both the universities were closed to women, as were the professions of medicine, the law, the Church, the army and the navy. Argument raged as to the nature and purpose of female education: many people thought that the only education necessary for girls was moral and religious training, which would help young women to subdue their unruly passions. Some women internalized this ideology and took it on themselves to advise their own sex, insisting that opportunities to become generals, politicians, legislators or advocates would be wasted on mere females. Women were even discouraged from talking politics in mixed company. Jane Austen was interested in politics and read solid books on history. Nonetheless, women were popularly said to be ruled by their hearts, not their heads. Voices were raised against such prejudice, and some people argued that girls needed to be taught to think. Others pleaded for the teaching of English grammar, pointing out that while the French language was a fashionable subject, most young ladies remained grossly ignorant of their own.

At home, the girls' education was probably much like that of the Bennet sisters in *Pride and Prejudice*. Elizabeth tells Lady Catherine they were always encouraged to read, and had all the masters that were necessary. When Jane was eleven her father was paying a drawing master. Jane's family considered her to be talented in that direction, and Cassandra and Henry both drew. Jane wrote in a letter when she was forty that she did not have her niece's 'fondness for masters'. Fanny Knight's music teacher, Mr Meyers, 'gives his three lessons a week – altering his days and his hours . . . just as he chooses, never very punctual and never giving good measure.' Jane herself learned the pianoforte in her teens. Jane was fortunate because the instruments were so expensive they were a rare luxury in country parsonages. When Frank Churchill in *Emma* gives a pianoforte to his secret fiancée Jane Fairfax, the gift is munificent indeed, an amenity the impoverished Mrs Bates and her daughter could never have provided.

If Mr and Mrs Austen could not afford to import many masters, the clever father and brothers filled the gap. James and Henry went to Oxford University, where James edited a periodical called *The Loiterer*.

An elegant hand was considered important for letter-writing. Jane's own letters are beautifully penned, their neat flowing handwriting sloping elegantly to the right. Only quill pens, which quickly wore down and needed recutting, were available to write with. Steel nibs did not come into general use until the mid-nineteenth century. In the circumstances, neat legible handwriting was important and the ability to write small made for economy in paper and postage. Members of Parliament had the privilege of sending mail for nothing, by signing letters above the address. This was called franking. Everybody else had to pay not when sending letters but on receiving them. When Jane was staying with maternal relatives at Stoneleigh Abbey in 1806, a Mr Holt Leigh, MP for Wigan in Lancashire, arrived and gave the family 'franks' for their letters so they could go for nothing.

In *Mansfield Park* when Fanny is pining for home, Edmund encourages her to write to her brother William. '. . . it will cost William nothing . . . when you have written the letter, I will take it to my father to frank.' Sir Thomas is an MP.

Payment was according to weight, which is why single sheets were used economically, and sometimes 'crossed' – turned upside down and written between the lines, or written in both directions so that one line of writing was at right angles to another. Two sheets of paper meant 'double postage'. Very penurious correspondents sometimes 'double-crossed' their letters. In November 1813 Jane received a 'black and red letter' from her brother Charles, written in black and crossed in red for clarity. Envelopes were hardly known and letters consisted of single sheets, folded and sealed with a thin wafer. Folding and sealing were necessary skills and while some people's letters were loose and untidy, Jane's were perfectly symmetrical, with the wafer always correctly placed. Although her own handwriting was neat and attractive, she thought it inferior to Cassandra's. 'I took up your letter again,' she wrote to her sister, 'and was struck by the prettiness of the hand, so small and so neat! I wish I could get as much on to a sheet of paper.' Another time she wrote, 'I am quite angry with myself for not writing closer; why is my alphabet so much more sprawly than yours?' Ladies did not write 'copperplate' roundhand: that was for ledger clerks. 'Ladies' hand', as it came later to be known, was a pointed style, enabling the reader to identify it as a woman's writing.

Jane was clever with her hands in general. 'An artist cannot do anything slovenly,' she wrote lightly in a letter. She excelled at spillikins, a game in which each player takes pieces of wood off a pile with a metal hook without disturbing the others.

From her mother Jane learned the then essentially practical skills of needlework, including embroidery. She was specially good at overcasting and became expert at satin stitch, no easy accomplishment. A sampler made when she was twelve can be seen at Chawton Cottage, as can a patchwork quilt, as exquisite in design as in workmanship. Made, of course, entirely by hand, this full-sized quilt, whose weight cannot be negligible, is assembled with tiny, almost invisible, stitches of perfect evenness and tension. Mrs Austen and her daughters were expert needlewomen indeed. Jane refers to collecting the pieces of material for it in a letter of May 1811. As an adult, Jane made many of her own clothes and on one occasion had to take an outfit botched by a dressmaker to pieces and remodel it herself. Sometimes she wished it were possible to buy clothes ready-made. In her day all clothes were sewn by hand by tailors and dressmakers, some more skilful than others. She preferred quality to quantity, but was forced to count her pennies.

Women rarely learned Latin or Greek, then the basis of male education. 'Literacy' at the time meant mastery of classical literature, not the ability to read English. The rare women who had shared their brothers' lessons in the ancient languages, before the boys were sent away to school, and who found these studies of interest, were advised to keep quiet about it. Perhaps Mr Austen, who taught Latin to his own boys as well as to paying pupils, and cared enough about his daughters' education to send them to boarding school, included them in these lessons, but if so Jane's brothers do not mention it. She knew enough Latin to write *'Ex dono mei patris'* (my father's gift) in the manuscript book her father gave her when she was fifteen. Wit was dreaded in women and clever women learned to keep their tongues under control. As the narrator of *Northanger Abbey* remarks, 'A woman especially, if she have the misfortune of knowing anything, should conceal it as well as she can.' Jane was well read in English literature: her favourite writers were William Cowper in verse and Dr Samuel Johnson in prose. Her copy of Johnson's *Rasselas*, volume two, survives, with her signature in it. She had read Henry Fielding's picaresque and outspoken novel *Tom Jones*, but preferred Samuel Richardson's *Sir Charles Grandison*, which she knew extremely well. She was familiar with Shakespeare and Milton, and in *Persuasion* Byron's poetry is mentioned. There was not much money to spare but the Austens always bought books.

Jane, like her character Fanny Price, was a quiet, shy girl. She was tall for her age and slender. When, in 1788, the family visited Great-uncle Francis, by now over ninety, at the Red House in Sevenoaks, her cousin Phila Walter cast upon her a cold eye. Phila was in her twenties and not very sympathetic to adolescents. She wrote to her brother that she preferred Cassandra, who talked well. 'The youngest (Jane) is very like her brother Henry, not at all pretty and very prim, unlike a girl of twelve. They all spent the day with us, and the more I see of Cassandra the more I admire – Jane is whimsical and affected.' It is noteworthy that both the writer Mary Russell Mitford, a granddaughter of Dr Russell, the Rector of Ashe, and Phila stigmatized Jane as affected: possibly Jane was experimenting with the face she presented to the world and wondering how to contain her own wicked wit within socially acceptable bounds. The implied judgment that Henry was not handsome either is surprising, as the surviving portrait shows him with fine features. The Austens were a good-looking family. Perhaps Jane, in her turn, did not care much for Phila, who was censorious and two-faced. Their cousin Eliza de Feullide, née Hancock, however, described Cassandra and Jane in their teens as 'perfect little beauties'. She reported to Phila when Jane was sixteen that Cassandra and Jane were both much grown and greatly improved in manners and looks. 'They are I think equally sensible, and both so to a degree seldom met with, but still my heart gives the preference to Jane.'

To be seventh in a family means that you can have only a limited share of attention. Cassandra was the elder girl and Jane grew up in her shadow, in a house full of boys, related and unrelated to them. Cassandra was always in demand at Rowling, Edward's first married home, a manor house provided by Elizabeth's relatives, and at Godmersham after he inherited in 1797, while Jane usually stayed behind. Jane may well have felt her clever brothers and Cassandra were more important, more highly valued, than herself. She was ten years younger than James, settled in his career as a clergyman, and possibly in awe of him.

She may have felt too that she could not compete in what, at home and outside it, seemed to be a man's world. The then current social morality discouraged assertiveness in girls, who were supposed to be cheerful and unselfish. The bluestockings of the mid-eighteenth century were no longer fashionable role models, if they ever had been. How could a girl with only reasonable prettiness and no fortune achieve recognition and respect? There were no competitive exams to challenge her, not even in music. Today's seventeen-year-olds prove themselves by taking exams and passing driving tests. Jane must often have felt crushed by her own lack of consequence in the world and the lack of opportunities to shine. In adult life she looked with amazement at the self-confidence of young people and asked half-humorously, 'What has become of all the shyness in the world?'

She took refuge in becoming a shrewd observer. In her writings from the age of fifteen onwards she took apart the excessive sentiment and far-fetched sensationalism of current pulp fiction, especially in her short epistolary novel, *Love and Friendship*. She enjoyed being witty about her neighbours and the words she puts into the mouth of Elizabeth Bennet in *Pride and Prejudice* have often been understood as applying to her own practice: 'I hope I never ridicule what is wise and good. Follies and nonsense, whims and inconsistencies *do* divert me, I own, and I laugh at them whenever I can.'

Pride and Prejudice is a Cinderella story. All Jane Austen's novels follow the romance pattern of happy marriage achieved after difficulties have been overcome. Her own life was very different, emotionally unfulfilled. She was far from unfeeling, but she cultivated detachment and avoided emotionalism. She became adept, in her letters and in her novels, at making jokes on painful subjects. It was her way of coping.

5

Flirtations and Scandals

THE AUSTENS WARDED off boredom with family jokes, conundrums, home-made verses, and theatricals in the dining room or the barn. James was fond of writing prologues and epilogues. In 1782, when Jane was just seven, he produced *Matilda*, a ranting blank verse tragedy by Thomas Francklin, set in the time of the Norman Conquest. Edward spoke the prologue, Mr Austen's pupil Tom Fowle the epilogue. Family mourning for their aunt Mrs Edward Cooper prevented festivities the next Christmas, but in July 1784 *The Rivals* by Richard Brinsley Sheridan was acted.

At Christmas 1786 Mrs Austen entertained Philadelphia Hancock, her married daughter Eliza de Feuillide and Eliza's little boy. Eliza had been considered too grave as a child, but now, in her twenties, was quite lively. She played every day on the pianoforte the Austens had borrowed for her. The visitors brought a present for Jane's eleventh birthday, a set of Arnaud Berquin's book, *L'Ami des enfans*. Jane had not met this cosmopolitan cousin before, and was enchanted with her and her social grace.

The following Christmas, when Jane was just twelve, her cousin Eliza played the lead in a domestic production of Susannah Centlivre's comedy *The Wonder: A Woman Keeps a Secret*. Eliza wrote to Phila Walter begging her to take part, but Phila puritanically objected to the idea of appearing in public. In the New Year the Steventon company performed *The Chances*, an old play by John Fletcher, adapted by David Garrick. This was a comedy set in sixteenth-century Naples, dealing with girls in disguise and their jealous lovers. When Jane was fifteen, the family performed Isaac Bickerstaffe's recently published *The Sultan*, with Jane Cooper as Roxalana and Henry as the Sultan. A proto-feminist English girl, the heroine teases the Sultan into giving up his harem and making her his sole Sultana. Jane Austen learned from the dramatic writers to write brilliantly witty dialogue. Aged fifteen, she wrote an absurdist playlet called *The Mystery*, dedicated to her father, and later, she adapted Samuel Richardson's novel *Sir Charles Grandison* into a five act drama.

Energetic Mrs Austen was in favour of the theatricals, saying she had no room for idle young people, though the plays gave Eliza, a married lady and mother of a baby boy, Hastings de Feuillide, the chance to flirt shamelessly with Jane's brothers James (then in his early twenties) and Henry (in his late teens), as Henry Crawford does with Maria and Julia Bertram in *Mansfield Park*.

In September the following year the Austens heard of a couple who had fallen in love while they were rehearsing an amateur production and eloped to Scotland. The Honourable Thomas James Twisleton, aged eighteen, ran away with Charlotte Anne Frances Wattell, also under age. The age of majority was then twenty-one. The play was *Julia* by the Irish dramatist Robert Jephson, friend of Dr Johnson and his circle. It may be that the name Julia stayed in Jane's mind, to reappear in *Mansfield Park*. Another link in the chain of associated ideas was that Thomas Twisleton's sister Julia had married a distant cousin of Jane's, James Henry Leigh, of Adlestrop Park. Twisleton's younger sister, the Honourable Mary-Cassandra, was an 'Adultress' Jane was to recognize at a dance in Bath in 1801, having homed in on Mary-Cassandra's likeness to Julia Leigh. Jane wrote:

> I am proud to say I have a very good eye at an Adultress, for though repeatedly assured that another in the same party was the *she*, I fixed on the right one from the first. A resemblance to Mrs Leigh was my guide. She is not so pretty as I expected . . . she was highly rouged, and looked rather quietly and contentedly silly than anything else.

The adultress was a year older than Jane herself, and had married at sixteen. Seven years later her husband, Edward Jervis Ricketts, discovered love letters to his wife from Charles William Taylor, and Mary-Cassandra went home to her mother. In June 1798 the Bishop of London granted Ricketts an Episcopal divorce, which did not allow remarriage; in January 1799 the House of Lords granted a civil one, which did. The hearing was newsworthy: Mary-Cassandra had been seen furtively visiting Taylor's house in Margaret Street and had boasted to her maid, in lurid detail, how much better he was in bed than her husband. The Austen sisters knew all about this. Indeed, Jane openly expressed opinions about scandals of which she had heard. She was far from being sheltered from learning of the immorality of society.

For example, Jane told Cassandra in a letter in January 1801 that Fulwar Fowle's wife Eliza, née Lloyd, had seen Lord Craven and 'found his manners very pleasing indeed. The little flaw of having a mistress now living with him at Ashdown Park seems to be the only unpleasing circumstance about him.' The mistress was fifteen-year-old Harriette Wilson, who later became a notorious courtesan. When Harriette fell on hard times, she wrote her memoirs and tried to blackmail her former lovers. Her price for silence was £200 (now worth at least 200 times as much) per lover. It was to Harriette that the Duke of Wellington is said to have uttered his famous challenge: 'Publish and be damned!' Lord Craven in 1807 married an actress called Louisa Brunton. When *Emma* was published in 1815, Jane Austen wrote that Lady Craven admired it very much, but did not think it equal to *Pride and Prejudice*.

Nearer home, the diminutive Revd Charles Powlett, curate of Winslade, who had tried to give Jane a kiss at a ball in January 1796, gave a rowdy party, disturbing the neighbours. His father was an illegitimate son of the third Duke of Bolton. Illegitimate children were numerous. Sometimes called 'accidental' or 'natural' children, they were often recognized and reared by their paternal relatives. Charles spent much time at his grandfather's seat, where he acquired expensive tastes and ran seriously into debt, finally leaving England for Brussels to avoid his creditors. He married a young, extravagant wife, who appeared at a ball 'both nakedly and expensively dressed'. She caused Jane some amusement by referring to her husband in Italian as her

'*Caro sposo*', a detail Jane was to put to use when she created the affected Mrs Elton in *Emma*.

Another Mrs Powlett caused even bigger ripples. Colonel Thomas Norton Powlett was a distant relative of Charles and had at the age of thirty-one married Letitia Mary Percival, ten years younger. When Jane was living in Southampton in 1808 she was shocked to learn that Colonel Powlett's wife had had an affair with Charles Sackville Germain, second Viscount Sackville, later fifth Duke of Dorset. This continued until after the Powletts had moved to Southampton where Mrs Powlett took communion with Cassandra and Jane. Twelve days before Jane wrote to tell her sister all about it, the Viscount and Mrs Powlett had been caught together. The *Morning Post* the previous day (21 June) had announced, 'Mrs P's *faux pas* with Lord S——e took place at an inn near Winchester.' Three days earlier it had announced, 'Another elopement has taken place in high life. A noble Viscount, Lord S, has gone off with Mrs P, the wife of a relative of a noble Marquis.'

Colonel Powlett brought an action for damages against Lord Sackville. The case was reported in the *Hampshire Chronicle* five weeks later. The story was this. Lord Sackville met Colonel and Mrs Powlett at the Stockbridge racecourse on 9 June, when Sackville overheard the Colonel arrange to go yachting with a friend the next day. Next morning, after the Colonel had gone to Southampton Quay, Mrs Powlett ordered post horses for her carriage and drove to the White Hart Inn, Winchester. When she arrived she took a room upstairs. Lord Sackville arrived soon afterwards, and was given a room downstairs where he ate a light breakfast, lounged at the open door of his room and chatted with the landlord, Mr Bell. Mrs Powlett came downstairs and walked about a little but said nothing. When she went upstairs again Lord Sackville soon followed her. They went into her room and closed the door. Mr Bell, growing suspicious, asked his wife to investigate. She knocked on the door, but was told not to come in. Mrs Bell went to another room with a connecting door and as it had been locked from Mrs Powlett's side insisted that it be opened. After some delay, it was. Shutters and curtains were closed, and Lord Sackville was huddled at the far side of the bed. Mrs Powlett indignantly demanded an explanation for the intrusion. Mrs Bell said nothing but when Mrs

Powlett grew shrill Mrs Bell accused her of immorality. Lord Sackville stepped forward and asked Mrs Bell to hush the matter up. Mrs Bell said this was impossible as one of her chambermaids knew all about it. Mrs Powlett burst into tears. Lord Sackville ordered Mrs Bell not to upset Mrs Powlett. He left the room and drove away in his carriage. Mrs Powlett went back in hers to Southampton. The subsequent court case resulted in Colonel Powlett being awarded damages of £3,000. Jane Austen was to use a similar story for the Henry Crawford–Maria Rushworth elopement in *Mansfield Park*, though in less salacious detail. In the novel there is merely a newspaper paragraph which uses initials.

During Jane's lifetime, divorce was rare and consequently newsworthy. Just before she died Jane wrote to her niece Fanny Knight, 'If I were the Duchess of Richmond, I should be very miserable about my son's choice. What can be expected from a Paget, born and brought up in the centre of conjugal infidelity and divorces? I will not be interested about Lady Caroline. I abhor all the race of Pagets.' Charles, fifth Duke of Richmond, was engaged to Lady Caroline Paget, whose father Lord Paget later became Marquis of Anglesey. He famously lost a leg at Waterloo, and the Duchess of Richmond, Lady Caroline's future mother-in-law, had given the celebrated ball on the eve of the battle.

In 1795 Lord Paget, Lady Caroline's father, had married Lady Caroline Elizabeth Villiers, daughter of the Earl of Jersey and a former mistress of the Prince Regent. Jane Austen detested the thought of both people. Lord Paget had an adulterous affair with Lady Charlotte Wellesley, sister-in-law of the Duke of Wellington. Lady Charlotte's husband was awarded £20,000 in damages and divorced his wife. Family and friends tried to mediate between Lord Paget and his wife, but he had run away with Lady Charlotte. The Pagets were divorced in 1810. Lord Paget remarried and fathered six children, in addition to four by his first wife. Here were conjugal infidelity and divorces indeed! Jane was not exaggerating.

There was a family connection, however, and the Austens owed the Pagets a favour. Jane's brother Charles served on the frigate *Endymion* under Captain Charles Paget, who became Admiral Sir Charles Paget and whose recommendation got Charles a promotion.

Jane knew the facts of service life. In *Pride and Prejudice* a private in the militia is flogged. Sailors on one of Frank Austen's ships were flogged for mutiny and sodomy. Both could be capital offences. Mary Crawford in *Mansfield Park* is making an outrageously rude joke when she says that as an admiral's niece she has seen enough of 'rears and vices'. She laughingly adds, 'Now, do not be suspecting me of a pun, I entreat.' Such brittle coarseness is completely in character.

Marital infidelity was not the only social vice of which Jane was aware. At the same time she spotted the 'Adultress', she added coolly, 'Mrs Badcock and two young women were of the same party, except when Mrs Badcock thought herself obliged to leave them, to run round the room after her drunken husband. His avoidance and her pursuit, with the probable intoxication of both, was an amusing scene.'

Drunkenness was common, and not only among men. This scene took place a few days after Jane's arrival in Bath when the family took up residence there in 1801. 'The waters' at Bath were considered good for gout, a common eighteenth-century complaint. Symptoms are painful swelling of the joints, restlessness, irritability, cramp, indigestion, constipation and thirst. It is commonly associated with heavy drinking, especially of port, but though its eighteenth-century prevalence may have been due to the drunken habits of the time, it has more recently been suggested that, like the gravel and kidney stones which also afflicted Jane Austen's contemporaries, gout may be in part caused by dietary deficiencies. Teetotallers can and do get gout. Whatever his drinking habits, Jane's maternal uncle James Leigh-Perrot suffered from gout, which was his original reason for visiting Bath. He had added 'Perrot' to his name in order to inherit a house and land. He knocked down the house, sold the land and built a new house, Scarlets, near Maidenhead.

Scandal of another kind touched the ultra-respectable Austen family when Mrs Leigh-Perrot was arrested for shoplifting on 8 August 1799. She walked down Stall Street, Bath, from their home in Paragon to Smith's haberdashers on the corner of Bath Street. Mrs Leigh-Perrot bought some black lace to trim a cloak. She gave the man a five-pound note. He took it with the goods to the back of the shop while she turned from the counter to the door to look for her husband. When the purchase was wrapped and her change given to her, she took

47

the parcel out of the shop. She walked towards the route her husband generally took on his way to drink the waters and soon met him. They stopped to pay a tradesman's bill and were on their way to the Post Office to post a letter when they passed Smith's, where Mrs Leigh-Perrot had bought her black lace an hour previously. Miss Elizabeth Gregory, part-proprietor of the shop, dashed out into the street.

'I beg pardon, madam, but was there by mistake a card of white lace put up with the black you bought?'

Mrs Leigh-Perrot said that as she had not been home and the parcel had not been out of her hand, Miss Gregory could examine it herself. Miss Gregory opened the parcel and found not only the black lace but a card of white edging which she took out and said, 'Oh, here it is.' She went back into the shop. Mrs Leigh-Perrot, writing to her cousin Mountague Cholmeley, said this did not surprise her as she assumed a mistake had been made in the shop. On the corner of Abbey Churchyard the young man who had taken the black lace away to wrap approached, stopped the couple and insisted on taking Mrs Leigh-Perrot's name and address. In some alarm, she gave it. Hearing nothing, she concluded a mistake had been cleared up but a few days later she received an anonymous, undated letter through the mail, addressed to 'Mrs Leigh-Perrot, Lace dealer'. It said, 'Your many visiting acquaintance, before they again admit you into their houses, will think it right to know how you came by the piece of lace stolen from Bath Street a few days ago. Your husband is said to be privy to it.'

Miss Gregory and her assistant had been to the Guildhall and laid charges of attempted theft against her, swearing they had seen her take the lace, worth one pound, and had found it in her possession. The Mayor and magistrates, who knew the couple, acted according to the letter of the law and Mrs Leigh-Perrot was committed to Ilchester Jail to await her trial at Taunton Assizes. The charge was serious as punishments for offences against property were heavy. If found guilty, this woman of fifty-five, deaf and bronchitic, could suffer the death penalty. In practice, the sentence would probably be commuted and she would be transported to Australia, then a giant penal colony, for fourteen years.

Her husband, two years older and accustomed to gentlemanly comfort, declared that if she was sent as a convicted criminal to Botany

Bay he would sell his land and houses and go with her. He was in poor health, with a foot enlarged by gout, and only able to walk with two sticks. He retained a barrister to defend her and drummed up witnesses prepared to swear that she was in no way unstable or dishonest. He moved to Ilchester to be with her. Their money and social position helped: they were lodged not in stinking cells but in the house of the jailer, Edward Scadding. 'Nothing can have been more respectful than his behaviour,' Mrs Leigh-Perrot reported to Mountague Cholmeley. But one of her worst miseries was seeing what her 'dearest husband' was going through: the 'vulgarity, dirt, noise from morning till night'. Her husband was in constant pain, and the only medical man available combined his profession with dealing in coals and manufacturing tiles, suggesting his practice was less than successful. Greasy toast laid on her husband's knees by the children, and a smoking chimney, did not help. Worse, Mrs Scadding licked her knife. Family and friends rallied round and visited but there was no privacy. Chambers, Mrs Leigh-Perrot's maid of long standing, had died, and Mrs Leigh-Perrot missed her attendance.

On 11 September, a month after the incident, an application for bail was made. But as Mrs Leigh-Perrot had been found with the white lace in her possession, bail was refused. Mrs Austen offered to send either or both of her daughters to keep their aunt company. Presumably this generous gesture was made with their agreement. If it was so, it involved heroic sacrifice on Jane's part, as she never liked her aunt very much. Mrs Leigh-Perrot, to her credit, refused, saying she could never allow 'these elegant young women' to be 'inmates in a prison'.

Mountague Cholmeley had promised to attend the trial but was laid up (or claimed to be) with the gout himself. The trial was held on 29 March 1800, eight months after the offence was said to have been committed. Mrs Austen again offered her daughters as support but their aunt again nobly refused. 'To have those two young creatures gazed at in a public court would cut me to the very heart.' Their brother James, always a favourite with the childless Leigh-Perrots, would have gone but his horse had fallen on him and he had a broken leg.

Charles Filby, who had served Mrs Leigh-Perrot at the haberdasher's, swore he had seen her take the lace and conceal it under her cloak. Cross-examined, he admitted he had been a bankrupt. Sarah Rainer, who also worked there, swore she had seen Filby pack the parcel and that he had put into it only black lace. Elizabeth Gregory swore she had found the white lace on Mrs Leigh-Perrot. The judge invited the prisoner to make her defence. At the time defence counsel were not allowed to address juries on their clients' behalf, only to examine witnesses for their own side and cross-examine those for the prosecution.

Speaking in her own defence, Mrs Leigh-Perrot argued that she was too rich to steal. She had inherited an estate in Barbados. (In old age she boasted to her great-nephew James-Edward Austen-Leigh that she dined with thirty families and employed a housekeeper, a cook, a housemaid, a footman, coachman, gardener, and a gardener's boy who also waited at table.) She claimed that the parcel's being still in her hand an hour after leaving the shop was in her favour. She called witnesses in her defence. One was John Crouch, a pawnbroker, who said he had had dealings with Filby. A Miss Blagrave said that on 19 September she had bought a veil at the shop but found two in her parcel when she got home. Five Berkshire neighbours and three Bath tradesmen testified to Mrs Leigh-Perrot's honesty.

The trial took six and a half hours but the jury stayed out for only fifteen minutes before bringing in a verdict of 'Not guilty'. There were emotional scenes in court and the case was reported in the *Bath Chronicle*. A pamphlet telling the story of the trial was published at eighteen pence.

The expense of bringing in character witnesses had amounted to £2,000. Mrs Leigh-Perrot said she shuddered to think that innocent people without resources had probably been hanged. The shop was in financial trouble. Mr Smith, the owner, had left his wife and gone bankrupt. Miss Gregory was his sister-in-law. The shop assistant Charles Filby was her lover and they possibly hatched a blackmail plot together.

Vindicated, the Leigh-Perrots went back to their house in Bath, though Mountague Cholmeley growled that 'infernal Bath' was a 'den of villains and a harbour of all sorts of swindlers'. Mrs Leigh-Perrot wanted her accusers put in the pillory, but her solicitor told her this was impracticable.

Despite the falsity of the accusations, a faint shadow hung about her. She was later suspected of stealing garden plants. A college friend of James-Edward Austen-Leigh, Alexander Dyce, wrote later in his copy of *Northanger Abbey* and *Persuasion* that the family were 'dreadfully shocked at the disgrace which she brought upon them' and that the lady had 'an invincible propensity to stealing'. If so, she was not the only rich woman to show this weakness. She was notoriously stingy. Six years later she exasperated Jane by failing to hand over a trifling sum she owed her, making only vague offers of payment in kind. Might it not be possible that Gregory and Filby, having seen her steal previously, planted the lace on this occasion in an attempt to get justice as they saw it?

Mrs Leigh-Perrot was disappointed when James-Edward, son, grandson and great-grandson of clergymen, followed them into the Church. She felt his good looks and charm could do better, and threatened financial sanctions if he persisted. She became capricious, sometimes saying she would leave her house, Scarlets, to him, sometimes promising to buy him a living, at other times denying him. However, she relented and made him her heir on condition he added the name Leigh to Austen. Thus he founded the family of Austen-Leighs. He always felt, however, that his great-aunt could and should have helped him earlier.

When Jane Austen was asked which of her characters she liked best, unhesitatingly she replied, 'Edmund Bertram and Mr Knightley', adding that she knew real English gentlemen were often very different. The conscientious clergyman, the brave sailor and the responsible landowner were her ideals: but she was clear-eyed enough to recognize how often the reality fell short.

6

The Marriage Market

HEN JANE WAS twenty-one, tragedy struck her sister. Cassandra had become engaged in 1795 to the Revd Thomas Fowle, a young man eight years older than she was. He had been one of her father's pupils from 1779–83, living in the house from the time Cassandra was six until she was ten. He was a friend of her brother James, and his father had been a college friend of Mr Austen. Like his tutor and doubtless on his recommendation Thomas went to St John's College, Oxford, in 1783. By 1788 he was holder of two curacies and in 1793 his cousin Lord Craven presented him with a living, the rectory of Allington, Wiltshire. He was also appointed Lord Craven's domestic chaplain. Tom may have proposed to Cassandra when he officiated at the wedding of her cousin and one-time schoolfellow, Jane Cooper, to Captain Thomas Williams in 1792 when Cassandra was nineteen. The engagement was eminently suitable. Thomas's father was Vicar of Kintbury. Thomas's brother Fulwar, also one of George's pupils, succeeded his father and lived at Kintbury till he died in 1840. Fulwar was married to his cousin Eliza Lloyd (pronounced Floyd), whose sisters, Martha and Mary, were friends of Jane. The name was pronounced in this way as the family were originally Welsh.

Mr and Mrs Austen must have been highly pleased with their daughter's prospects of happiness and Mr and Mrs Fowle were certainly pleased at the idea of having Cassandra as their daughter-in-law. But Tom's income was small and the young couple agreed to wait to marry until one of the livings Lord Craven held in Shropshire fell vacant. The engagement was never officially announced.

Lord Craven took his chaplain with him when he went as Colonel of the Buffs (3rd Foot) to help put down a slave revolt in the West Indies in 1795. Thomas, hesitating to offend his patron, did not mention the engagement to him and hastily made his will. The Buffs sailed in November but Lord Craven followed later in his private yacht accompanied by Tom, who wrote to Cassandra on 8 January 1796 that if the winds allowed they would sail from Falmouth the following Sunday. When people set off on long sea voyages they were incommunicado for months. Letters could be sent only when ships put into port or met at sea. People left at home could only wait patiently for the return of their loved ones. The return of travellers was necessarily unscheduled and news arrived slowly.

Tom caught yellow fever off San Domingo in February 1797, died and was buried at sea. The Austens, expecting to have him back with them at any time, did not hear of his death until a couple of months later. Lord Craven said afterwards that had he known Thomas was engaged to be married, he would never have taken him abroad.

Cassandra remained close friends with Thomas's parents for as long as they lived and with his brother Fulwar. Jane said her sister behaved with a degree of resolution and propriety which no common mind could evince in such a situation. Broken-hearted, Cassandra faced life with Christian stoicism. She went into full mourning as if she had been Tom's widow. James later wrote a poem in Tom's memory saying how much he had looked forward to officiating at the marriage of his sister and his friend.

Sense and Sensibility was begun at this time and Elinor's painful, disciplined self-command reflects Cassandra's. But how Cassandra must have regretted that 'sensible' decision to wait, that fruitless two-year engagement and the poverty which was the only reason for delay! Excessive caution led to disaster and a long life of loneliness for Cassandra, especially after the early death of Jane. It is hard not to see parallels between Cassandra's fate and the wistful unhappiness of Anne Elliot in *Persuasion*. Anne's misery was remediable in consoling fantasy whereas

Cassandra's life was ruined by her loss. Although Thomas Fowle left her £1,000 she would surely have preferred a husband to a legacy. Towards the end of *Persuasion* comes the famous passage:

> How eloquent could Anne Elliot have been, – how eloquent, at least, were her wishes on the side of early warm attachment, and a cheerful confidence in futurity, against that over-anxious caution which seems to insult exertion and distrust Providence! – She had been forced into prudence in her youth, she learned romance as she grew older – the natural sequel of an unnatural beginning.

Cassandra marked it and added in the margin, 'Dear dear Jane! This deserves to be written in letters of gold.'

Captain Wentworth in the novel had been made commander in consequence of 'the action off San Domingo' and had come into Somersetshire in the summer of 1806. Captain Wentworth, like Jane's brother Frank, was defending England's colonial territories in the Caribbean.

In her earliest surviving letter, written from Steventon to Cassandra on 9–10 January 1796, when Cassandra was staying with her intended parents-in-law at Kintbury, looking forward to her marriage, Jane writes of her own flirtation with Tom Lefroy, three weeks younger than herself. She mentions his birthday first, as almost coinciding with Cassandra's.

The ball Jane writes of was at the home of the rough Squire Harwood. Serious-minded James's dancing had improved. Cassandra had scolded Jane for behaviour which might give rise to gossip. Jane wrote teasingly:

> I am almost afraid to tell you how my Irish friend and I behaved. Imagine to yourself everything most profligate in the way of dancing and sitting down together. I *can* expose myself, however, only *once more*, because he leaves the country soon after next Friday, on which day we *are* to have a dance at Ashe after all. He is a very gentlemanlike, good-looking, pleasant young man, I assure you. But as to our having ever met, except at the three last balls, I cannot say much; for he is so excessively laughed at about me at Ashe, that he is ashamed of coming to Steventon, and ran away when we called on Mrs Lefroy a few days ago.

Next day Tom found the courage to return the call and Jane pretended to find fault with the colour of his morning coat. Dark colours for men were replacing the pastels popular in the earlier eighteenth century and young men were wearing their own hair instead of powdered wigs. Jane attributed Tom's old-fashioned taste for a light-coloured coat to his admiration for Henry Fielding's novel *Tom Jones*. Jane herself had spent all her own small allowance on pink figured silk for her ballgown and white gloves to wear with it. She joked, though there may have been an element of seriousness, that she half expected a proposal. 'I shall refuse him, however, unless he promises to give away his white coat.' But the evening ended without any declaration from the young man.

In her next letter (14 January) Jane drags in the mention of his name only to declare she does 'not care sixpence' for Tom. In the continuation next day Jane adds: 'At length the day is come on which I am to flirt my last with Tom Lefroy, and when you receive this it will be over. My tears flow as I write, at the melancholy idea.'

The reference to tears may be an exaggeration but there is no doubt Jane was hurt, if only in her pride. Among the music copied out by her own hand there is a heavy concentration of Irish airs, which may suggest some emotional involvement. However, she also had a lot of Scottish music and she knew no Scotsmen.

Nearly three years after Tom's departure Jane wrote to her sister, then at Godmersham, that Mrs Lefroy, Tom's aunt, had called:

> In spite of interruptions both from my father and James, I was enough alone to hear all that was interesting, which you will easily credit when I tell you that of her nephew she said nothing at all, and of her friend very little. She did not once mention the name of the former to *me*, and I was too proud to make any inquiries; but on my father's afterwards asking where he was, I learned that he was gone back to London in his way to Ireland, where he is called to the Bar and means to practise. She showed me a letter which she had received from her friend a few weeks ago ... towards the end of which was a sentence to this effect: 'I am very sorry to hear of Mrs Austen's illness. It would give me particular pleasure to have an opportunity of improving my acquaintance with that family – with a hope of creating to myself a nearer interest. But at present I cannot indulge any expectation of it.'

Mrs Lefroy was the bearer of not one, but two pieces of bad news. Not only had the charming, if bashful, Tom Lefroy been shunted out of Jane's orbit but the 'friend' referred to, another eligible young man, the Revd Samuel Blackall, had made it plain he could not 'indulge' any expectations of Jane. It is possible that Jane Austen gave him small encouragement. The letter to Cassandra, though, suggests she had cherished hopes or at least let her fancy play with agreeable possibilities. Mr Blackall was five years older than Jane, and had been a Fellow of Emmanuel College, Cambridge, before becoming Rector of North Cadbury in Somerset. He was married in 1813 to Susanna Lewis, ten years younger than himself.

Jane's letter to her sister continues:

> This is rational enough; there is less love and more sense in it than sometimes appeared before, and I am very well satisfied. It will all go on exceedingly well, and decline away in a very reasonable manner. There seems no likelihood of his [Mr Blackall's] coming into Hampshire this Christmas, and it is therefore most probable that our indifference will soon be mutual, unless his regard, which appeared to spring from knowing nothing of me at first, is best supported by never seeing me. Mrs Lefroy made no remarks on the letter, nor did she indeed say anything about him as relative to me. Perhaps she thinks she has said too much already.

Mrs Lefroy was the wife of the Rector of Ashe, the Revd Isaac Peter George Lefroy, and dignified with the courtesy title 'Madam' Lefroy. The family, of Huguenot origin, were worldly and intellectual. Anne Lefroy was better off than the Austens and did not need to manage her own dairy. She taught the village children to read and write, and to plait straw so that they could earn money by making hats. She vaccinated all her husband's parishioners herself. Her brother, Sir Samuel Egerton Brydges, rented Deane parsonage for two years. He said his sister had an exquisite taste for poetry and knew the works of Milton, Pope, Gray and Collins almost by heart, together with 'the poetical passages of Shakespeare'. Sir Samuel has been confused by some biographers with Sir Brook Bridges, whose daughter Elizabeth married Jane's brother Edward.

Jane looked on Mrs Lefroy as a dear friend, though whether she acted the part of a true friend in teasing her nephew out of his attraction to a penniless girl may be doubted. Jane's feelings were clearly piqued, not least her pride. She says she doesn't care about Mr Blackall or about Tom but we do not believe her. She protests too much. Tom became Lord Chief Justice of Ireland and lived to be ninety-three. He remembered Jane as the object of his youthful admiration all his life.

In old age, he was proud of the early friendship with the celebrated Jane Austen, but said he loved her with 'a boy's love'. He married a rich woman, Mary Paul, sister of a college friend, in 1799, and had nine children. He bought an estate in County Longford where his descendants still live.

Although Mr and Mrs Lefroy teased Tom out of his feelings of attraction to Jane and packed him off to London to study law at Lincoln's Inn under the watchful eye of his Uncle Benjamin they blamed the young man himself for precipitating this decisive course of action. They told their sons that Tom had behaved badly in paying attention to Jane when he knew he could not afford to marry for a long while yet. The Lefroys' predecessor at Ashe Rectory, later known as Ashe House, was the Revd Dr Richard Russell and some have wondered whether Lady Russell in *Persuasion*, who gives dangerously prudential advice to Anne Elliot, blighting her youthful romance at nineteen, owes something to 'Madam' Lefroy.

The young Jane had fantasized about marriage, scrawling imaginary entries for herself and various young men on a blank page in her father's church register, proclaiming the banns between herself and 'Henry Frederick Howard Fitzwilliam of London', entering a record of marriage between herself and 'Arthur William Mortimer' and giving as the names of the witnesses Jack and Jane Smith, 'late Austen'.

But marriage was not to be, for either sister. Jane may have reflected later that lack of money had cheated Cassandra of the happiness she had a right to expect, and had also driven Tom Lefroy away. There is another legend in the Austen family that Jane liked and was liked by another young man who died prematurely. The meeting is supposed to have happened at the seaside: either at Teignmouth, Sidmouth or Dawlish, some time in Jane's mid-twenties. Cassandra liked the young man and was persuaded he was worthy of Jane, that he was in love with her and that she would have accepted him. Cassandra was apt to judge people coolly yet she admired him as 'unusually gifted with all that was agreeable.'

He arranged to meet the sisters at a later date but instead of a reunion all they had of him was news of his death. This story was told to Caroline Austen, James's daughter, by Cassandra when she was an old woman. She told Caroline that he was pleasing and very good-looking. He is likely to remain another phantom romance in Jane Austen's life, untraceable.

Jane was also attracted to Edward Taylor of Bifrons, a manor house in Kent, improved from its Elizabethan origins to a smart new Georgian residence. The young man, a year younger than herself, was the son of the Revd Edward Taylor. On a visit to Kent in September 1796 Jane mentioned the house as being the 'abode of him on whom I once fondly doted'. Edward Taylor was a distant relative of Elizabeth Bridges, who by this time had married Jane's brother Edward.

Jane was admired by the Revd Edward Bridges, Elizabeth's younger brother. She first went to east Kent in 1794 when she was eighteen and two years later she danced with him at Goodnestone (pronounced Gunston), the Bridges family seat. Bridges playfully called her 't'other Miss Austen' and in 1805, when Jane and he were staying at Goodnestone, Jane told Cassandra: 'It is impossible to do justice to the hospitality of his attentions toward me; he made a point of ordering toasted cheese for supper entirely on my account.'

He seems to have proposed marriage, as Jane later implied they were still friends though she had not been able to accept his 'invitation'. He was later married unhappily to a woman who suffered from 'spasms and nervousness'. He got into the habit of taking refuge at Godmersham with his sister and brother-in-law.

Harry Digweed was a close friend and there is a family tradition that Jane Austen's bossy Aunt Leigh-Perrot persuaded Jane's father to leave Steventon for Bath because of a suspected romantic attachment between Jane and a Digweed. This seems improbable, as the Digweeds were perfectly eligible, though they only rented the Manor House, and it was no business of Aunt Leigh-Perrot's anyway. Be that as it may, George Austen perhaps thought his unmarried daughters would stand better chances of marrying if they met some new people. Harry married the feather-headed but lovable Jane Terry. The Terrys lived at Dummer House, near Steventon, a Georgian building which is still there.

Jane was also friendly with Charles Fowle of Kintbury, brother of Cassandra's fiancé. She asked him to buy some silk stockings on her behalf but withdrew the request when she realized she could not afford them. When he bought them anyway she was cross but they stayed on good terms until he died suddenly at the age of thirty-five. He practised as a barrister and was active in home defence in 1799 and 1804–5 when Napoleon threatened to invade England.

Other admirers were a Mr Heartley and John Willing Warren; Jane considered Warren ugly but pleasant. He was a college friend of her brothers James and Henry, often staying at Steventon Rectory, and he contributed to their magazine, *The Loiterer*. He was a Fellow of Oriel College, Oxford, and was later called to the Bar, becoming a Charity Commissioner.

According to family tradition Jane received a proposal from a young landowner called Thomas Harding Newman, who possessed three large estates, Nelmes and Clacton Hall in Essex and Black Callerton in Northumberland. He was four years younger than Jane Austen, a sporting gentleman who shot and kept his own pack of foxhounds. Thomas's eldest son, Dr Thomas Harding Newman, was for half a century the owner of the 'Zoffany' portrait, which may possibly be of Jane Austen's second cousin, Jane Motley Austen, who became Mrs Campion. Mrs Campion's brother gave the picture to Dr Thomas Harding Newman's stepmother, an admirer of Jane Austen's novels, while Mrs Campion was still alive, which suggests the portrait was not of Mrs Campion in youth but of some other girl.

About one proposal of marriage, however, there is no dispute. It came on 2 December 1802 from a man who was six years younger than Jane. Cassandra and Jane went on a visit to their old friends Catherine and Alethea Bigg, expecting to stay the usual two or three weeks. A week later, on a Friday, they turned up at Steventon Rectory where brother James had succeeded his father, now retired, all four women together in a carriage. Catherine and Alethea soon left after tearful and affectionate goodbyes.

James and his wife, Mary, were even more surprised when

Cassandra and Jane demanded that their brother should immediately take them to Bath where the family were now living. Well-brought-up women could not decently travel without a servant or a male protector and James had a carriage. He had to arrange for somebody to take his Sunday services for him at short notice. His sisters insisted, almost hysterically, that he must do it, though he could not understand what the panic was about. Eventually he received an explanation: Jane was running away from a suitor she had rashly accepted the previous evening. That morning she had changed her mind and told the young man so. To stay under the same roof after that would have been embarrassing so the sisters had fled.

Jane was forced to throw herself on James's mercy when she wanted to get back to Bath. A recurrent inconvenience for her was being dependent on lifts in other people's carriages. Respectable women did not travel alone by stagecoach. Too often her friends and relations were going in the wrong direction or not far enough. Except for a few months when Jane was in her early twenties, her father had no carriage, and when he set one up found he could not afford it. This was as bad as having no car today.

Jane's rejected suitor was Harris Bigg-Wither, brother of Alethea and Catherine Bigg. His father, Mr Lovelace Bigg, added 'Wither' to his name when he inherited property in 1789. The daughters remained the Misses Bigg. Harris was a well-off country gentleman, tall and well-built, but plain, awkward and unpolished. He stammered, and could never have matched Jane's intellect and cultivation. She dreaded marriage to a man of inferior understanding. Harris was, however, a sensible man and many girls would have been happy to marry him.

To Jane he offered the prospect of social position and comfort with sisters-in-law who were already her friends. But she could not sacrifice her integrity in a marriage of convenience, though in refusing him she was giving up the prospect of luxury as mistress of Manydown, a stone Tudor mansion built round a courtyard, and with a splendid ironwork staircase going up to a handsome reception room on the first floor. She sacrificed the prospect of sharing a grand park, with oaks, a cedar and the fashionable ditch known as a ha-ha (because it created a barrier which deceived the eye from a distance), for a life of pinching and scraping. She knew the house well, for it was near Basingstoke and she had often spent the night there after dances. Manydown was demolished in 1965.

As she was nearly twenty-seven, the age of Charlotte Lucas in *Pride and Prejudice* and of Anne Elliot in *Persuasion*, she recognized this proposal as a last chance and the temptation to accept must have been powerful. She was already an 'old maid' according to the standards of her day, when girls were thought to have done well if they married in their teens and those in their twenties were considered to have lost the bloom of youth. With the pressure to marry so intense in her society because unmarried daughters were a financial burden on their parents, her renunciation was courageous indeed.

Younger sons of good family, in Holy Orders and with no money, were plentiful in her circle: single men in possession of a good fortune were not. In Maria Edgeworth's novel *Patronage*, published in 1814, a book Jane Austen read, a husband's income of £2,000 entitled a woman to be called 'pretty well married' but to rate as 'very well married' she would need a man with £10,000 a year.

The gap between a five-figure income and the actual stipends earned by well-born, well-educated clergymen, the younger sons with no inheritance to look forward to, was enormous. A contemporary of Jane's described such young men as being 'shoved off about the world to scramble through it as best they could with nothing but their good blood to help them.' These were the potential husbands within Jane Austen's own reasonable expectations. To be addressed by a landowner was beyond them.

Cassandra later destroyed the letters covering the Bigg-Wither episode, but not before letting her niece Catherine Hubback, Frank's daughter, read them. Catherine gathered that Jane was much relieved when the affair was over, and that she had never been attached to him. Harris Bigg-Wither two years later married Anne Howe Frith, an Isle of Wight heiress, who bore him five sons and five daughters. Jane's letters between 1801 and 1804 are missing, either because they dealt with this matter which Cassandra considered private, or because Jane was generally disgruntled and Cassandra did not wish to be reminded of her sister's unhappiness. She was living at the time in Bath, where she was never even moderately contented.

It was a commonplace of the time that what was openly known as the 'marriage market' was overstocked with well-dressed spinsters, trapped at home with their parents with no hope of escape until an offer of marriage turned up. As Charlotte Lucas says in *Pride and Prejudice*, 'I am not romantic, you know. I never was. All I ask is a comfortable home.' There were many like her, whose hopes were doomed to disappointment. The problems of the Bennet girls in *Pride and Prejudice*, of embarrassing relatives and minimal dowries, are solved in fairy-tale fashion. In real life their chances of marrying well would be small, and Mrs Bennet's anxieties, however foolishly expressed, represent social and economic realities.

Jane was fond of joking that she would like to marry the poet the Revd George Crabbe. According to her nephew James-Edward Austen-Leigh, she enjoyed Crabbe's work 'perhaps on account of a certain resemblance to herself in minute and highly finished detail'. Jane wrote when the death of Crabbe's wife was reported in 1813 that she had only just worked out from one of Crabbe's prefaces that he was married. 'Poor woman! I will comfort *him* as well as I can, but I do not undertake to be good to her children. She had better not leave any.' This was a mere fantasy. Jane never met Crabbe.

Crabbe's verses depict the lot of the rural poor with grim realism. They were written as a corrective to the fashion for romanticizing cottagers' lives. Although Jane Austen does not foreground the poor in her books, they were all around her. As befitted the parson's daughter she gave them presents of clothing. She reported to Cassandra on 24 December 1798 that she had given 'a pair of worsted stockings to Mary Hutchins, Dame Kew, Mary Steevens and Dame Staples; a shift to Hannah Staples, and a shawl to Betty Dawkins; amounting in all to about half a guinea'. She was overjoyed when her prosperous brother Edward gave her £10 to spend among the cottagers at Chawton, her final home, and when his adoptive mother bequeathed £20 'to the parish'.

Just before she died, having reached the age of forty as a single woman, Jane, supported mainly by the charity of her brothers, wrote to her niece Fanny Knight, not yet transformed into Lady Knatchbull, 'Single women have a dreadful propensity for being poor – which is one very strong argument in favour of matrimony.' Earlier, though, she had warned Fanny that nothing could compare with the misery of being bound without love. Jane had seen a loving marriage between her own parents and knew its worth. Anything was better than marrying without affection, but on the other hand, as she was at pains to point out to Fanny, want of money, and sheets turned sides to middle were not inviting prospects. She comforted Fanny, who was in her mid-twenties and still single, by telling her not to be in a hurry: the right man would come at last.

The choice of the right marriage partner was crucial, for marriage was all but indissoluble. Divorce was possible only for the very rich, as it needed an Act of Parliament. Husbands could divorce unfaithful wives, as Mr Rushworth in *Mansfield Park* does after Maria runs away with Henry Crawford, but it was difficult for a wife, however ill treated, to be legally freed from a violent or dissolute husband. Once married, wives who had chosen unwisely had to put up with it.

Unless a separate 'settlement' was made upon her, as soon as she married all a woman's property and money became her husband's. Yet risky as marriage was, it was considered better than single life. A man could not honourably break an engagement: only the lady herself could 'release' him from it. A man who broke his engagement was inviting legal action by the lady for breach of promise. Loss of marriage prospects was taken seriously, as lifelong maintenance and enhanced social status were at stake.

Jane Austen was acutely aware of these problems long before they impinged on her personally. In her teens she began a novel called *Catharine, or the Bower* which starkly depicts the plight of women in her day. The heroine is an orphan living with a repressive aunt. Her only friends are the daughters of a neighbouring clergyman, reduced after his death to dependence on rich and stingy relatives. The elder has been shipped off, like Jane's aunt Philadelphia Hancock, to India with the 'fishing fleet' and is 'splendidly but unhappily married'. The younger has been taken by a titled relative as 'companion' to her daughters, an uncongenial and dependent position. The new parson and his wife are haughty and quarrelsome, well-born and ill-mannered. They had hoped for better things than a country living. The monotony of Catharine's existence is broken by a visit from a fashionable family with a snobbish, brainless daughter whose shallow accomplishments 'were now to be displayed and in a few years entirely neglected'.

This girl, who prefigures Isabella Thorpe in *Northanger Abbey*, imagines vaguely that it must be delightful to voyage 'to Bengal or Barbadoes or wherever it is', and be 'married soon after one's arrival to a very charming Man immensely rich'. Catharine's bower is the only place where she can think and pull herself together when she is depressed. Its symbolism is obvious. Jane did not finish this early story, but it shows the teenage writer able to see social situations with clarity. Another early work, *The Three Sisters*, written when she was about sixteen, deals with mercenary marriages.

Despite her youthful popularity, all Jane's relationships with men came to nothing. Her obstinate heart forbade her to marry except for love. The flippant, flirtatious teenager faded into a middle-aged maiden aunt, dowdy not because she chose to be – indeed she loved clothes – but because she was poor. In a society where dowries were looked for, her poverty may well have been one of the reasons she never married. The plots of Jane's novels and her refusal to marry for convenience make it plain that she believed in marrying for love, but she knew that in the real world most men had a way of falling in love with girls who brought money with them.

We have reason to be selfishly grateful that Jane Austen never did attach a husband. With a growing family she would have found it hard to concentrate, even if she had married a rich man. If she had married a younger son or a clergyman she would have been equally poor and rather more harassed. Instead of direct descendants, she left us the inimitable novels.

7

Brothers and Their Wives

JAMES, JANE'S ELDEST brother, followed his father to St John's College, Oxford, before becoming ordained. Clever and studious, his intellectual precocity enabled him to matriculate, that is to enter the university, at fourteen. His great-uncle the Master of Balliol invited him to dine. Dr Theophilus Leigh was by then well over eighty. At that time Oxford and Cambridge undergraduates wore academic dress, square tasselled caps and gowns, at all times in public. James, entering his great-uncle's lodgings, was taking off his gown as if it were an overcoat, as he did not yet know the etiquette. 'Young man,' said Dr Leigh, 'You need not strip. We are not going to fight.'

In 1786 James spent a year in Europe, visiting France, Spain and Holland. He was the most learned and scholarly of the Austen children.

James's first curacy was at Stoke Charity and his second at Overton, both within a few miles of Steventon. He kept his university terms, popping down at intervals to perform his clerical duties. Living in the small vicarage house at Overton, he went hunting with the Kempshott pack. At that time Kempshott Park was rented by the Prince of Wales (later Prince Regent and King George IV of England) and James was often in the field with royalty. Another hunting man, Mr William John Chute of the Vyne, presented James to the vicarage of Sherborne St John in 1792. While at Overton he did duty at nearby Laverstoke, where he met and fell in love with Anne Mathew, whose father, General Mathew, rented the manor house. James married in

1792, his father performing the ceremony. The bride's mother was Lady Jane Bertie, daughter of the second Duke of Ancaster and sister of the third. James was twenty-seven. A country clergyman was not much of a catch, but Anne was well over thirty with 'a great deal of nose', so the General accepted James as son-in-law and allowed the young couple £100 a year. James had, after all, expectations from James Leigh-Perrot. The Leigh family found him a living at Cubbington, Warwickshire. This brought the couple's combined income up to £300 a year. Although nominally vicar, James never went to Cubbington, but employed a curate. He and Anne lived for a while at Court House, Ovington, but James needed a permanent home to take his pale, slender bride to, so his kind father employed him as curate at Deane and allowed him to live there rent free.

This was generous, as the Deane house had previously been let to a tenant, Mrs Martha Lloyd. Mrs Lloyd and her unmarried daughters then moved to Ibthorpe (pronounced Ibthrop), about sixteen miles from Steventon and not far from Andover. Mrs Lloyd, a clergy widow, was the mother of Martha and Mary, close friends of Jane. Eliza Lloyd had married her cousin the Revd Fulwar Craven Fowle, who with his brother Tom (Cassandra's fiancé) had been one of George Austen's pupils. When Mrs Lloyd, Martha and Mary left Deane, Jane made Mary Lloyd a tiny 'housewife' or sewing set as a leaving present. This was a very small bag of white cotton with gold and black zigzag stripes. Inside was a strip of fabric pierced by tiny needles and fine thread. On a scrap of paper Jane had written:

This little bag I hope will prove
To be not vainly made,
For if you thread and needle want,
It will afford you aid.
And as we are about to part,
'Twill serve another end,
For when you look upon the bag,
You'll recollect your friend.

Settled at Deane, James and Anne lived above their modest means: she kept a close carriage and he a pack of harriers. They had spent £200 on furnishing the house.

Great-uncle Francis Austen had died the previous year, aged ninety-three, and left £500 to each of his nephews. Now Charles had left home for the Naval Academy the pressure was less and Mr Austen cut down on the number of his pupils. Inflation meant that his charges had almost doubled, and were now £65 a year. Jane and Cassandra could have a spare bedroom next to theirs as a sitting room, always called the dressing room. The walls were cheaply papered and the furniture scanty, but Jane preferred it to the parlour downstairs as being more comfortable and elegant. She also now had a pianoforte. The room housed the sisters' oval workboxes in Tonbridge-ware with ivory barrels holding reels of sewing silk.

James and his parents lived not much more than a mile apart and he liked to drop in nearly every day. Anne, after a pregnancy which forced her to spend whole days in bed, gave birth safely to a daughter, Anna. Her mother-in-law, presumably summoned by James, got out of bed in the middle of the night and walked along the muddy lane by the light of a lantern to help her granddaughter into the world. Mrs Austen was a practical woman. Anna's godparents were her great-uncle and great-aunt, the Duke of Ancaster and his Duchess, and her grand-father, General Mathew, who gave the sum of twenty guineas to be divided between the nurse and the maidservants. Seventeen-year-old Jane, now aunt both to James's daughter, Anna, and Edward's daughter, Fanny, wrote messages to her new nieces. When France declared war on Britain in February 1793 the generous General bought James an army chaplaincy. It was not intended that James should go to war, but that he should draw a salary and pay a substitute.

James's wife died suddenly when his little girl was two years old. Anne ate her dinner normally but collapsed afterwards. An emetic was administered but it did not help. She lived only a few hours and was dead before the doctor arrived. He told James there was some internal 'adhesion of the liver' which he thought had probably rup-tured.

The young widower's grief was intensified because little Anna wailed constantly for 'Mama'. James, overwhelmed and feeling help-less, sent the child to his mother and sisters to bring up. Anna loved her aunts Jane and Cassandra and left affectionate reminiscences of them. They bought her a little cherrywood chair. Her grandfather

Mathew was very proud of her and once whisked the little girl away from her aunts to a grown-up dinner party.

After an inconclusive attraction to his cousin Eliza de Feuillide, who preferred her 'dear liberty and dearer flirtation' as she put it after she was widowed in 1794, James was married again in 1797 to Mrs Lloyd's daughter Mary, whose face was seamed with smallpox.

Eliza de Feuillide wrote to her cousin Phila Walter that Jane was much pleased with James's match, which was natural as Jane had known Mary and liked her for a long while. 'Despite being neither rich nor handsome, she is sensible and good-humoured,' said Eliza. Not only were the Lloyds old family friends but Mary was cousin to Tom Fowle, who was going to marry Cassandra and who had been promised a living in Shropshire by Lord Craven. The ties of love and friendship were being satisfactorily bound.

Mrs Austen wrote Mary a letter of welcome, 'I look forward to you as a real comfort to me in my old age, when Cassandra is gone into Shropshire and Jane – the Lord knows where.'

Jane grew to like Mary less as time passed, judging her to be grasping and manipulative, referring to her coolly in letters as 'Mrs JA'. Mary could be generous with time and trouble but was extremely careful with money. General Mathew for the sake of his granddaughter Anna continued to allow James the £100 a year he had given with his daughter Anne. Mary never overcame her fear of the General and doubtless was touchy about having taken his daughter's place as James's wife. Mary was not a secure or happy person. She may have felt, like other second wives, that she could not compete with James's first wife; Anne had been so aristocratic. Mary had a sharp, abrupt way with her and a hot temper even with her own children. Although she was not actively cruel to Anna she had no crumbs of affection to spare, and favoured her own children, James-Edward and Caroline.

James was careful not to annoy Mary by making a fuss of his elder daughter and so remained remote from the child. He was, like many fathers, chiefly interested in his son. Anna's father never mentioned his first wife and there was no portrait of her. All the child could remember was a pale, slim lady in white. Although intelligent and warmhearted, Anna was largely disregarded. Not surprisingly she grew up moody and difficult. The poor child's life was twice disrupted, first by her mother's death and then at four years old by her removal from her doting grandmother and aunts to a stepmother's care. Understandably she made rebellious gestures. She horrified her family in 1808, when she was sixteen, by having her hair chopped off like a boy's, which they looked on as a mutilation, though in fact Anna was merely following the latest fashion and her relatives had not caught up. At the same early age, anxious to assert her independence, she became engaged to marry, though she later broke it off. Anna never really accepted her step-mother. When in disgrace at home Anna sometimes took refuge with her aunts. Aunt Jane wrote down stories at Anna's dictation before the little girl could write.

James soon reverted to his former habit of visiting his parents be-fore breakfast, despite Mary's reproaches. She was jealous and suspi-cious. Heavily pregnant with her first child, she was suffering from rheumatism and longing to give birth. Mary's sister Martha was with them. Mary had hired an inexperienced girl 'to be her scrub' but James feared the girl would not be strong enough for the work.

Jane's letter of 17 November 1798 tells Cassandra, 'I believe I never told you that Mrs Coulthard and Anne, late of Manydown, are both dead, and both died in childbed. We have not regaled Mary with this news.' Next day Jane added that Mary's baby had been born the previous night, a fine little boy, and everything was going on very well. Anna had been packed out of the way to the Lloyds at Ibthorpe.

When Jane visited James's new son the baby was asleep but she was told that his eyes were large, dark and handsome. Jane was critical of Mary's domestic arrangements: she was untidy, she had no dressing gown, her curtains were too thin. Seeing all this, Jane shuddered that she had no ambition to have a baby herself. Was there an element of sour grapes?

This baby was to become the Revd James-Edward Austen-Leigh, known as 'Edward', a name confusingly shared by his uncle and that uncle's eldest son. Mr Austen-Leigh drew on the memories of his half-sister, Anna Austen Lefroy, and his younger sister, Caroline Austen, for his *Memoir*, when he was more than seventy years old and Vicar of Bray. He attempted when in his teens to write fiction and it was to him that

Jane's famous (though not entirely serious) letter about working on 'the little bit (two inches wide) of ivory' was written.

Edward, Jane's third brother, left home to live at Godmersham Park, where he had long been a favourite, when he was sixteen and Jane was eight. Instead of going to Oxford like his brothers James and Henry he was sent on the Grand Tour, a liberal education for rich young men. He may have spent some time at a German university, though his weakness in Latin suggests that he had no particular gift for languages. Travel and sightseeing probably suited him better than a rigorous course of study. The only one among the brothers who did not care for field sports, although he could easily have afforded to practise them, he found his greatest pleasure in attending to his estates. We are reminded of Mr Knightley in *Emma*. Edward's adoptive mother, old Mrs Knight, relinquished her estate to him four years after her husband died in 1794, keeping only £2,000 a year for herself.

Edward changed his name to Knight in 1812 after Mrs Knight, who had always been most affectionate and generous to him, died. Jane wrote of him: 'I know of no one more deserving of happiness.' She rejoiced that his income was so good, she told Cassandra, adding wistfully that she was as glad as she could be 'at anybody's being rich but you and me'. It cannot have been easy to see one brother elevated to wealth while she was eking out a meagre allowance and other brothers were struggling.

When Jane stayed at Godmersham she luxuriated in ease and elegance and could not imagine anybody being less than happy there. Guests drank French wines which Jane appreciated as being better than the mead, orange wine and spruce beer made in her home at Steventon. Cassandra was the petted favourite at Godmersham as she and Edward were dear to each other. It was when she was on these visits that she and Jane exchanged letters full of news.

Edward had been the first of the Austen brothers to marry. His bride was the beautiful Elizabeth Bridges, daughter of Sir Brook Bridges, baronet. They were a fertile family: Elizabeth was one of thirteen children and she gave birth to eleven. The eldest daughter of Edward and Elizabeth was Fanny, born 1793 and Jane's favourite niece, who begged her spinster aunt for advice on marriage. The right man did come at last for Fanny, as her Aunt Jane had predicted, and at twenty-seven Fanny married Sir Edward Knatchbull, a morose widower twelve years older than herself with six children, and she bore him nine more.

In gentry and professional families the size of the Austens' it was taken for granted that one or two of the sons would enter the Church. Opportunities elsewhere were not numerous and provincial doctors and lawyers had low status. George Austen sent his first and fourth sons, James and Henry, to Oxford so they could become clergymen, though Frank, who was deeply religious, might have been a wiser choice. Frank, after a spell ashore at Ramsgate, when he was raising a corps of 'sea-fencibles' against invasion in 1815, was known in the navy as 'the officer who knelt in church'.

By the time Henry graduated from Oxford war was raging against France. He was not old enough to be ordained so he joined the Oxfordshire militia, the equivalent of today's Territorial Army, as lieutenant, rising to captain, paymaster and adjutant. He considered joining the regular army but became deputy receiver of taxes for Oxfordshire and had to visit that county several times. Henry eventually did go into the Church after the bank in which he was a partner failed and after the death of his wife. He had married in 1797 when Jane was twenty-one.

His wife was Eliza de Feuillide, widowed daughter of his father's sister Philadelphia Hancock. She was sophisticated, musical and dazzlingly pretty, with enormous eyes and a pointed elfin face surrounded by powdered curls. Eliza may just possibly have been the child of her godfather Warren Hastings, through whom she inherited the £10,000 he had given her mother's husband. She was ten years older than Henry but as his first cousin knew him and the rest of the family intimately.

In 1787 Henry had stayed at Eliza's smart house in London's Orchard Street. He was only sixteen and she was a glamorous society matron but it is probable that he first fell in love with her and with her lifestyle at that time. He was already six feet tall, handsome and personable. Ten years later they were married.

Eliza shrewdly judged that Henry was better suited to be a soldier than a parson. On her second marriage she wrote telling her godfather Warren Hastings that Henry had been for some time in possession of a comfortable income. She had resisted him for two years but was now persuaded by his excellent temper and understanding, his affection for herself and for her little boy, together with his skilled management of her finances. She had also resisted Henry's by then widowed elder brother James. In 1801 Henry gave up the army and the couple lived in Upper Berkeley Street, Portman Square, 'quite in style' as her envious cousin Phila Walter, still single herself, put it. Eliza was enchanting, though she was frivolous and flirtatious and undomesticated, for which Phila could not forgive her. Eliza the socialite had married not one but two attractive husbands while Phila was still single. Eliza, whose son had meanwhile died, was afraid that Henry had a galloping consumption but he outlived her.

Eliza's life had been sensational. Carefully educated with a French companion and sent to the Continent at fifteen after her father died, she learned to speak the language like a native. In 1780 she visited Versailles and watched King Louis XVI of France and his Queen Marie Antoinette at dinner. Through her eyes we get a first-hand glimpse of the *ancien régime*. The Queen, she wrote to her cousin Phila, was a fine woman with a beautiful complexion and elegantly dressed:

> She had on a corset and petticoat of pale green lutestring covered with a transparent silver gauze, the petticoat and sleeves puckered and confined in different places with large bunches of roses, and an amazing large bouquet of white lilac. The same flower, together with gauze, feathers, ribbon and diamonds intermixed with her hair. Her neck was entirely uncovered and ornamented by a most beautiful chain of diamonds, of which she had likewise very fine bracelets; she was without gloves, I suppose to show her hands and arms, which are without exception the whitest and most beautiful I ever beheld. The King was plainly dressed; he had however likewise some fine diamonds. The rest of the royal family were very elegant . . . There is perhaps no place in the world where dress is so well understood and carried to so great a perfection as in Paris . . . Powder is universally worn . . . heads in general look as if they had been dipped in a meal-tub.

In her next letter Eliza insisted the Queen's complexion was natural. 'Rouge is, I acknowledge, much worn here, but not so universally as you imagine; no single ladies ever make use of it, and were they to do it, would be much disapproved of.' Later Eliza described the celebrations for the birth of the Dauphin in 1782, when the King and Queen appeared in clothes embroidered with jewels. The scene was just like the enchanted palaces in the *Arabian Nights*. In 1784 Eliza watched a pioneer ascent in a hot-air balloon. Eliza's life was vastly different from the lives of the Austens at Steventon. No wonder Henry was captivated by her.

Eliza's first husband was Count Jean Capotte de Feuillide, whom she married in 1781. During the honeymoon she had boasted to her cousin Phila Walter that he was amiable in both mind and person and 'literally adores me', although Eliza confessed that she was not in love with him. Eliza described herself as 'mistress of an easy fortune with the prospect of a very ample one . . . the advantages of rank and title, and a numerous and brilliant acquaintance'.

Only the last claim turned out to be true. The Count lived in hopes of getting hold of some property in due course. Meanwhile he was financially embarrassed. In 1784 he obtained a grant of 5,000 acres of marshland from the King on condition he drained it. The work was completed in a year and a half and building works were set in hand. Eliza's mother managed to stretch their £600 a year. The Count and Eliza lived in a rented château. Although Eliza described him in a letter as 'aristocratic and *royaliste*' there is some doubt about his title. If she was disillusioned she never admitted it.

When accused in 1794 he tried to save his skin by claiming, perhaps truthfully, to be of humble origin but was not believed. He had returned to France in 1788 under the impression that the seething turmoil was beginning to calm down but Eliza stayed in England because her little boy was sickly (indeed, malicious Phila Walter thought him retarded and hoped he was not going to be like 'poor George Austen'), and because Eliza's mother, Philadelphia Hancock, was failing. The Bastille was stormed in 1789. In 1791 the Count returned to England for a brief while. A soldier, he received messages from France that he had overstayed his leave and that if he remained in England his property would be confiscated so he went home in a doomed attempt to save it.

Civil commotion had spread from France to England. After Eliza's husband left for Paris her carriage was caught in a London riot. A mob was demolishing houses and fighting mounted Guardsmen. 'The noise of the populace, the drawn swords and pointed bayonets of the Guards, the fragments of bricks and mortar thrown on every side, one of which had nearly killed my coachman, the firing at one end of the street . . . alarmed me,' she wrote to Phila.

Eliza's husband could not get away from Paris. In 1794 he attempted to bribe a witness who had accused the Marquise de Marboeuf of producing a famine by planting the wrong crops on her land. He and the Marquise were executed on the same day. Eliza, who had, it is said, been in France with her husband at the time, fled, according to family tradition, to the coast and safety in England along with French refugees, though this story seems too romantic.

Widowed Eliza showed an admirable toughness and coolness. After the Peace of Amiens she returned with Henry, by then her second husband, to France in March 1802 hoping to recover some of the Count's property. Napoleon Bonaparte, First Consul of France, had ordered that all English travellers should be arrested. Eliza's perfect French enabled her and Henry to escape undetected. She dealt with the travel arrangements, telling people that her husband, muffled and bundled up in the back of the carriage, was a helpless invalid.

The story of her cousin's husband's fate left Jane Austen with a horror of France and of revolution. The family politics were Tory and Jane's values were in the main conservative.

After Eliza and Henry came back to England they settled in London and Henry became a banker. Eliza died in 1813. Two years after her death Tilson's bank, in which Henry was a partner, collapsed. Henry followed his father and eldest brother into the Church, taking curacies at Farnham and Bentley near Alton in his native Hampshire. He was witty and wrote good sermons but never fulfilled his early promise. At nearly fifty he married Eleanor Jackson. He never had any children.

In later life he grew pompous and the word-picture he left of his sister Jane is a whitewash, describing a woman too good to be true. He says her real characteristics were 'cheerfulness, sensibility and benevolence' when we know that she was often fighting depression and anger and could be detached to the point of malice. 'Pictures of perfection make me sick and wicked,' she said. As for 'sensibility', she wrote a novel which illustrates the eighteenth-century conviction that excessive emotional indulgence can be dangerous. But Henry and Jane were very close, which may be the reason behind his rose-tinted view of her.

8

The Butterfly and the Poker

TWELVE YEARS YOUNGER than Jane Austen, another writer, largely forgotten in our own day but celebrated in hers, was Mary Russell Mitford, author of *Our Village*, a series of fictionalized sketches of country life. Her mother, Miss Russell, later Mrs Mitford, knew the Austen family at Steventon when Jane was a child, and Miss Russell's father was Rector of the neighbouring parish of Ashe. Her daughter, Miss Mitford, wrote in *Our Village*, 'Nothing is so delightful as to sit down in a country village in one of Miss Austen's delicious novels,' but in her letters she allowed herself to be more acid. She reported that her mother had described the young Jane Austen as 'the prettiest, silliest, most affected husband-hunting butterfly she ever remembers'. Cattily she describes Jane as 'an old maid (I beg her pardon – I mean a young lady).' Jane was forty at the time.

Jane's letters when a young woman certainly show a healthy streak of frivolity. There is some dispute as to whether Mrs Mitford, who left the district when Jane was eleven, ever saw Jane Austen after she reached her teens or whether Mrs Mitford relied on gossip. Both she and her daughter were plain and dumpy, which may have coloured the mother's judgment.

Jane mixed with landed neighbours and did her best to conform to their lifestyle, to be a socialite, enjoying parties and dances from her mid-teens onwards. A graceful and accomplished dancer, she was proud of being able to dance all evening without fatigue. She objected to partners who danced badly. As she grew older partners were less easy to find. She sometimes reported sitting out without being asked to dance, and pretended she did not mind.

Miss Mitford added:

> A friend of mine who visits her now, says that she has stiffened into the most perpendicular, precise, taciturn piece of 'single blessedness' that ever existed, and that, till *Pride and Prejudice* showed what a precious gem was hidden in that unbending case, she was no more regarded in society than a poker or a firescreen, or any other thin, upright piece of wood or iron that fills the corner in peace and quietness. The case is very different now: she is still a poker – but a poker of whom everyone is afraid.

One wonders why Miss Mitford's informant Miss Hinton bothered to visit Jane at all when we learn that Miss Hinton's brother-in-law was contesting Jane's brother Edward's rights of inheritance from his adoptive family, the Knights. The Hintons, being near neighbours, kept up a pretence of civility. If Jane was reserved with this false friend she was right to be wary. Excessive familiarity, gush and superlatives were considered vulgar, as we see from the empty-headed characters in the novels. Jane was brought up in the English stoical tradition in which one kept one's griefs to oneself and presented a cheerful face to the world. It was selfish to burden others with personal problems. To do so was to fail in consideration, in what Jane called 'good breeding' and 'decorum'. As she grew older, Jane grew more and more reserved with strangers though still warm and lively within the family. Her brother Frank described her as cheerful when she was a young woman. He admitted she had sometimes been accused of haughtiness but said her wit and drollery kept those close to her in fits of laughter. Her brother Henry, who loved his sister and knew her better than most, wrote after her death: 'She was tranquil without reserve or stiffness; and communicative without intrusion or self-sufficiency.' Whatever false picture Henry may have painted of Jane elsewhere, at least here he can be thought to be reliable.

Miss Mitford, while finding Jane's novels 'delicious', originally thought *Pride and Prejudice* wanting in elegance. In her opinion, only an entire want of taste could produce a heroine so pert and so worldly as Elizabeth Bennet. 'Worldly' was a word of condemnation used by people who prided themselves on being strictly religious.

There is some evidence that Jane's own religious and moral principles grew more rigid as she aged. If she did end up like a poker, she enjoyed her time as a social butterfly, going to dances in private houses and monthly assemblies at the Town Hall in Basingstoke. Entertainments were few, and people travelled considerable distances over rough tracks in order to enjoy themselves in company. In the absence of street lighting, balls were given for preference on moonlit nights. As the daughter of a clergyman with a well-born wife, Jane mixed occasionally with the aristocratic Bolton, Dorchester and Portsmouth families, and was invited to grand balls in Kent as an appendage of her rich brother Edward.

By her late thirties Jane could smile at social butterflies herself: 'Dear Mrs Digweed! I cannot bear that she should not be foolishly happy after a ball.' In her early twenties, balls provided her with activity, social contacts and gossip. A ball was not necessarily a grand affair: the word could be applied to a small private dance. When she was twenty-three, Jane wrote to her sister about a ball where there were thirty-one people, only eleven of them female. She listed her partners. Another time she reported that a ball had 'nearly sixty people' and sometimes there were seventeen couples, but 'there was commonly a couple of ladies standing up together.' This meant partnering each other, a desperate expedient. Jane Austen loved dancing and flirting.

On the evidence of *Northanger Abbey* (written in the late 1790s), it was the custom to dance two dances and then change partners. Two dances meant the twice up and down of the minuet which was danced at the beginning of every formal ball. It was slow and solemn, dignified rather than jolly, incorporating formal bows and curtsies, moving with measured paces, forwards, backwards and sideways, with complicated gyrations. One couple would open the ball. Not everybody was confident of his or her skill and ladies indicated their willingness to perform by wearing a particular kind of lappet on their headdresses.

The dances were hornpipes, quadrilles, cotillions and minuets, country dances, Scotch jigs and reels. Some were danced lengthwise, which kept the gentlemen and ladies in separate rows, offering small opportunity for flirtation, or even conversation. Some were square dances and others round dances. At the Coles' party in *Emma*, published 1816, a space is cleared for dancing:

> Mrs Weston, capital in her country dances, was seated, and beginning an irresistible waltz; and Frank Churchill, coming up with the most becoming gallantry to Emma, had secured her hand and led her up to the top.

The most important lady present had the honour of starting off the dance: later in the story Emma has to give way to the newly married Mrs Elton. Quarrels about precedence were commonplace. Although the most distinguished lady was supposed to lead, embarrassment was sometimes avoided by drawing lots. Partners were sometimes chosen by the same method.

The waltz was invented in Vienna in the late 1780s, swept through France, and arrived in England about 1812. Old dances were performed to the new tunes. A book published the same year as *Emma* gives instructions for 'that new and elegant system of dancing called Country dance Waltzing or Waltz Country dancing', whereby figures were still performed in sets. Lessons in the new dance were advertised. The tunes arrived before the new way of dancing did.

Lord Byron wrote a long poem to the new dance, which he rhymes with 'salts':

> Morals and minuets, Virtue and her stays,
> And tell-tale powder, all have had their days,

he says, summing up social trends.

> Endearing Waltz! – to thy more melting tune
> Bow Irish jig, and ancient rigadoon.
> Scotch reels, avaunt! and country-dance forego
> Your future claims to each fantastic toe!
> Waltz – Waltz alone – both legs and arms demands,
> Liberal of feet, and lavish of her hands;
> Hands which may freely range in public sight
> Where ne'er before – but pray 'put out the light' . . .
> The breast thus publicly resigned to man,
> In private may resist him – if it can.

The poet suggests that such heated intimacy on the dance floor is likely to lead to promiscuity. As Byron's poem emphasizes, the 'seductive' and even 'voluptuous' waltz was considered exciting, even immoral, because it offered unprecedented opportunities for grasping a partner round the waist, instead of leading her by the hand.

A waist without stays, according to the fashion of the day, was erotic, and at this time women were throwing their stays away. The natural waistline was abandoned until 1818, the year after Jane Austen died. According to Byron, morals were abandoned as well. At the turn of the century women's clothing became loose, comfortable and flimsy. Fashion victims damped their muslin gowns to make them cling to the body. They were starting to wear knickers, as men gave up knee-breeches for trousers. Rigid boned bodices ('stays') and hooped skirts gave way in the 1790s to high-waisted straight dresses modelled on Greek and Roman styles and to our eyes remarkably like maternity dresses.

Wigs and hair-powder had disappeared, except for the stubbornly old-fashioned, and loose curls under large hats became fashionable. Heavy brocades went out of style and instead muslin (fine cotton) was widely popular, plain or patterned: the spotted, the sprigged, the mull (plain) or the jackonet (slightly heavier than mull) and the tamboured (embroidered), as we learn from *Northanger Abbey*. White was considered the most elegant colour: in *Mansfield Park* Edmund Bertram praises his cousin Fanny's taste when she wears white to a ball. The lower orders, though, were not encouraged to ape their betters. In the same novel, the young people's aunt Mrs Norris is gratified to learn that two housemaids had been sacked for presuming to wear white gowns.

Although in Jane's fictions women who think about nothing but clothes are laughed at, she took a keen and normal interest in bonnets and gowns and pelisses (overcoats) herself, the more so as a new dress was a rare and important purchase, involving serious consideration and planning, as cash was always short.

9

Dancing and Shopping, 1796–1800

VEN IF SHE was as socially invisible as Miss Mitford in-sisted, Jane had the honour of opening an evening's dancing in Kent with Edward Bridges when she was twenty. At a small private hop ladies took turns to play the pianoforte and at this party Lady Bridges, her daughter Elizabeth and an Anne Finch played for different dances. Miss Finch was the unmarried sister of George Finch-Hatton of Eastwell, a nearby estate. Jane was mixing with the landed gentry, but agonized whether to tip the servant five shillings or half a guinea.

In September 1796 Jane visited her brother Edward and his wife, who were living at Rowling, part of the estate of Goodnestone Park in Kent, then belonging to Elizabeth's brother, where their first four children were born. Poignantly, in the event, Jane talked to friends of Cassandra's engagement. This was when she went to Bifrons and contemplated with a melancholy pleasure the abode of Edward Taylor.

Frank, who was with her, received good news: he had been appointed to serve on the *Triton*, a new 32-gun frigate commanded by Captain John Gore, and so had to leave for London. Jane was left hoping her father would fetch her home from London as she could not stay in the city alone. She had small hope that Henry would be coming her way. She wanted to travel by stagecoach but Frank would not let her.

We do not know how she eventually got home, as letters for the next eighteen months are missing. It was during this period that Cassandra's fiancé died and was mourned and Cassandra must have felt the letters too personal and painful to keep. However the journey was managed, it would have been uncomfortable and probably slow. The usual speed of travel was six or seven miles an hour and the only vehicles were drawn by horses. When John Thorpe in *Northanger Abbey* boasts that he defies any man in England to 'make my horse go less than ten miles an hour in harness', he is exaggerating. The argument that follows his claim suggests that the actual speed on the twenty-three-mile journey from Tetbury to Bath was more like six and a half. Jane writes of covering the distance between Sittingbourne and Rochester in Kent, some eleven miles, in an hour and a quarter but she says the driver drove exceptionally fast. The next stage to Dartford, a slightly shorter distance, on a muddy road and with indifferent horses took them just over two and a half hours. The journey from London to Godmersham in East Kent in 1808 took ten and a half hours. Mr Darcy in *Pride and Prejudice* says fifty miles on a good road should not take more than a morning, but morning meant from breakfast at ten o'clock till dinner time in the late afternoon or evening. Writing in 1814 to her niece Anna who was trying to write novels, Jane Austen advised her that characters had to be two days going from Dawlish to Bath, as they were a hundred miles apart.

It was around this time that the sisters, never particularly well dressed because lacking money, in the opinion of younger members of the family adopted the style of middle age unnecessarily soon. Cassandra and Jane took to caps, then worn by married women, widows and ageing spinsters, in their early twenties. This was not due to carelessness, as they were both fussy about neatness, but because Jane preferred wearing a cap to the bother of hairdressing. In a letter to her sister she says her hair is not much trouble except for washing and cutting. She wore it plaited and pinned up at the back. Hair was arranged at home, though for special occasions, such as the dances which made up so important a part of social life, a maid might be called upon. Anne ('Nanny') Littleworth attended to Jane's hair when, aged twenty-three, she went off to a ball. Jane never had a personal maid of her own.

Anne worked for Jane's parents as a general servant and was

married to brother James's coachman. Jane spells the name 'Littlewart', probably the way it was pronounced. When 'Nanny' was ill in bed with fever and a pain in her side the Austens were forced to employ char-women. Eventually they found a new maid whom they were determined to like, though she would have to be taught about dairy work. She was a good cook, was strong, and claimed to be a good needlewoman. Clearly a servant in a modest household had to be versatile.

Three days after her twenty-third birthday Jane grumbled that the forthcoming ball in Hampshire would be 'stupid': people were get-ting 'so horribly poor and economical in this part of the world' that she had no patience with them. Kent was 'the only place for happiness' as 'everybody' was rich there. A new acquaintance was agreeable but, per-versely, Jane found this irritating: she didn't want people to be too agreeable because she couldn't be bothered to like them too much. She was growing restless. Her eyes were becoming weaker and she eventu-ally needed spectacles. When she was unable to read or sew she prac-tised her music. Life was passing her by.

Jane and Cassandra had their six-monthly allowance of ten pounds each to spend and Jane was planning new winter clothes. She had bor-rowed the trimming for a cap from Cassandra while Cassandra was away. She put a narrow thread of silver round it twice without any bow and instead of the black military feather suggested by Cassandra planned to put in a coquelicot (poppy red) one instead.

In January 1799 Jane went with her brother Charles, who only just managed to be home in time, to Lord Dorchester's ball at Kemp-shott Park. Charles enjoyed as much social life as he could when he was on shore and Jane manoeuvred to get him invitations to balls at great houses where the middle classes were occasionally allowed in. But of-ten his naval duties prevented his attendance.

Jane decided against her white satin cap and borrowed a fashion-able 'Mamelouc' cap, a kind of fez with a trailing scarf, from James's wife Mary, who had been given it by her cousin Charles Fowle but thought it too smart for a country parson's wife. The Battle of the Nile in 1798 had made everything connected with Egypt all the rage. Con-temporary fashion plates showed Mamelouc cloaks and robes in flow-ing red cloth. Hats were decorated with 'Nelson rose feathers'. The very smartest ladies wore green morocco slippers bound with yellow and laced with crocodile-coloured ribbon. Jane wore her green shoes and took her white fan. A provincial lady, Jane delighted in being up to date.

She spent the evening chiefly among the Bigg sisters of Manydown and their party, but despite her fashionable get-up was rarely asked to dance. Who was she, after all, however grand her mother's antecedents, but Parson Austen's younger daughter, a girl with no fortune except her still-hidden talent? A good-looking officer of the Cheshires, people told Jane, wanted very much to be introduced to her but to her regret did not bother to put this wish into effect. Lord Bolton's eldest son was such a bad dancer that though he politely asked her Jane preferred to sit out. She stayed with Martha Lloyd at Deane. Jane and Martha shared the bed and talked till two in the morning while the baby James-Edward and his nurse made do with the floor.

The next ball Jane went to was a couple of weeks later with only eight couples in the room, and twenty-three people altogether, including the vulgar Jervoises, a neighbouring family, and the noisy Terrys. Charles was by then at Deal, having been made second lieutenant. He had been home for something more than a week. Now that he no longer powdered his hair and had it cut short, following the new fashion, he was agreed to be handsome. The *Tamar* was in the Downs and Charles, returning to Deal, was rather hoping to be too late for her before she sailed so he might get a better station. He took one of the night coaches and Jane would have liked to go with him but did not want to come back by herself. She dreamed of going part of the way and dropping in at Godmersham, now Edward's home.

Jane and Cassandra went occasionally to visit their maternal uncle James Leigh-Perrot and his wife in Bath. Jane wrote an early version of *Northanger Abbey*, set in that city, before she went to live there in 1801.

In May 1799 she and her mother, together with Edward and Elizabeth and two of their five children, went to Bath for four weeks and five days, three months before Mrs Leigh-Perrot's unfortunate experience over the piece of lace. They travelled by sound roads and had good horses as far as Devizes, where at five o'clock they sat down to asparagus, lobster and cheesecakes. Jane took an endearing pleasure in her food. The rest of the journey was less comfortable. It was raining when they arrived and their first view of Bath was gloomy. They stayed at 13 Queen Square, which they were very happy with despite dirty quilts. There was a picturesque view of the left side of Brock Street, broken by three Lombardy poplars in the garden of the last house in Queen's Parade. The landlady, Mrs Ann Bromley, was a fat woman in mourning black, and a little black kitten ran about the staircase.

On the way they called on the Leigh-Perrots, who lived at 1 Paragon, but Jane's uncle was not well enough to see them. Jane found their own situation far more cheerful than Paragon. The new papers were full of arrivals, so Jane looked forward to socializing and to public breakfasts every morning in Sydney Gardens, large pleasure grounds which had been laid out four years earlier. Edward was at Bath for his health, drinking and bathing in the waters and trying a new treatment, 'electricity', which Jane said was not expected to be of much use. She was convinced however that the effect of the waters could not be negative. Nevertheless a month later Edward's appetite had failed him and he felt nauseous and feverish. The family wondered whether these might be symptoms of gout, though the apothecary put them down to Edward's having eaten something that disagreed with him. Gout must have been on the family's minds; gouty Uncle James Leigh-Perrot had walked too far and could now only get about by sedan chair. Most of the time he sat at home with his swollen feet wrapped in flannel. Edward, though, was not too ill to have bought a pair of black coach horses for sixty guineas on the advice of his neighbour in Kent, Mr Evelyn.

The shops in Bath were tempting. Jane was delighted with a new lace-trimmed cloak and laid out money on Cassandra's behalf for one like it. Flowers, she noted, were very much worn but fruit was better. Jane had seen grapes, cherries, plums and apricots on hats. Elizabeth had a bunch of artificial strawberries. At the most expensive shops a plum or greengage cost three shillings, cherries and grapes about five. Jane went looking for something cheaper, which she did not find, but was consoled by the gift of a pretty hat from Elizabeth, half straw, half narrow purple ribbon. She persuaded herself that it was more natural to have flowers growing out of the head than fruit, anyway. Three shillings could buy four or five sprigs of flowers, after all.

Rarely indeed could Jane afford to buy what she hankered for. Usually shortage of cash forced her into compromises and she persuaded herself she liked them. Sometimes penny-pinching led her into making mistakes. Cassandra and Jane had intended buying a veil for their sister-in-law Mary as a joint gift and Jane found one for half a guinea but she made a bad bargain, for the muslin on closer inspection was thick, dirty and ragged. Hoping Cassandra would approve, she changed it for a black lace one that cost sixteen shillings, more than half as much again.

The letters from this trip tell of various trivial but entertaining incidents. She met a young bespectacled Mr Gould who had just gone to Oxford University, and was diverted to learn that he was under the impression that Fanny Burney's novel *Evelina* had been written by Dr Johnson.

Edward, Elizabeth, Jane and the children all went to a grand gala concert with fireworks, which surpassed Jane's expectations, and to the theatre to see *Bluebeard* and *The Birthday Day* by Kotzebue, German author of *Lovers' Vows*, the play rehearsed in *Mansfield Park*.

Edward's children dictated letters to their Aunt Cassandra, written out by Jane. Fanny, aged six, said she was very happy at Bath but would be glad to get home and see her three younger brothers, George, Henry and William. Had the chaffinch's nest in the garden hatched? She was afraid her papa was not much better for drinking the waters. Little Edward, a year younger, relayed a message from his grandmama, hoping that the white turkey was laying and that the black one had been eaten. He liked gooseberry pie and gooseberry pudding very much. Was it the same chaffinch's nest as the one they had seen before they came away? 'And pray will you send me another printed letter when you write to Aunt Jane again, if you like it,' he added.

Jane added a postscript of her own saying they would be back at Steventon the following Thursday for a very late dinner, later than her father would like but she wouldn't mind if he ate earlier. 'You must give us something very nice, for we are used to live well,' she wrote, for food was as absorbing an interest as were clothes.

In October 1800 Jane was writing from home to Cassandra at Godmersham. The weather was fine and warm for the time of year and Jane had been walking to visit relatives and friends. At Oakley Hall, seat of the neighbouring Bramston family, they ate sandwiches 'all over mustard' and admired Mr Bramston's porter [beer] and Mrs Bramston's transparencies. Mrs Augusta Bramston was in fact Mr Bramston's sister, unmarried, but dignified with the courtesy title of 'Mrs' in the eighteenth-century way. Jane was promised two roots of heartsease pansies, one purple and one yellow. Edward had given Jane some money for charitable spending. In the village they bought ten pairs of stockings and a shift for Betty Dawkins, one of Jane's poor. Betty wanted this undergarment more than the rug first thought of. Betty was duly grateful, sending Edward 'a sight of thanks' for his generosity.

In November 1800, Jane heard from Frank, who had written from the *Peterel* off Cyprus, having provisioned at Jaffa in Palestine, on 8 July 1800. He was off to Alexandria. Frank's career was advancing well. He had been made Commander of the *Peterel* in 1798. Jane had heard from Charles and was to send the shirts his sisters were sewing for him six at a time as they were finished. His ship, the *Endymion*, was waiting for orders. Mrs Austen was happily dressing a doll for Anna. James's wife Mary was delighted with a mangle, a gift from Edward, though the new maid had 'jilted' her and gone elsewhere. Mangles were new technology and a boon to women, who until then had to wring water by hand out of wet clothes and household linens. The mangle, which consists of rollers for squeezing water out of wet washing before it is hung out to dry, was invented the year Jane Austen was born.

Later that month Jane went to Lord Portsmouth's ball at Hurstbourne Park in a gown she had borrowed from her aunt Mrs Leigh-Perrot. The morning after, her hand shook from drinking too much wine. Jane danced only nine dances out of twelve and was prevented from dancing the rest purely for want of a partner. This neglect riled her. Her tone about the evening and the other women is bitchy.

One girl was 'vulgar, broad-featured'; the Misses Maitland, nieces of her late sister-in-law, Anne Mathew, were only 'prettyish', resembling poor dead Anne in having 'a good deal of nose'. 'There were very few beauties, and such as there were, were not very handsome . . . Mrs Blount was the only one much admired. She appeared exactly as she did in September, with the same broad face, diamond bandeau, white shoes, pink husband and fat neck.' A pregnant girl had danced away with great activity, having somehow got rid of a good part of her child and 'looking by no means very large'. Her husband, however, was ugly, 'uglier even than his cousin John' (the pleasant but plain John Warren). Jane reported that General Mathew, James's first father-in-law, had the gout and his daughter Mrs Maitland the jaundice. 'I was as civil to them as their bad breath would allow me,' writes Jane with a shudder of the three Debary sisters, whom she did not care for at all.

Charles was home, looking well and handsome. Jane had a new dress which she was more and more pleased with. Charles did not like it but Mr Austen and Mary did and Mrs Austen had come round to admitting it wasn't so ugly after all. So eventually did Charles. James liked it so much that if Cassandra was willing to sell hers in the same pattern Mary would buy it. Jane spent a pleasant day with the Lefroys at Ashe, where fourteen sat down to dinner in the study because the dining-room chimney had been damaged in a storm. There were whist and casino games. James and Mrs Bramston took turns at reading Dr Edward Jenner's pamphlet on the cowpox, while the Revd Henry Rice and Miss Lucy Lefroy, who were engaged to be married, 'made love'.

The celebrated Dr Jenner of Awre in Gloucestershire promoted vaccination with cowpox vaccine against the then scourge of smallpox. He was to meet Jane's niece Caroline in November 1813 at Cheltenham, then a spa (or as it was then called, a 'spaw') town where invalids went to drink mineral waters. Having some doubts that Caroline's previous vaccination was effective, he revaccinated her himself. 'I had therefore the honour,' wrote Caroline, 'of a second operation from the hands of the great discoverer himself; and at the end of the whole process, he pronounced it had been all right before.'

On 21 November another letter from Frank arrived dated 2 October. He wrote from Larnica in Cyprus after leaving Alexandria and was ignorant, as far as his sisters could tell, of his recent promotion to the rank of post-captain.

Around that time Cassandra went with Edward and Elizabeth to stay with Lewis and Fanny Cage of Milgate in Kent. Fanny was Elizabeth's sister. On the way home Cassandra spent three weeks with Henry and Eliza in London. Jane went to stay with Martha Lloyd at Ibthorpe. Martha had asked her to bring books. Jane replied sharply that she was coming to talk, not to read. She could do that at home. She was reading Robert Henry's *History of Great Britain*. A week later Cassandra was at Godmersham and Jane still at Ibthorpe.

At home, Steventon Rectory garden was being replanted with beech, ash and larch. The bank along the elm walk was sloped down to receive thorns and lilacs. There was a new suggestion for planting that part of the garden: should it be a little orchard, with apples, pears and cherries, or would larch, mountain ash and acacia be better? If Jane was bored with her life, she at least expected her home to be permanent until she should leave it for a home of her own. The weather was bad so even such 'desperate walkers' as Jane and Martha could not go for their usual promenades. They were cooped up all day from morning till night, literally as well as metaphorically. Life crawled on from day to day with little thought of change. The blow was yet to fall.

10

Exile, 1801

*L*ATE IN THE year 1800 George Austen decided to retire, leaving James to take care of the combined parishes of Steventon and Deane. Like Sir Walter Elliot in *Persuasion*, but in circumstances even less favourable, he removed to Bath. Jane was shattered at the loss of her beloved childhood home which, like the farm labourer's tied cottage, merely went with the job. Jane never lived in a secure home of her own. She had been away on the visit to Martha Lloyd and her mother at Ibthorpe, eighteen miles away, when the decision was arrived at but the information was delayed.

One day as Jane and Cassandra came in from a walk their mother announced with her usual briskness, 'Well, girls, it is all settled. We have decided to leave Steventon and go to Bath.' Jane was almost twenty-five; Cassandra, nearly three years older, had hoped to leave home as a bride. But as dependent daughters they had no choice other than to move with their parents. Their father always spoke of his grown daughters as 'the girls': 'Have the girls gone out?' he would say.

Mary Austen was waiting to greet Cassandra and Jane after their walk. When Jane received the edict she is said to have fainted. She resented having decisions affecting her future made above her head and behind her back. Mary was shocked to see such distress, though Jane was unaware of Mary's sympathy for her and suspected Mary of having an eye to the main chance, elbowing Jane's father out of his own rectory to make way for James. Jane complained to Cassandra that James and Mary could not wait for his parents to go and were seizing everything by degrees. She refused an invitation to celebrate their fourth wedding anniversary at Ibthorpe. Any stick would do to beat Mary with: Mary was to take Jane's mother's place at Steventon and enjoy its spacious garden while the Austens went into exile in one of Bath's narrow town houses. Jane's forebodings were perhaps justified. James did up the rectory endlessly with what Henry's wife, Eliza, called 'alterations and embellishments' but when, years later, Edward became its owner and wanted to install his own son as rector, he decided it was fit only to be demolished and a new rectory built elsewhere. So much for the novelist's birthplace.

Jane loved the countryside and said she was convinced that beauty of landscape must be one of the joys of heaven. The removal from the old house, spacious now her brothers had all left home, the garden, the wood walk and the fields, together with increased and not easily negotiable distance from friends, was horribly painful to her. She felt uprooted. The gipsyish life which she was to lead with her mother and sister for nearly a decade afterwards did not suit her at all and stopped her writing.

However close and affectionate the family, it is natural for adults to seek independence. Jane Austen was no worse off than other women of her generation and class, but she was trapped and she knew it. Again and again she writes of women with no money who can escape their cramped lives only by a good marriage: Elinor and Marianne Dashwood in *Sense and Sensibility*, Jane and Elizabeth Bennet and Charlotte Lucas in *Pride and Prejudice*, Fanny Price in *Mansfield Park*. Emma Woodhouse in *Emma* is a spoiled provincial princess with an independent fortune but in the background there is the danger of governessing hanging over Jane Fairfax. It was said that portionless girls became governesses if accomplished, milliners if not. Governesses were downtrodden, isolated and underpaid. It is not clear whether or not Anne Elliot in *Persuasion* has a marriage portion, but in situation she resembles Jane Austen most closely. A single woman, her youth gone, she is forced to leave her childhood home and friends for Bath because her father is moving there. Anne hates everything about it. Creative writing, including comedy (and Jane Austen is a brilliantly funny writer), is often fuelled by pain and anger, the grit that makes the pearl.

The Leigh-Perrots invited the Austens to stay with them, at least initially, but Jane was determined to be independent. The aunt and uncle were delighted that the Austens were coming to Bath. However, they suspected something must lie behind the precipitate decision, and this was when Jane's aunt speculated that Jane must be growing attached to William Digweed; but even if it had been so, neither her parents nor William's would have had reason to object. William was the fourth Digweed son. Some letters over the Christmas period that year seem to be missing. Possibly Jane poured out her grief and rage to Cassandra at this time, for Cassandra was at Godmersham. If so Cassandra suppressed the letters.

Paragon, where the Leigh-Perrots lived, is the eastern side of a curved street on the slope of a steep hill. On the opposite side, called Vineyards, the terraced pavement was raised, to protect pedestrians from the mud and horse manure of the streets. In Jane's day Paragon had only twenty-one houses, as those at the end of the row were known as Axford Buildings. Not far away is Camden Place, described by a contemporary writer as a 'superb crescent composed of majestic buildings'. Readers of *Persuasion* will remember that Sir Walter Elliot chose Camden Place to live in when he left Kellynch Hall in Somerset for Bath because it had 'a lofty and dignified situation, such as became a man of consequence.'

There were three parts of Bath under consideration by the Austens: Westgate Buildings (where Anne Elliot's widowed friend in *Persuasion*, Mrs Smith, lived in penury); Charles Street; and some of the short streets leading from Laura Place or Pulteney Street. In *Persuasion* Viscountess Dalrymple and her daughter take a house in Laura Place. Mr Austen hankered after Laura Place and its environs but Jane expected, rightly, that the area would be too expensive. She fancied Charles Street as the buildings were new and near the Kingsmead fields. Charles Street led from the Queen Square chapel to the two green park streets. Mrs Austen liked Queen Square, and wanted the corner house in Chapel Row which opened into Prince's Street, though she knew it only from outside. Jane thought it would be very pleasant to be near Sydney Gardens and have access to the Labyrinth every day. The Labyrinth no longer exists. She guessed that Mrs Leigh-Perrot would want them near her in Axford Buildings but, as Jane put it, the Austens hoped to escape.

Meanwhile their goods had to be disposed of. Most of the pictures, especially the Scriptural ones and a 'battlepiece', were to be left at Steventon for James, though Cassandra's drawings and two paintings on tin would go with her. There was some doubt about the French agricultural prints in the best bedroom, which Mrs Austen said had been given by Edward to her daughters but Jane could not remember: she asked Cassandra whether she or Edward knew anything about them. Perhaps he had brought them home from his Grand Tour. The plan was for Mrs Austen and the girls to go ahead followed by the father about three weeks later. They were taking their beds with them but not the rest of the furniture. Transport costs were too high. They thought of taking the better pieces, the sideboard or the Pembroke table, but Jane decided that it was not worthwhile to take the chests of drawers. They would buy new, and bigger, ones made of deal and have them painted to look neat. The total value of their furniture was estimated at £200.

Mrs Austen did not feel her health would permit her to furnish the new home and Jane had promised that Cassandra would see to everything. Jane wanted Cassandra to be with her on the journey but Cassandra was going to the Lloyds. Martha had promised to visit Steventon in March and was more cheerful than she had been. Martha was in her mid-thirties. Her sisters Mary and Eliza were both married and she herself lived with an ailing widowed mother. Acquaintances continued to marry and have children while Martha and the Austen daughters stagnated. Young Lady Bridges was pregnant with her first child: Jane commented that she was 'in the delicate language of Coulson Wallop, *in for it!*'

Jane reported on two forthcoming weddings with forced jocularity. In both cases the brides-to-be were widows. Mrs John Lyford was to 'put in for being a widow again' by marrying a Mr Fendall, a banker in Gloucester of very good fortune. Jane cheered herself up though by remembering that Mr Fendall was considerably older than his fiancée and encumbered with three small children. Mrs Lawrell was going to be married to a Mr Hinchman, a rich East Indian. It seemed unfair to Jane that women who had once achieved independence by marriage should be getting second bites at the cherry, and to men of wealth at that, while her own plight was inescapable.

There were other irritations. Peter Debary of the 'endless' Debary family, whose sisters' bad breath Jane had commented on, had turned down the curacy at Deane under James because it was too far from London. Jane commented sarcastically that he might have said that about Exeter or York, Glencoe or Lake Katrine: but Hampshire? Mr Debary had shown himself 'a Peter in the blackest sense of the word'. She meant he was 'black Peter', a name for the knave of spades, possibly alluding also to St Peter's denial of Christ. Mr Austen thought of offering the job to James Digweed but he was already earning £75 a year and the Deane curacy was worth only £50.

For once Jane alluded in a letter to public affairs: 'The threatened Act of Parliament does not seem to give any alarm.' This was a proposal to peg the price of wheat to ten shillings the bushel as a disastrous harvest the previous autumn was causing hardship. Napoleon had risen to power in 1799 and Britain could not rely on imports to feed itself. The farmers opposed the measure as they stood to lose by it, and it was defeated. Jane added that her father was doing everything he could by raising his tithes and she hoped he would soon have nearly £600 a year. Out of that he would have to pay James for the curacies of Steventon and Deane, maintain four people and pay wages to the servants.

On 5 January 1801 Jane wrote to Cassandra, who was staying at Godmersham, that her mother intended to keep two maids in Bath: 'a steady cook, and a young and giddy housemaid, with a sedate, middle-aged man, who is to undertake the double office of husband to the former and sweetheart to the latter. No children, of course, to be allowed on either side.' The word *sweetheart* had a stronger meaning than we would attach to it. We wonder whether the letters Cassandra destroyed included similar naughty jokes. Menservants, adulterous or otherwise, turned out to be beyond the family's means except temporarily. They generally kept a cook and a housemaid.

Neighbours bought up Mrs Austen's poultry. Jane hoped the lands her father had farmed would not fall into the hands of Mr Harwood or Farmer Twitchen but would go to a neighbour, Mr Holder. John Bond, now too old to do more than look after sheep, had to be found a job, not too strenuous. John himself was unconcerned, confident of getting another place as a farmer had told him he would take him on if he ever left the Rector's employ. Mr Holder did take over the farm and employ John Bond, who was relieved to keep his home. This did not satisfy Jane, who thought John would have been better off working for Harry Digweed. Harry would probably have supplied him with a more permanent dwelling and kept a horse for him to ride about on.

A visit by Cassandra to London had been put off so she had to forego the opera and miss seeing the celebrated actress Mrs Jordan. Jane told her sister rather tartly that both Cassandra and her mother had chosen to offer advice as to how Jane should dispose of her possessions: '. . . but as I do not choose to have generosity dictated to me, I shall not resolve on giving my cabinet to Anna till the first thought of it has been my own.' She was growing prickly.

'Do as you like,' Jane snapped at her sister. 'I have overcome my desire of your going to Bath with my mother and me.' When Cassandra's company no longer seemed desirable to her she was in a bad way. Jane turned instead to Martha, who had come to Steventon early in January. She and Jane were at work sorting Mr Austen's books, as there were 500 to be got rid of. Jane wanted James to take them at half a guinea each but they were sold at auction. Jane passed on her own children's books to Edward's daughter Fanny, now eight.

James had dined with them and written a letter to Edward, filling three sides, 'every line inclining too much towards the north-east,' Jane said critically. The note of impatience with James and Mary continued: 'This morning he joins his lady in the fields of Elysium and Ibthorpe.' Even more irritably she wrote to Cassandra, 'It gives us great pleasure to know that the Chilham ball was so agreeable and that you danced four dances with Mr Kemble . . . Why did you dance four dances with so stupid a man?'

Mary wanted Cassandra to bring home from Godmersham a pattern of the jacket and trousers that Elizabeth and Edward's sons wore. Her own little James-Edward was getting too big for frocks. Mary would really have liked one of their old ones but Jane thought this hardly 'doable'. As Elizabeth and Edward had four boys by this time jackets and trousers were probably handed down till worn out. Mary thought her son, James-Edward, was not out of doors as often as he ought to be and she was engaging another servant to look after him.

The Austen parents had a servant problem: Anne Littleworth's

husband did not want her to give up work at a time of high un-
employment and although in some ways Jane would have liked to keep
her on, it might be better, she thought, if Mrs Littleworth could find
something nearer her husband and child than Bath. Perhaps the Henry
Rices could employ her? There were not many places, remarked Jane,
that she was qualified for.

Jane comments wickedly on the illness of Edward's adoptive
mother, the widowed Mrs Knight, pretending to disbelieve a rumour
that the elderly Mrs Knight had had an illegitimate baby. 'I do not believe she would be betrayed beyond an *accident* at the most.' Does Jane
mean by 'accident' a miscarriage, induced or otherwise? She tended to
harp on immoral sexual relations and upon pregnancies. Heartlessly
Jane remarks that the Wylmots, of Ashford, Kent, being robbed 'must
be an amusing thing to their acquaintance'. Frustrated at every turn,
she took refuge in making sport of her neighbours and in envy of other
people's good fortune. Edward, already rich, had received a legacy of
£100!

Jane would need two new summer dresses and asked Cassandra to
buy some of the materials. She wanted two lengths of brown cambric
muslin, seven yards for their mother and seven and a half for Jane herself ('it is for a tall woman') preferably in different shades of brown.
Jane was intending to buy her other new fabric, 'yellow and white
cloud', when she went to Bath. The weather had been muggy that winter but now late in January there had been snow.

Between 25 January and 11 February 1801 Jane's letters are missing. Her next was from Manydown to Cassandra at 24 Upper Berkeley
Street, Portman Square, London, where she was staying with Henry
and Eliza, Edward having conveyed her there. Only recently had
Henry given up his commission in the militia and set up as an army
agent and banker. Jane reported that she had received a letter from
Charles, who had arrived from Lisbon on the *Endymion*, having had a
royal passenger, the Duke of Sussex, sixth son of King George III of
England. The Duke had asthma and needed to winter in warmer
climes than Britain. The sailors found the Duke 'fat, jolly and affable'
and apparently much attached to his morganatic wife, Lady Augusta
Murray, daughter of the Earl of Dunmore. When the letter was written the *Endymion* was becalmed but Charles had been hoping to reach

Portsmouth soon. He had received the letter with the news about leaving Steventon before he left England and was much surprised. He was now reconciled and planned a visit to Steventon while the rectory was still theirs. As an unmarried sailor he regretted the loss of a settled home ashore. Because Cassandra had been to see the exotic animals at Exeter Exchange, one of the sights of London, Jane added playfully that these were all the particulars of Charles's letter worthy of travelling into 'the regions of wit, elegance, fashion, elephants and kangaroons [*sic*]'. Australia had only recently been discovered so kangaroos were a novelty.

On leaving Manydown Jane took satisfaction in the opportunity of travelling back at no expense, as the Bigg family carriage would be taking Catherine Bigg to Basingstoke. Such things as travelling cheaply were a serious consideration to the cash-strapped Jane. The coach fare from London to Southampton, for example, was sixteen shillings. Catherine thought of fetching Cassandra back to Hampshire but if so Cassandra's visit would have to be stretched. Perhaps Henry could send his carriage a stage or two and Cassandra could be met by a servant. James had offered the use of his carriage but as he had no reason for going to London this would inconvenience him. Probably Cassandra travelled by Henry's carriage part of the way.

There were other farewell visits to be paid and received. Jane called on the Revd Henry Dyson, curate of Baughurst, Hampshire. Mrs Dyson 'as usual looked big'. She was expecting the seventh of their twelve children. Jane was always interested in pregnancies. Their house seemed to have 'all the comforts of little children, dirt and litter'.

The Austens were leaving their established friends to live among invalids and the elderly as, by 1801, the smart set were deserting Bath for Brighton. Lady Saye and Sele and her daughter, the 'adultress' Mary-Cassandra Twisleton, now divorced, were moving to Bath too. Because Bath was being invaded by the new rich and social climbers like Miss Augusta Hawkins of Bristol in *Emma*, who met her husband, Mr Elton, at Bath, society people avoided public gatherings and kept to themselves at private parties. The public assemblies which Jane had attended as a girl, and which Catherine Morland in *Northanger Abbey* enjoyed, were no longer smart places to see and be seen.

Jane decided to make the best of things. 'The Basingstoke balls are certainly on the decline,' she declared. She found something interesting in the bustle and activity of going away and looked forward to spending summers by the sea or in Wales. There was talk of spending the summer at Sidmouth. The increased mobility she decided was an advantage which she had often thought of 'with envy in the wives of soldiers or sailors'. She had grown restless and told Cassandra she was not, after all, sacrificing a great deal in quitting Hampshire. She was, we suspect, whistling in the dark.

There are no surviving letters between February and the following May. Jane made herself useful to her father by copying baptisms and burials into the registers at Steventon and Deane. Few parish registers have been recorded by a hand so distinguished.

11

Bath, 1801

ON 4 MAY 1801 Mrs Austen and her daughter Jane set off for Bath in their hackney chaise. Jane at least must have cast several longing, lingering looks behind at the tall elms and sycamores and the meadows full of wild flowers.

The journey from Steventon in Hampshire to Bath in Somerset, about eighty miles, took all day. They lunched on beef but could only eat a small portion. The second part of the journey from Devizes to Paragon took more than three hours and they arrived at half-past seven. They were kindly received with cups of tea. Hardly had she been in the dining room two minutes when Jane's uncle interrogated her about the naval careers of Frank and Charles.

Next day she wrote to Cassandra, who was at Godmersham:

> The first view of Bath in fine weather does not answer my expectations; I think I see more distinctly through rain. The sun was got behind everything, and the appearance of the place from the top of Kingsdown was all vapour, shadow, smoke and confusion.

All in Bath was noise, dust and bustle with numerous dashing equipages, barouches and curricles, passing and repassing, carts and drays, with sedan chairs for invalids, the gouty and ladies with no carriages. Traffic jams were frequent. In the season, on a Sunday in the Crescent, a contemporary was mildly shocked to see young women walking alone or in groups with neither servants nor chaperones, talking and laughing at street corners, and, worst of all, sometimes walking alone with young men. Street cries of milkmen, muffin men and sellers of newspapers rang out. In wet weather the clatter of pattens could be heard. When it rained people could take their exercise in the Upper or Lower Assembly Rooms with the view from the ballroom of the River Avon winding among green meadows and wooded hills.

Bath lies about a hundred and twenty miles to the west of London. It is famed for its natural hot springs. According to legend a British prince called Bladud was cured by the waters of leprosy before the Romans set foot on the British Isles. The magnificent Roman bath and two pagan temples near the Abbey churchyard were not excavated till 1871. After the Romans left Britain the Saxons built a new town and their own church, which was rebuilt by the Normans. This building was destroyed by fire in 1137 and the Abbey dates from the fifteenth century. In the sixteenth century Queen Elizabeth granted Bath a charter. The city expanded to include Barton Fields to the West and Walcot in the east. Jane Austen's parents had married at Walcot parish church. It was demolished in the mid 1770s and a new church built.

Neo-classical Bath as we have it, Britain's earliest and arguably most successful example of town planning, was built between 1705 and 1810. During those years the streets were paved and lit. Formerly a small dirty town infested with muggers, then called footpads, Bath rose in importance as a provincial centre of fashion second only to London during the eighteenth century and reached its peak in the 1750s. The novelist Fanny Burney described it as 'a city of palaces, a town of hills and a hill of towns'. The town was attractive to people in reduced circumstances because living was cheaper there than in London. Jane wrote to Cassandra when she had been three days in Bath that meat was only eightpence a pound, butter twelve pence and cheese ninepence halfpenny. She was shocked however at the 'exorbitant' price of fish: a whole salmon cost two shillings and ninepence. Food in Bath was not as fresh as their own produce had been, and needed ready cash. Bath offered luxury shops, though: England's first ice-cream parlour was opened there in 1774.

Bath is beautiful, even today, surrounded by sprawling suburbs. In Jane Austen's day it nestled among wooded hills and the view from Beechen Cliff, mentioned in *Northanger Abbey*, must have been glorious. The architect John Wood, who died in 1754, designed Queen Square, the North and South Parades, and the beautiful Circus built by his son of the same name. The Circus, dating from 1754, is a circle of houses with classical columns of the three orders, Doric, Ionic and Corinthian, supporting a continuous frieze. The Royal Crescent, Bath, is a neo-classical monument to the age of reason. It was built of local stone, a soft creamy colour, though to Anne Elliot in *Persuasion* Bath offers merely a 'white glare'. Jane's feelings of exile from and nostalgia for the country home where she was born are projected onto her sad and lonely heroine. Anne finds the clatter and yells of Bath exhausting.

By the time Jane Austen went to Bath to live it was less of a social magnet than a retirement town. It was noticeably inhabited by single people, especially, as a foreign visitor ungallantly put it, 'superannuated females'. On the other hand, it offered advantages to those with cultivated tastes, with some possibility of congenial society concentrated in a small area instead of widely scattered as in country districts. There were concerts and other entertainments, and a theatre where David Garrick, Sarah Siddons and other great actors had appeared. Richard Brinsley Sheridan's *The Rivals*, which had been coldly received in London, was a runaway success in Bath. Kotzebue's *Lovers' Vows*, the play rehearsed but never performed in *Mansfield Park*, was played six times at the Theatre Royal while Jane Austen was living in Bath. The city offered excellent shops, circulating libraries, a hospital and 'the waters'. There were numerous inns and ample stabling, as important an amenity then as parking space today. A contemporary writer observed that lodgings in Bath were elegant and plentiful. He suggested that a ten-minute walk was adequate to find somewhere suitable. But the Austens had great difficulty in finding a comfortable place to live. They soon confirmed that the fashionable streets such as the Royal Crescent and the Circus were well beyond their means. The houses in King Street were too small.

In her first letter from Bath Jane writes of walking with her uncle to the famous Pump Room, where he had to drink a glass of the waters, then believed to be medicinal. On the way they passed down Broad

Street and High Street, past the magnificent west front of Bath Abbey, flanked by a pair of Jacob's ladders, angels ascending and descending, carved in stone. The new Pump Room, built in 1795, and now a restaurant, has four tall fluted pillars crowned with Corinthian capitals supporting a sculptured pediment, and the clock by Thomas Tompion dating from 1709. Inside, the Pump Room is a lofty oblong space with tall windows, and a semicircular arched recess at each end. At the western end the gallery for musicians is still in occasional use today, though nowadays there is a stage where music is played by a trio. In the eastern apse still stands a statue of Beau Nash, arbiter of Bath fashion, which Jane must have seen.

Richard Nash was born in 1674 and died in 1762, thirteen years before Jane was born. But his edicts lingered. In 1705, when the first pump room was built, he became master of the ceremonies at Bath and made it the leading fashionable watering place. He wrote new rules for balls and assemblies, abolished the wearing of swords in places of amusement, forbade duelling, persuaded gentlemen to abandon boots for shoes and stockings, tamed refractory sedan chair men, and laid down a tariff for lodging. On one occasion, when an uncouth country squire attempted to enter the ballroom in boots, Nash asked him disdainfully why he had not brought in his horse as well, since 'the beast was as well shod as his master'. Nash's influence was a civilizing one, polishing the rough manners of the provincial gentry.

Catherine Morland in *Northanger Abbey*, drafted originally in the 1790s, goes to public assemblies and is introduced to her partner Henry Tilney by the master of ceremonies, a Mr King. Mr King was a real person, Master of the Ceremonies at the Lower Rooms from 1785 to 1805, when he became Master of the Ceremonies for the Upper Rooms. His regime was as strict as that imposed by Beau Nash.

Balls at the Assembly Rooms (destroyed by fire in 1820) began at six o'clock and ended at eleven. About nine o'clock the gentlemen were expected to treat their partners to tea and at the end of the evening hand them into the conveyances which were to take them home. Monday's balls were devoted to country dances. At the 'fancy-ball' on Thursday, when strict evening dress was not required, two cotillions were danced, one before and one after tea. The cotillion was a French dance with elaborate steps, figures and ceremonial. To perform the dance ladies wore shorter skirts than usual with their overdresses picturesquely looped up. Overdresses eventually went out of style when the high-waisted straight-skirted gowns came in. In Jane Austen's time cotillions were presided over by a French prisoner of war, Monsieur de la Cocardière.

Henry Tilney in *Northanger Abbey* says a country dance is 'an emblem of marriage'. Catherine disagrees. She says, 'People that marry can never part, but must go and keep house together. People that dance only stand opposite each other in a long room for half an hour.' Catherine enjoys the gaieties Jane Austen tasted as a teenager. Anne Elliot in *Persuasion*, unrevised when Jane Austen died in 1817, attends only private parties. The heyday of public mixing was over. Anne finds Bath society as dull and insipid as Jane did, mixing with her uncle and aunt's elderly friends. For all Jane's dislike of the town she kept in touch with developments. *Persuasion* is set in 1814 during the brief lull in the French war. The penultimate chapter of *Persuasion* takes place partially in Union Street, which was not built till after Jane had left Bath for Chawton. Queen Square had become unfashionable by the time Jane wrote her last novel. Henrietta and Louisa Musgrove look down on it.

Jane soon noticed the warmer climate in the west of England: she was warmer in Bath without a fire than at Steventon with an excellent one. She hoped to persuade Mrs Lloyd to settle in Bath, for this would bring Martha's companionship and Jane loved Martha. Jane was having her new dress made by Mrs Mussell the seamstress and for once has left a detailed description so we know exactly what it was like. It was to be:

> a round gown, with a jacket and a frock front, like Catherine Bigg's, to open at the side. The jacket is all in one with the body, and comes as far as the pocket holes; about half a quarter of a yard deep I suppose all the way round, cut off straight at the corners, with a broad hem. No fullness appears either in the body or the flap; the back is quite plain . . . and the sides equally so. The front is sloped round to the bosom and drawn in – and there is to be a frill of the same to put on occasionally when all one's handkerchiefs are dirty – which frill *must* fall back. She is to put two breadths and a half into the tail, and no gores, gores not being so much worn as they

were; there is nothing new in the sleeves, they are to be plain, with a fullness of the same falling down and gathered up underneath, just like some of Martha's – or perhaps a little longer. Low in the back behind, and a belt of the same.

Cassandra was making Martha a bonnet and Jane asked her to make Martha a cloak of the same materials. 'They are very much worn here, in different forms – many of them just like her black silk spencer, with a trimming round the armholes instead of sleeves; some are long before, and some long all round like C Bigg's.' Later Jane undertook to order a gown for Cassandra but warned that although Mrs Mussell had made the dark gown very well she did not always succeed with lighter colours: 'My white one I was obliged to alter a great deal.'

Jane and her mother had ordered a new bonnet apiece, both white straw trimmed with white ribbon. Jane was perhaps relieved to find her bonnets looked very much like other people's and quite as smart. Cambric muslin bonnets were being worn and some of them were pretty but Jane was not going to buy one till Cassandra turned up. Bath was 'getting so very empty' that there was small need to exert herself. She drank tea, played cribbage and walked by the canal.

News of the Steventon sale arrived from Mary: sixty-one and a half guineas for the three cows pleased Jane but to get only eleven guineas for the tables was a blow. Eight guineas for her pianoforte, she told Cassandra, was about what she had expected. She was more anxious to hear about her books as she had heard they had gone well. She was impatient to hear the rest, as all she had learned anything about was the cows, bacon, hay, hops, tables and her father's chest of drawers and study table.

The Austens looked at a house in Seymour Street but the rooms were cramped, the biggest being fourteen feet square. Jane dressed up and went with her uncle and aunt to the Upper Rooms. Before tea four couples danced while a hundred people watched. Jane thought the gathering 'shockingly and inhumanly thin'. It was at this dance that she spotted Miss Twisleton the adultress. Jane planned to have another gown made in case they should go to the rooms again the following Monday, though she did not enjoy these occasions. She was soon bored and irritable. Next day, after just a week in the city, she was already writing to her sister, who was with the Lloyds at Ibthorpe:

Another stupid party last night; perhaps if they were larger they might be less intolerable, but here there were only just enough to make one card table, with six people to look on, and talk nonsense to each other. Lady Fust, Mrs Busby and a Mrs Owen sat down with my uncle to whist within five minutes after the three old *Toughs* came in, and there they sat with only the exchange of Admiral Stanhope for my uncle till their chairs were announced. I cannot anyhow continue to find people agreeable; I respect Mrs Chamberlayne for doing her hair well, but cannot feel a more tender sentiment. Miss Langley is like any other short girl with a broad nose and wide mouth, fashionable dress and exposed bosom.

These people were all strangers and Jane did not easily attach herself. Nevertheless she was about to accompany Mrs Chamberlayne and Miss Langley to the village of Weston, then a mile and a half from Bath. This walk was spoken of as Bath's Hyde Park or Kensington Gardens.

Jane made conversation with Edward's Kentish neighbour, old Mr William Evelyn, who thought more of horses than of anything else, and she teased Cassandra by pretending to have flirted with him. Cassandra was shocked and reproved her sister for indiscretion. Wearily Jane explained she had been making the most of the story: she had only seen the man four times. Later he and his wife took Jane out for rides in their phaeton, which she found 'bewitching'. In her letter Jane made the best 'copy' she could out of her dull social life, but the time in Bath was the low point of her experience. Aunt Leigh-Perrot had taken umbrage because a Miss Bond was offended that Mrs Leigh-Perrot had left Bath without saying goodbye, though the two ladies were not on visiting terms. Jane Austen described it as 'the oddest kind of quarrel in the world'.

The proposed walk to Weston took place but everybody except Jane and Mrs Chamberlayne begged off. Mrs Chamberlayne was a good walker and climbed energetically up Sion Hill, arousing Jane's competitive side. 'I could with difficulty keep pace with her – yet would not flinch for the world.' They stopped for nothing, marching on in the hot May sunshine, as if, Jane said, they were afraid of being buried alive. After this exhibition of mettle Jane was forced into a grudging admiration. A few days later they went walking together again and Jane managed to keep up with her. Such friendship as there was came to an end when the Chamberlaynes left Bath a few days afterwards. A Mrs and Miss Holder invited Jane and her mother to drink tea, and although Mrs Austen's cold made it necessary for her to turn down the invitation, Jane went. It was the fashion to dislike them, Jane told Cassandra, but they were so polite and their white gowns looked so nice that she was won over, if only for the satisfaction of disagreeing with her Aunt Leigh-Perrot, who turned up her nose at the fashionable white gowns as 'absurd pretension in this place'. Jane warned Cassandra that Miss Holder had an idea that Cassandra was remarkably lively: 'therefore get ready the proper selection of adverbs, and due scraps of Italian and French.' Miss Holder talked pathetically of her dead brother and sister. Death was never far away.

A girl called Marianne Mapleton, whom Jane had met on her visit to Bath in 1799, had died. 'Many a girl on early death has been praised into an angel, I believe, on slighter pretensions to beauty, sense and merit than Marianne,' wrote Jane, adding in the next sentence that the auctioneer Mr Bent seemed *bent* on being detestable, valuing the family books at only £70. Jane called on the Miss Mapletons the day after Marianne was buried to inquire after the family, not expecting to be let in, but found herself welcomed by Marianne's pale and dejected sisters.

Another house the Austens looked at had damp in the kitchen and carried with it reports of discontented tenants and putrid fevers. Large houses in desirable situations within their means tended to be in poor condition. Affordable accommodation, compared with Steventon, was poky. Jane and her mother looked at houses in New King Street but they were also too small. Others were damp and an offer to raise the kitchen floor at 12 Green Park Buildings was not acceptable. Though the water might be out of sight it could not be sent away, as Jane remarked. At the end of May Mr Austen came back from Godmersham, having collected Cassandra from Kintbury on the way.

The family eventually moved into 4 Sydney Place at the end of Pulteney Street, flanking a part of the Sydney Gardens, which greatly pleased Jane. At that time Sydney Place was on the outskirts of the city, near open countryside. They had found the house, which now bears a plaque saying she lived there, as the result of an advertisement in the *Bath Chronicle* of 21 May. While the landlord was redecorating the

Austens travelled. The roomy, commodious house had a pretty drawing room on the first floor with three tall windows which offered a view of the Gardens, with their sloping lawns and handsome trees. A green bank was crowned with a pillared classical pavilion. The Kennet and Avon Canal passed under an old stone bridge. On gala nights there were music, singing, cascades, transparencies, fireworks and illuminations. Jane watched some fireworks which she described as 'really beautiful' and she found the accompanying illuminations very pretty. The Austen parents thoroughly enjoyed their retirement and the cheerfulness of town life.

The Austens went to Sidmouth for part of the summer of 1801 at the invitation of the Revd Richard Buller, a former pupil of Jane's father. Mr Buller's vicarage was at Colyton in east Devon and he was recently married to a girl called Anna Marshall. Jane was growing sensitive about still being single herself and feared she would be embarrassed by displays of affection between the newly married couple but her fears were groundless. She even kept up a correspondence with Mr Buller afterwards. In 1805 he turned up in Bath, in bad health, and died at thirty. Jane also went to Dawlish where she found the library 'pitiful and wretched'. The following year they went to Ramsgate and to Tenby and Barmouth in Wales and from there Mr and Mrs Austen and Charles, who had joined them, journeyed back to Hampshire, reaching Steventon on 14 August.

Frank had been appointed Captain of HMS *Neptune* in 1801, but in 1802 the temporary Peace of Amiens meant he and his men were paid off. He was at Portsmouth. His parents, with James and Mary, visited to see his fine ship but Jane and Cassandra were at Godmersham for a stay of several weeks. Edward now had seven children. Charles brought his sisters back to Steventon on 28 October.

He had received £30 as his share for capturing a privateer and was expecting £10 more. He had bought gold chains and topaz crosses (now in the Jane Austen museum at Chawton) for Cassandra and Jane. Jane pretended to scold but immortalized the gift in *Mansfield Park* as a present to Fanny Price from her sailor brother, William.

On 25 November 1802 Jane and Cassandra went to visit Catherine and Alethea Bigg at Manydown, expecting to stay two or three weeks. On 2 December came Harris Bigg-Wither's proposal to Jane.

Seen in the context of her age, her dissatisfaction with life in Bath or trailing round with her parents, and her pinched life of poverty, her refusal of this opportunity is dazzling in its integrity. Her sister-in-law Mary, handing the story down to Caroline, said the young man was 'very plain in person . . . nothing but his size to recommend him'. Caroline added, 'I have always respected her for the courage in cancelling that yes the next morning. All worldly advantages would have been to her – and she was of an age to know *this* quite well. My aunts had very small fortunes and on their father's death they and their mother would be, they were aware, but poorly off. I believe most young women so circumstanced would have taken Mr W and trusted to love after marriage.' Caroline's mother Mary thought Jane had made a mistake in changing her mind. We may think the decision was correct, and also, given the background, heroic.

It was at this time that Eliza, whose son Hastings de Feuillide had died in 1801, went back to France with Henry in an attempt to lay claim to her first husband's land. For what may, if report be true, have been the second time in her life she was forced to flee. Had her command of the French language been less than perfect, she and Henry would have been interned until the end of the war, which was still far from over.

In spring 1803 hostilities broke out again. The Austens were at Bath and Frank and Charles returned to active service, Charles to his previous job as first lieutenant of the *Endymion*, Frank to Ramsgate to organize volunteers for coastal defence. There he met and became engaged to Mary Gibson. They waited to marry until he had some more prize-money and did not do so until 1806. Jane visited her brother at Ramsgate where she was observed by Sir Samuel Egerton Brydges, brother of 'Madam' Lefroy. He was the author of an autobiographical novel, *Fitzalbini*, which Jane had found feeble when she read it in 1798. He described her as 'fair and handsome, slight and elegant, with cheeks a little too full . . . Even then I did not know she was addicted to literary composition.' Although between 1795 and 1799 Jane had drafted three novels, in Bath her literary output ceased almost completely.

12

Lyme and Bath, 1804–5

*T*N SEPTEMBER 1804, after Mrs Austen had recovered from a bout of illness, the family, accompanied by Henry and Eliza, went to Lyme, the beauty spot on the Dorset coast which figures so memorably in *Persuasion*, inspiring a lyrical outburst on landscape in the Romantic manner unique in Jane Austen's fiction. It was on this holiday that Cassandra, at a picnic, made the sketch of Jane seen from the back, wearing a blue gown and bonnet. This was their second visit, as they had also been at Lyme on 5 November the previous year when there was a catastrophic fire caused by Guy Fawkes Day celebrations.

Jane was early attracted by the writings of William Gilpin, a clergyman who toured Britain in the 1770s, describing and illustrating the beauties of the countryside. An artist of considerable skill, he popularized the concept of the picturesque, which had originated in France and Italy and was nourished by the experience of sublime scenery on the Grand Tour. Gilpin was born in Cumberland, which formed his taste for landscape. Nature for Gilpin was God's work of art and therefore superior to any work of man. Natural scenery was a suitable object of reverence, lifting the contemplative mind through rapture up to the Deity.

Jane writes emotionally about the wooded cliffs of Lyme in *Persuasion*, despite having made fun of Marianne Dashwood's romantic enthusiasm for landscape in *Sense and Sensibility* and of Catherine Morland for her ignorance of picturesque vocabulary in *Northanger Abbey*.

'Picturesque' to Gilpin meant merely something which would look good in a picture but by the 1790s enthusiasm for scenery and gardens artfully arranged to look like wildernesses with artificial ruins had generated new descriptive jargon.

Lyme is 150 miles south-west of London, at the mouth of a narrow valley opening on a spectacular cliff-lined coast and fine sandy beaches. The town was first known as Lyme Regis (Latin for King's Lyme) in 1316. As early as 1234 it was an important port. Jane Austen writes of Charmouth, which lies in a valley between the hills, with its 'sweet retired bay backed by dark cliffs' and its fragments of low rock among the sands. She could take a pathway along the top of the Church Cliffs, now so badly eroded that the cliff and its church have crumbled.

The Austens drove from Bath by way of Shepton Mallett, Somerton, and Crewkerne, joining the Lyme road where an old inn, the Hunter's Lodge, stood. They passed through the cheerful village of Uplyme and down the long hill towards the charming old main street of Lyme, which seems to be, as Jane put it herself, 'almost hurrying into the water'. Halfway down the street their chaise turned into a lane which ran westward and finally made a steep descent to the harbour. At the end of the little parade nearest the harbour on a grassy hillside was the long, rambling white cottage where they stayed. It had low ceilings and small windows, and a staircase so steep and narrow as to be dangerous. There were two doors, on different levels. In front was the entrance, with dining room and kitchen; at the top of the house the bedrooms opened out on to the bank behind.

On the middle floor was the drawing room, with a lovely view through its projecting bay window of the sea and harbour with the Cobb to the west and the picturesque chain of cliffs to the east. The Cobb is a massive, semicircular stone pier with upper and lower causeways. The steep flight of steps mentioned in *Persuasion* and known locally as 'Granny's teeth' is still there. It dates from at least the early fourteenth century and figured in the 1995 film version of Jane's novel.

Nearby, and visible from the projecting bay window of the drawing room, was a small white cottage perched on the corner of a sea wall near an old pier. This cottage was probably the original of the one in the novel where the Harvilles settled. Unlike other houses in

sheltered Lyme, it was exposed to rough weather and would have necessitated Captain Harville's 'contrivances against winter storms'. Jane
Austen's brother Frank thought Captain Harville was drawn from
himself. Only from the windows of that house could Captain Benwick
have been seen after Louisa Musgrove's accident, 'flying past the
house' and towards the town itself for a surgeon.

When the poet Lord Tennyson visited Lyme later in the century
his friends were anxious to point out where the Duke of Monmouth
landed. The Duke was the illegitimate son of King Charles II of England. Monmouth raised an army and tried to seize the throne when
Charles's brother succeeded as James II but was eventually beheaded
for treason in 1685. In one version of an often-told story, Tennyson
said, 'Don't talk to me of the Duke of Monmouth. Show me the exact
spot where Louisa Musgrove fell!'

The Parade runs from the harbour to the old town. A stretch of
firm sand served as a short cut for the horse-drawn wagons bringing
freight up from the harbour to the town. Just beyond some thatched
cottages stood the Assembly Rooms, perched on the eastern promon-
tory of the bay and surviving till 1927. The Assembly Rooms, with music provided by three violins and a violoncello, opened their doors on
Tuesdays and Thursdays. The subscription was fifteen shillings and
sixpence. Subscribers paid two shillings for balls, one shilling for card
assemblies; on other nights tea and coffee cost sixpence, and sixpence
was charged for cards, chess or backgammon. Everybody else was
charged double.

It was about this time that Jane met the young man she may have
been in love with, but who died. Cassandra knew the details but passed
on to her niece Caroline only the vaguest possible outline. This is frus-
trating, as Caroline herself had a remarkably full and accurate memory.

Cassandra had gone to Weymouth. Henry and Eliza, who had
moved from Upper Berkeley Street in London to a little terrace house,
16 St Michael's Place, overlooking the then open fields of Brompton,
had travelled down to Lyme with Jane and her parents. Jane wrote to
Cassandra at Ibthorpe on 14 September to say she hoped Cassandra
had reached Mrs Lloyd's already. Jane sympathized with her sister's
disappointment that there was no ice at Weymouth. Before refrigera-

This portrait was at one time believed to be by Zoffany and to show the young Jane Austen, but the dates do not fit. It may be of a distant cousin, also named Jane Austen

Retouched image of Jane Austen. Softened and falsified,
this version of Cassandra's drawing sentimentalizes Jane.
It was done in watercolour by a Mr Andrews

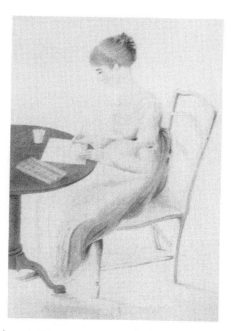

Fanny Knight, aged seventeen, drawn by her aunt Cassandra Austen

Lady Knatchbull, mother of the first Lord Brabourne. As Fanny Knight, eldest child of Jane Austen's third brother, Edward, she had been Jane Austen's favourite niece. In old age she wrote to her younger sister Marianne that her aunts, Cassandra and Jane, were not altogether 'refined'

Jane Austen's father, the Revd George Austen,
known at St John's College, Oxford, when he was a Fellow,
as 'the handsome proctor'

The Revd James Austen, Jane's eldest brother. Although Jane admitted he was 'good and clever', in later life she found James irritating, and regretted that too many of his opinions were 'copied from' his less clever second wife, Mary

Jane Austen's third brother, Edward, adopted at sixteen. He inherited fine estates, Godmersham in Kent and Chawton in Hampshire, and in 1812 changed his name to Knight. His eldest child, Fanny, was Jane Austen's favourite niece

Henry Austen, Jane's fourth brother, with whom she had a close rapport. He was six feet tall and charming, but his career was chequered. Starting in the militia after Oxford, he became a banker, but the business crashed and he was eventually (as his costume here shows) ordained

Francis Austen, Jane's elder brother, born between Cassandra and herself.
Frank showed initiative as a small boy and joined the Navy at eleven,
rising to become Sir Francis and Admiral of the Fleet

Charles Austen, eighth and youngest child of George and Cassandra Austen.
To Jane and her sister, he was their 'particular little brother'. Charles followed
Frank into the Navy and rose to become an admiral

This scene shows the 'adoption' of Edward Austen by Mr and Mrs Thomas Knight. George Austen stands behind his son, while the boy holds out his hands to his new 'mother', who was always kind and affectionate to him

Godmersham Park in East Kent, home of Jane Austen's rich brother, Edward Knight. When she stayed there, Jane could drink French wines and forget 'vulgar economy'

Manydown Park, the house Jane Austen could have been mistress of, had she not refused Harris Bigg-Wither's marriage proposal. It was demolished in 1965

Hurstbourne Park, owned by the Earl of Portsmouth, who had been a pupil boarding with Jane Austen's father. Jane went to his annual ball there in November 1800

Anna Austen, who married Ben Lefroy. Anna was the elder daughter of
Jane Austen's eldest brother James. It was said by many people that the
heroine of *Emma* resembled Anna in appearance

Laura Place seen through the gateway of Sydney Gardens. From J C Nattes's 'Bath, Illustrated by a Series of Views' 1806. Mr Austen hankered after Laura Place, but it was too expensive for the Austen family

Sydney Gardens, Bath, also by J C Nattes. Sydney Gardens had recently been opened as a pleasure ground when the Austens moved to the city

Jane Austen's workbox at Chawton Cottage, made of wood lacquered in black and gold. Jane, her mother and sister were all accomplished needlewomen

Expertly sewn with almost invisible stitches of perfect evenness and tension,
this patchwork quilt, made by Jane Austen, her mother and her sister,
hangs today in Chawton Cottage

The bedroom shared by Jane and Cassandra in Chawton Cottage,
their last home together, as it is today

The drawing room at Chawton Cottage today. Jane practised
on the pianoforte every morning before making the breakfast

Walking costume, 1815. The pelisse (overcoat) shown is trimmed with lace.
Made by hand, such trimmings were costly. In 1809 Jane Austen was relieved
to learn that a new pelisse could be had for as little as seventeen shillings,
but buttons were expensive

The waistline remained high throughout most of Jane Austen's adult life.
Here are a ballgown which Fanny Knight might have worn and a smart
walking costume of 1815

tion winter ice was stored underground but supplies seem to have run out that summer. She was sorry too that Cassandra had arrived too late to see the Royal Family embark on the Royal Yacht the previous Wednesday. Jane had had a slight fever: there was a lot of it about. A Miss Anna Cove had been saved, according to her mother, from serious illness by the administration of an emetic. Mrs Austen had been playing cards. The game was Commerce. With characteristic dryness, Jane writes:

> We are quite settled in our lodgings by this time, as you may suppose, and everything goes on in the usual order. The servants behave very well and make no difficulties, though nothing certainly can exceed the inconvenience of the offices, except the general dirtiness of the house and furniture and all its inhabitants . . . I endeavour as far as I can to supply your place, and be useful and keep things in order; I detect dirt in the water decanter as fast as I can . . .

Jane also gave medicine to Jenny the cook, which Jenny threw up. It was the custom for ladies to prescribe for servants. The Austens had taken their other servant, Molly the maid, with them. A manservant, James, had been recruited locally, probably by Henry. Jane was delighted with him. Mrs Austen's shoes had never been so well polished and the silver plate had never looked so clean. He waited well at table, was attentive, handy, quick and quiet: 'He is quite an Uncle Toby's annuity to us.' Jane was alluding to the novel *Tristram Shandy* by Lawrence Sterne. In the book the narrator's Uncle Toby has £120 a year besides his army half-pay. James's wages would have been at most £20 a year so the implication is that he did the work of half a dozen. James could read and Jane exerted herself to find reading matter for him: 'Unfortunately he has read the first volume of *Robinson Crusoe*. We have the Pinckards Newspaper however, which I shall take care to lend him.' James was not only a reader, he was also eager to see the world and wanted to go to Bath. He had accompanied Mr and Mrs Austen to a ball at the Assembly Rooms a little after eight o'clock. At half-past nine Mr Austen walked home accompanied by James with a lantern. The lantern was not necessary as the night was moonlit but as Jane observed it was likely to prove a convenience. Mrs Austen and Jane stayed till about ten thirty. How they got home Jane does not say.

She is more interested in telling Cassandra about her lack of dancing partners:

'Nobody asked me the first two dances,' she wrote mournfully. 'The next two I danced with Mr Crawford – and had I chosen to stay longer might have danced with Mr Granville, Mrs Granville's son – whom my dear friend Miss Armstrong offered to introduce to me – or with a new, odd-looking man who had been eyeing me for some time, and at last without any introduction asked me if I meant to dance again.' Jane could only account for such shocking familiarity by guessing he might be Irish. She suspected him of being connected with the son and son's wife of an Irish viscount, 'bold, queer-looking people, just fit to be quality at Lyme'. Irish Tom Lefroy had not been bold enough to please her. Now she took offence at a man's attention which she sneered at as a typically Irish breach of good manners.

She is equally acid about Miss Armstrong, whom she regarded coolly even though Miss Armstrong imagined herself to be a 'dear friend'. Miss Armstrong seemed to like people rather too easily. Jane perceived in her 'no wit or genius' though Jane allowed her to have sense and some degree of taste with 'very engaging' manners. 'Like other young ladies, she is considerably genteeler than her parents; Mrs Armstrong sat darning a pair of stockings the whole of my visit.' Jane begged Cassandra not to mention this to their mother for fear that she might do the same. Later she softened towards Miss Armstrong, who gently reproached her for coolness. Jane realized the girl was lonely and regretted her own bad manners.

Although she loved the seaside Jane never learned to swim. There were no swimming pools and sea-bathing was a new pastime. Men swam in ponds and rivers but ladies did not. Bathing was done from the bathing machine, a little cabin on wheels drawn by a horse into the water. Sea-bathing, even in winter, was prescribed as a remedy for various complaints – asthma, cancer, consumption, deafness, ruptures, rheumatism and madness. Jane found sea-bathing so delightful and Molly so pressing with her to enjoy herself that she stayed in rather too long and grew tired. Jane had few opportunities for pleasure. Despite parties and dances and tea-drinking her life was a dull one and she frequently expressed boredom and irritation.

The lease on the house at 4 Sydney Place in Bath had expired and the Austens did not renew it. When the household reassembled in Bath it was in 27 Green Park Buildings, which they had considered un-suitable when they viewed it in 1801.

Bad news arrived that December. Mrs Lefroy, sister of Sir Samuel Egerton Brydges and friend of Jane Austen's youth, was killed at the age of fifty-five when her horse threw her. Meeting James Austen in Overton that morning, she had complained that the animal was so stu-pid and lazy that she could not get him to canter. Something startled him and he bolted. Mrs Lefroy's servant caught at the bridle but missed his hold and Mrs Lefroy was fatally injured. She was by all ac-counts charming and gracious and her death was a great shock to Jane, who missed her badly. The accident happened on Jane's twenty-ninth birthday, while the Austens were in Bath. Later Jane wrote a poem to commemorate the fourth anniversary of Madam Lefroy's death. Thir-teen stanzas long, it begins:

> The day returns again, my natal day;
> What mixed emotions with the thought arise!
> Beloved friend, four years have passed away
> Since thou wert snatched forever from our eyes.
>
> The day, commemorative of my birth
> Bestowing life and light and hope on me,
> Brings back the hour which was thy last on earth.
> Oh! bitter pang of torturing memory.
>
> Angelic woman! past my powers to praise
> In language meet, thy talents, temper, mind,
> Thy solid worth, thy captivating grace!
> Thou friend and ornament of humankind.

Worse was to come. A month after Anne Lefroy's death, on 21 January 1805, Jane had to write giving Frank the news that their father had died at the age of seventy-three after a forty-eight-hour illness. She wrote in fact two letters, the second on the following day when she re-alized that Frank would have reached Portsmouth. She assured her brother that Mr Austen had not suffered much and had gone almost in his sleep. She was of course going to write to Edward at Godmersham and to Henry at Brompton. 'His tenderness as a father, who can do jus-tice to?' she wrote. She informed Frank that James was due to arrive the next day and that the funeral would be on the following Saturday, at the church on the site of the one in which Mr Austen had been married forty years earlier. Charles was at Halifax, Nova Scotia, aboard HMS *Indian* and could not come home for the funeral. Henry was at Godmersham and left at once for Bath, though Edward could not come.

James at once urged his mother to come and live with him and Mary at Steventon but she wanted to stay near her brother in Bath. Mr Austen's income died with him and Mrs Austen had only £140 a year. Even those modest payments were sometimes delayed. The daughters had no money of their own, apart from the interest on Cassandra's legacy. Jane was totally dependent. Edward, who had not supported his mother when his father was alive, offered a subsidy of £100 a year. With nine children of his own already he could hardly spare more. James, Henry and Frank each chipped in £50. Frank offered £100 but Mrs Austen would accept only half that sum. Frank wanted his generosity to be kept secret but Henry, characteristically officious, overruled him. Charles, only twenty-five years old and with his way to make, was not expected to help. Mrs Austen wrote to Mrs Leigh-Perrot that her sons were 'good' to her. But the widow and her daughters were far from comfortably off. 'My mother will have a good £400 per annum,' wrote Henry to Frank. Later he remembered that with Cassandra's income, this would come to £450. But three people had to live on that. Henry expected his mother to take furnished lodgings and reduce her establishment to just one female servant. This was living uncomfortably near the bone.

Jane forwarded to Frank a compass and sundial in a black shagreen (artificially roughened leather) case which had been their father's, together with a pair of scissors. Soon Henry was able to congratulate Frank on his command of the *Canopus*, an eighty-gun ship, which Henry the banker calculated would be worth £500 a year.

James wrote to Frank about their mother: 'Her future plans are not quite settled, but I believe her summers will be spent in the country amongst her relations and chiefly I trust among her children – the winters she will spend in comfortable lodgings in Bath. It is a just satisfaction to know that her circumstances will be easy . . . You will I am sure forgive Henry for not having entirely complied with your request for secrecy . . .' Henry was a blabbermouth, later revealing the author-ship of his sister's novels although they were published anonymously.

On 25 March 1805 the three women moved out of the house in Green Park Buildings and into lodgings at 25 Gay Street. This was halfway up the hill leading to the Circus and not far from the Royal Crescent. They were neither happy nor comfortable. Even Mrs Austen wanted to leave.

Cassandra left almost immediately for Ibthorpe to stay with Martha Lloyd and her mother, though she was indisposed herself. Old Mrs Lloyd was sinking and Jane's letter expressed the hope that her end would be as peaceful and easy as their own father's had been. Jane was sure that Cassandra's support would be invaluable to Martha and Mary, who was with them.

Jane told her sister that she and her mother were much in demand for quiet evenings drinking tea and that this would benefit them eco-nomically. 'Our tea and sugar will last a great while. I think we are just the kind of people and party to be treated about among our relations; we cannot be supposed to be very rich.' Jane and her mother had been to 'see Miss Chamberlayne look hot on horseback'. Seven years and four months ago they had been to the same riding house to see Miss Lefroy's performance. 'What a different set we are now moving in!' wrote Jane sadly. Bath had two riding schools where horses could also be hired: Ryles's in Monmouth Street, and Dash's in Montpelier Row, which also boasted a court on which to play real (royal) tennis.

The weather was bright and hot, and the walk in the Crescent had been curtailed. They went into the field nearby and passed Stephen Terry, part of the noisy family at one of the balls Jane attended in 1799, and his fiancée Miss Seymer. Her elegance was famed, but neither her dress nor her air had anything of the dash or stylishness people had talked of: quite the contrary, in fact. She looked very quiet and her dress was not even smart, Jane commented. The Austen women at this low point in Jane's life could not rise to being smart themselves, either in dress or in lifestyle. They were destitute.

An affectionate and entertaining letter had come from Henry. That it was enjoyable to read was no credit to him, Jane said, as in her fond eyes he could not help being amusing. He was grateful for a screen Jane had embroidered and did not know which delighted him more, the idea or the execution. His wife Eliza 'of course goes halves in all this' and sent a message of warm acknowledgment of the sisters' gift of a brooch. Henry had mentioned having sent a letter to Frank, who was in Gibraltar, from his fiancée, Mary Gibson, via General Tilson, then waiting at Spithead. Jane wondered whether it might be possible to reach Frank through another intermediary. Henry also proposed to meet his sisters on the coast, an expedition Jane looked forward to as 'desirable and delightful'. 'He talks of the rambles we took together last summer with pleasing affection,' she added.

On 16 April, while Cassandra was still at Ibthorpe, old Mrs Lloyd died. Martha's mourning clothes were late being delivered. Mourning black was essential for a respectable appearance. Martha was invited to live with Mrs Austen and her daughters to share expenses. Jane had always been fond of Martha, preferring her to her sister Mary, and what Jane called 'our partnership with Martha' seems to have been a success.

Mrs Stent, who had shared a home with Mrs Lloyd, was an early friend, rather down on her luck. On 21 April 1805 Jane wrote, 'Poor Mrs Stent! it has been her lot to be always in the way; but we must be merciful, for perhaps in time we may come to be Mrs Stents ourselves, unequal to anything and unwelcome to everybody.' Jane was nearly thirty, unmarried, worried about affording tea and sugar and living in rented rooms. Her future did not look promising.

She filled her letter to Cassandra with chatter about crepe sleeves and a head-dress of crepe and flowers, 'but I do not think it looked particularly well.' Her Aunt Leigh-Perrot owed her money but was reluctant to pay in hard cash, offering instead tickets to 'the Grand Sydney-Garden Breakfast' which 'Perrot' would buy if Jane asked him. Jane felt bound to refuse this grudging offer.

This incident shows Jane Leigh-Perrot in an unpleasant light, unwilling to pay an impoverished niece a small sum (it was only for a cap) from her own resources and making vague and insincere promises on behalf of her husband. One wonders whether a rich woman capable of such contemptible meanness might not perhaps have been guilty, after all, of stealing lace from a haberdasher's shop. Jane was so irritated that she made up her mind not to invite her aunt and uncle to any more evening tea-drinking but soon relented. Good manners won, despite tea being so expensive.

Mrs Austen had boasted to Mrs Leigh-Perrot that a sloop, a vessel of ten to eighteen guns under a commander, was reserved for Charles in the east. Mrs Leigh-Perrot exaggerated this into a frigate, a much larger ship commanded by a captain. Jane was waiting to hear from Charles himself. Although Uncle Leigh-Perrot's gout was worse he and his wife were planning to go to Scarlets, their house in the country.

Also in Bath as a visitor was Jane's godfather, the Revd Samuel Cooke, vicar of Great Bookham in Surrey, and his wife, Cassandra, cousin to Jane's mother. Their daughter Mary and son George went with Jane on long walks. George was 'very kind and talked sense to me every now and then in the intervals of his more animated fooleries with Miss Bendish, who is very young and rather handsome,' wrote Jane. She had reached the age when she was too old to be flirted with and had to look on while young girls received all the attention. This got under her skin: 'there was a monstrous deal of stupid quizzing, and commonplace nonsense talked, but scarcely any wit; – all that bordered on it, or on sense came from my Cousin George, whom altogether I like very well.'

Cousin George had a career at Oxford as tutor at Corpus Christi College, where his students included Thomas Arnold, later head-master of Rugby School and architect of the reformed nineteenth-century public school system with its cult of moral earnestness. Jane sometimes visited the Cookes, who lived not too far from the famous beauty spot Box Hill, the scene in *Emma* for the heroine's thoughtless attack on poor Miss Bates. While in Bath Jane Austen started, but did not finish, *The Watsons*, with characters called Tom Musgrave, Emma Watson and a small boy called Charles, who is saved from humiliation when Emma agrees to dance with him. This motif, with the sexes reversed, was used a decade later in *Emma*, when Harriet Smith is rescued by Mr Knightley after Mr Elton has rejected her. Jane Austen knew the misery of being at dances and waiting in vain for a partner.

Although she approved of George (so long as he was not neglecting her to talk frivolously with good-looking young girls) she had less time for his brother, the Revd Theophilus Cooke. When she met him later in London he struck her as having to offer only 'nothing-meaning, harmless, heartless civility'. We are reminded of Sir Walter

Elliot's eldest daughter Elizabeth in *Persuasion*, expert at saying 'the proper nothings' and exemplifying superficial, meaningless politeness. Miss Elliot's 'heartless elegance' gives 'a general chill'. In a society which valued polished manners, polite insincerity cannot have been rare but must have been useful as a social lubricant, preferable to the rough manners of the earlier part of the century.

Jane reported on visits and being visited: 'When I tell you that we have been visiting a Countess this morning, you will immediately with great justice, but no truth, guess it to be Lady Roden.' Lady Roden's relatives, the Ordes, had intermarried with the Hampshire Powletts. Her second son, James-Bligh Jocelyn, then fifteen, was in the navy and Charles, currently first lieutenant of the *Endymion*, had shown kindness to him.

It was not however Lady Roden but Lady Leven. 'On receiving a message from Lord and Lady Leven through the Mackays declaring their intention of waiting on us, we thought it right to go to them. I hope we have not done too much, but the friends and admirers of Charles must be attended to.' The well-born but financially constrained Austen women knew the importance to a man's career of the right contacts. Lord and Lady Leven were 'very reasonable, good sort of people, very civil, and full of his [Charles's] praise'.

Jane's account throws interesting light on the manners of the era:

> We were shown at first into an empty drawing room, and presently in came his Lordship, not knowing who we were, to apologize for the servant's mistake, and tell a lie himself, that Lady Leven was not within. He is a tall, gentlemanlike looking man, with spectacles, and rather deaf; after sitting with him ten minutes we walked away; but Lady L. coming out of the dining parlour as we passed the door, we were obliged to attend her back to it, and pay our visit over again. She is a stout woman, with a very handsome face. By this means we had the pleasure of hearing Charles's praises twice over . . . There is a pretty little Lady Marianne of the party, to be shaken hands with and asked if she remembers Mr Austen.

Marianne had the title 'Lady' prefixed to her Christian name because she was the daughter of an earl.

Tom Chute had fallen from his horse and Jane joked that she was waiting to know how it had happened before she started pitying him as she 'could not help suspecting it was in consequence of his taking orders; very likely as he was going to do duty or returning from it'. Her jokes were increasingly forced.

In June that year Jane and Cassandra had a respite at Godmersham where they played at school with the children. Cassandra was Miss Teachum the governess, Jane Miss Popham the teacher, Aunt Harriot Bridges Sally the housemaid, Miss Anne Sharp, the Godmersham governess, was the dancing master, the apothecary and the sergeant, while Grandmama Austen played Betty Jones the pie-woman, and the children's mother, Elizabeth, acted the bathing woman. They all dressed in character, and children and adults alike all enjoyed themselves.

After dessert they acted a play called *Virtue Rewarded*. Fanny was the fairy Serena and her cousin Anna the Duchess of St Albans. All this, followed by a bowl of syllabub in the evening! No wonder the children had happy memories of fun with Aunt Jane. As for Miss Sharp the governess, Jane became her friend. Miss Sharp kept in touch with Mrs Austen and Cassandra until the 1820s.

The children had another jolly day on 30 July. Cassandra, Jane, Fanny and Anna, with Edward's sons Edward, George, Henry and William, acted *The Spoiled Child* and *Innocence Rewarded*. Dancing followed. Possibly at this time Jane dramatized her favourite novel *Sir Charles Grandison* in collaboration with Anna. Mrs Austen and Anna left Godmersham the next day but Cassandra and Jane stayed on, dining out and attending balls in Canterbury. Henry turned up as well.

In August Jane was writing from Godmersham to Cassandra who was at Goodnestone with Edward's in-laws. The Godmersham party had visited Eastwell, where they played cribbage. Eastwell was a controversial new house in bastardized classical style by the architect Joseph Bonomi, who is mentioned in *Sense and Sensibility*. Bonomi had been commissioned by the Finch-Hatton family in the 1790s to build them a new house. It has been criticized as deliberately improper, in that its immense portico had five columns instead of the correct four or six, there was no frieze on the entablature, and the Ionic columns supported a 'coarse Michelangelesque cap'. This was Jane's first visit.

The Misses Finch had assumed that Cassandra would find it dull at Goodnestone, and Jane wished they could have heard Mr Bridges's solicitude on the subject and have known all the amusements planned to divert her. Miss Hatton at Eastwell had little to say for herself: her eloquence lay in her fingers, which were 'most fluently harmonious'.

Jane had written to Frank and played battledore and shuttlecock (an early version of badminton) with Edward's seven-year-old son William. 'We have frequently kept it up *three* times and once or twice *six*,' she told her brother.

The 'two Edwards' had been to Canterbury to see Mrs Knight, who was cheerful but weak. Edward's eldest boy, Edward, was unwell. His younger brothers were expected to return to school without him while he went to Worthing with the grown-ups, in case the fashionable cure of sea-bathing should be recommended. Jane had found Cassandra's white mittens. Jane's sister-in-law Elizabeth had proposed that Jane should take Cassandra's place at Goodnestone for a few days and Jane intended to turn up there. If her presence was inconvenient she could return in the carriage with Cassandra.

We learn that Mr Hall the hairdresser charged Elizabeth five shillings to do her hair and five shillings for every lesson to her maid. Jane considered he went off with 'no inconsiderable booty', to say nothing of the pleasures of being at Godmersham with food, drink and lodging, the benefit of country air and the company of the servants. He charged Jane only half a crown to cut her hair. Jane commented that he clearly respected either her youth or her poverty, adding that she had been looking into her affairs and was likely to be very poor. She could not afford to tip Sackree, the children's nurse deputed to look after her as temporary lady's maid, more than ten shillings. Strictly speaking, on a country house visit she should have distributed about £5 among the servants but this was totally beyond her means. She said wryly that as she was about to meet Cassandra at Canterbury, she need not have mentioned this. 'It is as well, however, to prepare you for the sight of a sister sunk in poverty, that it may not overcome your spirits.'

When Jane wrote again three days later on 30 August 1805, the sisters had changed places: Cassandra was at Godmersham, Jane at Goodnestone farm with Harriot Bridges. Jane did not want to stay too long, for fear of running out of clothes. She hoped Edward would be able to fetch her on Monday (she was writing on Friday) or Thursday if wet. She was glad young Edward was better.

It was Elizabeth's unmarried brother Edward Bridges who paid her hospitable attentions, ordering toasted cheese for supper specially to please her, but if he did propose to her, he was refused.

She enjoyed walking over the house and grounds at Rowling. That day the First and Second Grenadier Guards marched from Deal for Chatham, the First Coldstream and First Scots Guards from Chatham for Deal. Edward was nervous that the partridges would be disturbed, as shooting was due to begin on the Monday. Jane thought the 'evil intentions of the Guards' were certain. Troop movements on this scale are not surprising. The danger of invasion was only just past, as Napoleon's orders for the march from Boulogne back to the Danube were not issued till 22 August and the camp at Boulogne was being abandoned on the day Jane Austen was writing. She thanked Cassandra for recommending the Revd Thomas Gisborne's *An Inquiry into the Duties of the Female Sex*, which she was rather surprised to find she liked.

Early in September Cassandra and Jane stayed with Elizabeth's sister Sophia, Mrs William Deedes, at Sandling, near Folkestone. Sandling had an unusual feature: one of the sitting rooms was oval in shape, with a bow window at one end. There was a fireplace with a window, the centre window of the bow, exactly over the mantelpiece. William Deedes was Colonel of the South Kent volunteers and from 1807–12 Member of Parliament for Hythe.

By mid-September Godmersham was full again, and the sisters left for Worthing to join Mrs Austen and Martha Lloyd. They bought fish on the beach and Jane won seventeen shillings in a raffle.

Meanwhile Frank on the *Canopus* had won the approval of Admiral Horatio Nelson, who described him as an excellent young man. Frank was involved in the blockade at Cadiz and after Nelson arrived in the *Victory* on 28 September, the *Canopus* was ordered to 'complete supplies' at Gibraltar. Then she protected a convoy en route to Malta. Hearing that the enemy fleet was coming out of Cadiz, Frank made haste to rejoin the main British fleet but contrary winds prevented his reaching the battle of Trafalgar, fought on 21 October 1805. Although he did not care for fighting for its own sake he was disappointed. He wrote to Mary Gibson on 27 October:

> Alas, my dearest Mary, all my fears are but too fully justified. The fleets have met, and, after a very severe contest, a most decisive victory has been gained by the English . . . but I am truly sorry to add that this splendid affair has cost us many lives, and amongst them the most invaluable one to the nation, that of our gallant, and ever to be regretted, commander in chief, Lord Nelson, who was mortally wounded by a musket shot, and only lived long enough to know his fleet successful . . . To lose all share in the glory of a day which surpasses all which ever went before, is what I cannot think of with any degree of patience . . .

In January 1806 Mrs Austen, Jane and Martha went to Steventon, where Jane gave her seven-year-old nephew James-Edward *The British Navigator, or, A Collection of Voyages Made in Different Parts of the World.*

Mrs Austen left Steventon for Bath on 29 January, taking Anna with her, and found temporary lodgings in unfashionable Trim Street, meanwhile looking round for something better. Jane and Cassandra spent three weeks at Manydown, and came home to unexpected riches: Mrs Lillingston of Bath, a friend of Mrs Leigh-Perrot, had made Mr Leigh-Perrot her executor and left money to him, his wife and his nieces. Jane and Cassandra received £50 each. Jane's share was stretched to last her a whole year. Mrs Austen had hoped to find lodgings in St James's Square, but somebody else was negotiating for the whole house, so she expected disappointment.

Frank came to the rescue. He had been in the action off San Domingo and when he docked at Plymouth early in May he had prize money, a gold medal and a silver vase presented to him in recognition of his achievements. He could now afford to marry, though still not rich. He offered them a share in his home at Southampton, then a fashionable watering place. He would not be far from the dockyard at Portsmouth. Jane would put her knowledge of Portsmouth to good use when she came to write *Mansfield Park*. She left the detested city of Bath with happy feelings of escape.

13

Stoneleigh Abbey, 1806

FRANK MARRIED MARY GIBSON at Ramsgate on 24 July 1806 and came to Godmersham for their honeymoon on 26 July. Fanny wrote in her diary on Tuesday 29 July 1806, 'I had a bit of a letter from Aunt Jane with some verses of hers.' They read:

> See they come, post-haste from Thanet,
> Lovely couple, side by side;
> They've left behind them Richard Kennet
> With the parents of the bride!
>
> Canterbury they have passed through;
> Next succeeded Stamford-bridge;
> Chilham village they came fast through;
> Now they've mounted yonder ridge.
>
> Down the hill they're swift proceeding,
> Now they skirt the park around;
> Lo! The cattle sweetly feeding
> Scamper, startled at the sound!
>
> Run, my brothers, to the pier gate!
> Throw it open, very wide!
> Let it not be said that we're late
> In welcoming my uncle's bride!

To the house the chaise advances;
Now it stops – they're here, they're here!
How d'ye do, my Uncle Francis?
How does do your lady dear?

Fanny was just into her teens, an age when girls are hypercritical. If Jane's reputation had rested on her talent as a poet we should never have heard of her. These doggerel verses may have had something to do with Fanny's later conviction that her aunt was ever so slightly common.

In August 1806 Jane and her mother visited their relative the Revd Thomas Leigh of Adlestrop. Mrs Austen was proud of being a Leigh. Her family had owned Adlestrop Park in Gloucestershire near the Oxfordshire border since the Reformation. The original house, built by her great-grandfather, was knocked down halfway through the eighteenth century and replaced with a neo-Gothic building in the newest fashionable style. The occupant was a first cousin once removed, James Henry Leigh, married to the Honourable Julia, daughter of Lord Saye and Sele. Mrs Austen did not look to these grand relatives for hospitality but, as always, feeling at home in clerical company went to the rectory alongside where her cousin Thomas, an elderly widower, lived with his maiden sister, Elizabeth, who was Cassandra's godmother. Thomas, on visits to Steventon, had customarily tipped the children, and Jane and Cassandra had visited Adlestrop in July 1794.

The Revd Mr Leigh had grandiose ideas. He had commissioned the famous improver, Humphrey Repton, to enclose the village green, move the cottages, make a new entrance to the rectory and open up the back of the house. A new garden had been landscaped, abutting the garden of Adlestrop House. A stream of water was diverted through a flower garden, down the hill over ledges of rock and into a distant lake. It was visible equally from the mansion and the parsonage. From *Mansfield Park* we learn that Repton's fees were five guineas a day. Five pounds had been three months' allowance for Jane while her father was alive and was a lower servant's annual wage. The improvements at Adlestrop Rectory are remarkably similar to the ones suggested by Henry Crawford in the novel to Edmund Bertram, who drily answers that he will have to be satisfied with more use and less beauty.

While the Austens were at Adlestrop Rectory the grandest relative of all, the Honourable Mary Leigh, died on 2 July 1806 at Stoneleigh Abbey in Staffordshire. In her will she left the mansion and huge estate to the cadet branch of the family, the Adlestrop Leighs. They were to go to the Revd Thomas Leigh for his lifetime, then to Mrs Austen's brother James Leigh-Perrot, and eventually to James Henry Leigh of Adlestrop Park. Neither Revd Thomas Leigh nor James Leigh-Perrot had any children and neither was young. The family lawyer expected that the two old men would relinquish their claims if paid off with reasonable sums. What, at their time of life, could they want with an ancestral pile? The lawyer, who should have looked at the rectory to see the scale of Thomas Leigh's territorial ambition, had mistaken his man. The natural heir was James Henry Leigh but Thomas Leigh seized on his legacy as a piece of glorious good fortune and set off for Staffordshire at once, whirling his guests with him.

Between Kenilworth and Leamington, the Stoneleigh Abbey estate is superbly sited, the Avon winding through its pleasure grounds and deer park. Originally a Cistercian monastery founded by King Henry II, whose escutcheon is on the gatehouse, it is still occupied. Abbeys and other religious houses passed into the hands of Protestant gentry in the sixteenth century when Henry VIII abolished the Roman Catholic monasteries. The Leighs, who had the place from 1561, had been on the Royalist side in the English Civil War in the seventeenth century, when the Cromwellians cut off the head of King Charles I. Seven years before he met his grim fate, the King rested at Stoneleigh Abbey in 1642. He had marched to Coventry on his way to Nottingham but found the gates of the city shut against him. Harassed and exhausted, the King tried his luck instead at Stoneleigh and received a warm and loyal welcome with generous hospitality from his devoted subject Sir Thomas Leigh. In 1836 a flower painting at Stoneleigh was found to have been painted over a portrait of King Charles I by Sir Anthony Van Dyck. The Leighs supported all the Stuarts and from the time the Catholic Stuart King James II fled from England in 1688, the successive Lords Leigh refused to sit in the House of Lords or have anything to do with public life. This fastidious aloofness lasted well into Jane Austen's lifetime. In her *History of England from the Reign of Henry IV to the Death of Charles I* 'by a partial, prejudiced and ignorant historian', written when Jane was fifteen, she followed family tradition in passionately defending the Stuarts, especially Mary, Queen of Scots, and vilifying King Henry VIII and his daughter Queen Elizabeth I.

Stoneleigh had been added to between 1714 and 1726, when the huge west wing was built. The estimate for erecting it, exclusive of materials and gear such as ladders and ropes, the demolition of the old building and the digging of new foundations, was £545 for three storeys or £463 for two. The three-storey option was chosen. Sumptuous interior decorations cost extra.

When Mrs Austen and her daughters visited in August 1806 they ate fish from the pond and venison from the park, with pigeons, rabbits and poultry from the estate, in a large and noble parlour hung round with family portraits. It was a long way from cold souse and orange wine at Steventon. Mrs Austen was impressed by the size of the house, so big that neither she nor the new owner could easily find their way about. Mrs Austen jokingly suggested setting up signposts. There were forty-five windows in the front and a long flight of steps leading to a large hall. On the right was the dining room and within it the breakfast room where the guests usually sat. The Austens enjoyed the spot as, together with the chapel, it had the best view.

Mrs Austen had expected grandeur but was overwhelmed by beauty. 'I had pictured to myself long avenues, dark rookeries and dismal yew trees,' she wrote to James's wife Mary. Instead, she found large and beautiful woods full of delightful walks. The kitchen garden and orchard, over four and a half acres, had so much fruit that it rotted on the trees despite the depredations of blackbirds and thrushes.

To the left of the hall was the best drawing room, with a smaller one inside. These rooms were rather gloomy, with brown wainscot and dark crimson furniture. Behind them was the old picture gallery and the state bedroom, also gloomy, with a high dark crimson velvet bed. This may have been the one in which the ill-fated King Charles I slept. Behind the hall and the parlours were a passage that crossed the house, three staircases and two small sitting rooms. There were twenty-six bedrooms in the new part of the house and many good ones in the old. Another gallery displayed modern prints on a buff-coloured wallpaper and there was a large billiard room. The house was kept spotless. 'If you were to cut your finger I do not think you could find a cobweb to wrap it up in,' wrote Mrs Austen, alluding to an ancient remedy mentioned in Shakespeare's *A Midsummer Night's Dream*.

They enjoyed their visit, enlivened by the arrival of their agreeable relative George Cooke, and Jane had many a good laugh at the irritating Lady Saye and Sele, a relative of theirs, who visited. She was the mother of 'the adultress'. Lady Saye and Sele was the widow of Lord Saye and Sele, who had committed suicide by cutting his throat after stabbing himself with a sword and trying to drown himself.

When Mrs Austen and her daughters were with her, Lady Saye and Sele was offered some boiled chicken. She refused, adding pathetically that after her husband had destroyed himself she had eaten nothing but boiled chicken for a fortnight, and had not been able to touch it since.

Lady Saye and Sele was self-absorbed and less than tactful. In 1782 she had met the novelist Fanny Burney, already a celebrity, and insisted, 'I must introduce you to my sister, Lady Hawke ... She has written a novel herself, so you are sister authoresses! A most elegant thing! It's called *The Mausoleum of Julia*. Lord Hawke himself says it's all poetry!'

Lady Saye and Sele, unaware that her sister's outpourings were hardly comparable with Fanny Burney's artistic and professional achievement, gushed to the best-selling author of *Evelina* that Lady Hawke's effusion was to be *privately* printed, naturally. Probably this crass woman was equally patronizing to the young Jane Austen, then totally unknown, but whose fame was to eclipse even that of Fanny Burney.

While in Staffordshire, Mrs Austen and the 'girls' called on Mrs Austen's nephew, the Revd Edward Cooper, who with his sister Jane had often stayed at Steventon (they had no mother, she having died in an epidemic). He became curate at Harpsden, Mrs Austen's girlhood home. Unfortunately Edward was less than likeable and in his pomposity and insensitivity seems to have borne some resemblance to Mr Collins in *Pride and Prejudice*. When her brother Edward Knight's wife Elizabeth died two years later Jane hoped that Edward Cooper would not send 'one of his letters of cruel comfort'. He had recently published a volume of his sermons. His eldest son, Edward-Philip Cooper, although not yet twelve, was already precociously pompous, composing sermons and domineering over his brothers and sisters. When Edward-Philip was sent to Rugby in 1809 Jane hoped that being just one raw schoolboy among others would do him good and rub the corners off.

While at Stoneleigh the Austens visited Warwick Castle. It was Stoneleigh Abbey, though, with its ancient grandeur, that offered Jane Austen 'copy'. It became a partial model for Sotherton in *Mansfield Park*. Thomas Leigh held family prayers every morning in the old chapel, hung with black in honour of the departed owner. Then came breakfast, which consisted of chocolate, coffee or tea, plum cake, pound cake, hot rolls, cold rolls, bread and butter. Mrs Austen restricted herself to dry toast. Such matters were seen to by the house steward, 'a fine, large, respectable-looking man'. Mr Leigh was busy with his agent, Joseph Hill, a great part of the day. We think of Sir Thomas Bertram in *Mansfield Park*, who spent the morning after his arrival from Antigua with his steward. Mr Hill was a correspondent of Jane Austen's favourite moral poet, William Cowper.

Mrs Austen was impressed with the dairy, doubtless looking back to the one she had managed during her early married life. Awed, she told James's wife Mary that one servant was called the baker and did nothing but bake and brew beer. A household on this scale might employ as many as forty servants at an annual cost of some £7,000. Stoneleigh employed eighteen menservants, as well as a large complement of females. The new master had to fit them all out with mourning clothes.

This visit to Stoneleigh was Jane Austen's main experience at first hand of high life. Her relatives lived in a genuine stately home, even grander than Godmersham, with a lifestyle to suit. It was a far cry from lodgings at Bath or the small house in Southampton where Mrs Austen and the girls later shared a home with Frank and his wife. Mrs Austen must have hoped that this childless cousin, newly enriched, might do something for her, a struggling widow with two unmarried daughters past the age when they were likely to get husbands. She relied even more, however, on her brother James Leigh-Perrot, whom she had followed to Bath.

Jane too expected a legacy and was bitterly disappointed with the outcome. To her dismay and that of her brother Henry, the Revd Thomas Leigh, coming late into property and wealth, at the age of seventy-two took on a new lease of life, dashing about the countryside between Adlestrop, Stoneleigh and London. He retained his Adlestrop stipend, employing a curate to do the actual work.

His elderly sister, Elizabeth Leigh, coming from a quiet rectory in the Gloucestershire countryside, was bewildered to find herself mistress of the grandeurs of Stoneleigh. Her idea of hospitality was reading sermons aloud to her guests. When Jane's brother James and his family visited on 28 August 1809 she wandered disconsolately around the house trying to find out which of the eighty bedrooms had been set aside for Caroline and the maid allocated to her. She knew Caroline was supposed to be put near her mother, Mary, but couldn't find the mother's room either. She went into several rooms, turning down bedclothes to see whether or not sheets had been put on the beds. Eventually she asked if the little girl, then only four years old, might stay up till after prayers at nine o'clock and then she promised to find out from one of the housemaids where the guests had been put. Disoriented, Elizabeth had gone up the wrong staircase. It never occurred to this innocent lady, fresh from a country rectory, simply to ring the bell for her housekeeper.

Henry was gloomily convinced that Thomas Leigh would live for ever. Still infected with the fashionable rage for 'improvement', Thomas went so far as to make enquiries about landscaping the Stoneleigh gardens, a hobby only possible for the seriously rich. James Leigh-Perrot decided cash in the hand was better than an inheritance in the bush, so was trying to sell his claim for immediate profit. He settled for £24,000 down, and claimed an annuity of £2,000 from James Henry Leigh, plus two buck and two doe deer every year from the Park.

Jane took a dim view of this calculation, considering it to be mean, a 'vile compromise'. Thomas lived on another seven years, leaving not a penny to his cousin Mrs Austen or her dowerless daughters. Uncle James Leigh-Perrot lived on till 1817, the year of Jane Austen's own death. He left everything to his wife. At her death £24,000 was to go to James Austen, who was his executor, descending to his heirs, and £1,000 each to James's brothers and sisters. James died in 1819 and did not live to collect. In June 1808 Jane wrote bitterly to Cassandra, 'Indeed I do not know where we are to get our legacy, but we will keep a sharp lookout.' She was not joking. Mrs Leigh-Perrot did not die till 1836, when £1,000 went to each of Mrs Austen's surviving children. Only Edward, Henry, Cassandra, Frank and Charles were left. The residue went to James's son, James-Edward, later author of the *Memoir* of his Aunt Jane.

14

Southampton, 1806–9

WHEN IN 1806 Mrs Austen and her daughters left Bath for good, they went first to Clifton, now part of Bristol, with 'happy feelings of escape'. In October they went to Steventon, where Frank and his young wife had been staying, and from there they all moved to Southampton, then a city of 8,000 people, to share a house. When Frank was home, the house must surely have been crowded, but when he was at sea the company of her mother-in-law and sisters-in-law was intended to be welcome to his wife.

After temporary lodgings they moved into a rented house on a corner of Castle Square in 1807. The Revd James-Edward Austen-Leigh remembered it, half a century later, as having a pleasant garden bounded on one side by the old city wall. The top of this wall, reached by steps, was wide enough to walk along, offering an extensive view of the river and its wooded banks. At that time there was a castellated folly in the square, built by the second Marquis of Lansdowne, an eccentric who welcomed the French Revolution and collected portraits of its heroes. The original castle, dating from the eleventh century, had been incorporated into a new mock-Gothic palace in 1804. The Marquis was the Austens' landlord. The Marchioness had a light phaeton drawn by six or eight little ponies decreasing in size and graduated in colour from dark brown through light brown to bay and chestnut. The two leading pairs were managed by young postillions, the two pairs nearest the carriage driven 'in hand'. This elaborate procession practically filled up the square. To the small boy looking out of the window of the house lived in by his grandmother and his uncle and aunts, this was a fairy equipage. For Mary Russell Mitford, who visited Southampton in 1812, the town deserved to be the capital of fairyland. It certainly had its picturesque aspects. Newly fashionable bow windows had been added to the old houses. Southampton, at the mouth of the River Itchen, had until Brighton surpassed it in popularity been a fashionable watering place, with sea-bathing and mineral springs. The castle and Frank Austen's house are long demolished. The site was cleared in 1818, and in 1823 Zion Chapel replaced them. Jane's memories of Southampton were unromantic: she had nearly died there during her schooldays. In an early extravaganza, written when she was fourteen and a half, Jane has one of her characters refer to 'the dissipations of London, the luxuries of Bath, and the stinking fish of Southampton'. However, it was nearer Steventon than Bath and on the coast.

Portsmouth, the naval town so well evoked in *Mansfield Park*, was eighteen miles away. In January 1807 Jane entertained Captain Edward James Foote RN, a relation by marriage of Sir Brook Bridges, to a boiled leg of mutton, underdone and barely edible. Captain Foote particularly disliked it, but he was so good-humoured and pleasant that Jane 'did not much mind his being starved'. He gave them all a most cordial invitation to stay at his house in the country. Later Captain Foote was impressed with the Portsmouth scenes in *Mansfield Park*.

After being so far away from her childhood home Jane looked forward to being once more within visitable distance by her eldest brother. Steventon was twenty-three miles away. He did come; not every day, as he had done when they were at Steventon and he was at Deane, only a mile and a half away, but roughly once a week. Unfortunately, his appearances were unpredictable, and Jane complained that although she knew she ought to enjoy the visits of so good and clever a man the truth was that he irritated her by walking about the house, banging doors and ringing the bell for a glass of water. She wished James were more like self-contained Frank. Frank, considerate and kind, gentle in his manner, was used to cramped quarters on board ship and knew how to keep himself occupied; he knotted fringes, cut out patchwork and even worked in silver. Bookish James had no such

131

resources. The church records show James to have been less conscientious than his father. The registers are not so well kept, and he called in surrogate celebrants more often. The 'improvements' to her former home may have aroused Jane's envy or perhaps her regret.

James was suffering a diminution of income. Anna's grandfather General Mathew had died, so James lost the allowance of £100 a year. However, Lord Craven offered James a caretaker appointment, a living worth £300 a year, until a young protégé was ready to be ordained and take it up. James refused, as to him this arrangement smelled of simony (the buying and selling of benefices, an offence against ecclesiastical law). Mary could not understand this principled rejection and did not forgive her husband. There are several of Jane's letters missing from this period, which suggests that Cassandra censored further criticisms of James and Mary.

In January 1807 James, Mary and their toddler, Caroline, were staying at Southampton and Jane had provided rice pudding and apple dumplings. Cassandra was away at Godmersham and had been at Canterbury with Mrs Knight. Frank's wife Mary was expecting a baby, and James's wife Mary had invited Mrs Austen to stay with them in Steventon at the expected time of the birth. Jane was also invited, but because of her hostile feelings towards James's Mary she hesitated.

There were circulating libraries at Ford's in the High Street next to the Market House and at Skelton's at 22 High Street, in addition to a third kept by a Mr Baker. Jane's fastidious taste rejected *Clarentine*, a novel by Sarah Harriet Burney, half-sister to the more famous Fanny, published in 1798. She was surprised to find how foolish it was. She recalled liking it less on a second reading than on the first and decided it would not bear a third. It was full of unnatural conduct and forced difficulties, wrote the woman who had already drafted three distinguished novels herself but as yet published nothing. Jane was disgusted with a new book *Alphonsine, or Maternal Affection* by Madame de Genlis. Not only was the translation poor but 'indelicacies' made the Austens give up reading it aloud in the evenings after twenty pages.

They were much happier with Charlotte Lennox's *The Female Quixote, or, the Adventures of Arabella*, already fifty-five years old. Jane found it as enjoyable as she had remembered, and Frank's young wife, to whom the book was new, enjoyed it too. Jane added sourly that 'the other Mary' had little pleasure from that or any other book. 'Mrs JA' got on Jane's nerves and she found it a matter of regret that too many of clever James's opinions were copied from his less-clever wife. Mary was debating whether she could economize on a journey in order to buy little Caroline a new pelisse. Even so, she talked less about poverty than formerly, Jane observed.

Jane was amazed that her mother was not too disappointed at getting none of the Leigh money but was enjoying the comfortable state of her own finances which to her agreeable surprise left her with a balance of £30 to begin the new year. Mrs Austen had begun 1806 with £68 and was now beginning 1807 with £99, and that after spending £32 on stocks. Frank too had been settling his accounts and making calculations and they all felt they could manage though they hoped the rent would not go up. Frank supported his mother and sisters, his wife and himself, on £400 a year. Of course they still had servants. At this time their cook, Jenny, was away with her own relations and their dinners had suffered from having only Molly's head and Molly's hands to provide them. She was not as good at frying as Jenny.

'Our acquaintance increases too fast,' wrote Jane. Admiral Bertie and the Lances had been added to their circle, and Mrs Lance had offered to introduce them to some more people, but Jane and Frank declined. Jane did not think the Lances would come often. They were rich and lived in a handsome style. The Austens gave Mrs Lance to understand they were far from being rich themselves and Jane thought that Mrs Lance would soon drop them as not worth knowing. Jane was restless and gloomy again and her letters were full of strained wisecracks. A cramped house in Southampton was even less lively than Bath. Even so, Edward's eldest son, Edward, was going to the ancient boys' college at Winchester and Jane said there would always be a spare bed for him at Southampton.

They did not find it easy to avoid company, though, as many local people turned out to be connections. Mrs Maitland in Albion Place was sister to Anne Mathew, James's first wife. A Mrs Harrison, née Austen, was a distant cousin. There was Captain Sir Thomas Williams, whose first wife had been their cousin Jane Cooper, as well as numerous other naval officers who all knew Frank.

That February Jane wrote to Cassandra at Godmersham that she had managed to find some fish, four small soles that cost six shillings, to send to Kintbury. She sent them back in the basket that had brought poultry to Southampton. Jane rather resented her sister's extended absence and said she had more Sorrys than Glads to report. She complained that she saw nothing to be glad about, unless she rejoiced that Mrs Wylmot, a neighbour of Edward's in Kent, had another son and that Lord Lucan had taken a mistress, both of which events were of course joyful to the actors.

Mrs Austen would knit a rug for Cassandra as soon as she returned to choose the colours and the design. Jane teased her sister by saying that Frank and Mary needed her at home in order to help them buy household goods. Jane threatened Cassandra they would spite her by choosing knives that would not cut, glasses that would not hold, a sofa without a seat, and a bookcase without shelves. A dressing table was being made out of a large kitchen table belonging to the house, for which they had the permission of Lord Landsdown's painter, who lived in the castle. 'Domestic chaplains have given way to this more necessary office, and I suppose whenever the walls want no touching up, he is employed about my lady's face,' Jane joked.

The garden was being put in order by a man who charged less than the first one they had asked to estimate. They were to have currants, raspberries and gooseberries, and a laburnum. Jane asked specially for a syringa, for the sake of the line by William Cowper in his long poem, *The Task*: '. . . Laburnum rich/In streaming gold; syringa ivory pure'. She asked Cassandra to bring flower seeds from Godmersham, especially mignonette. Jane was gratified to hear that they were envied their house by many people and that their garden was the best in town.

But while she took pleasure in the garden, Jane's view of society was almost as sour and scornful as it had been in Bath. She put forward a grim view of a recent engagement between a Miss Jackson and a Mr Gunthorpe, predicting she would be very unhappy because of his unpleasant personality and the disapproval of both sets of parents. Of another possible match, she opined that a widower with three children had no right to look higher than his daughter's governess. She snarled, 'Mr Waller is dead, I see; I cannot grieve about it, nor perhaps can his widow very much.' Another malicious comment was called forth when a distant cousin, John Austen, inherited a fortune stemming from old Francis Austen. 'Such ill-gotten wealth can never prosper!' What annoyed her was that it was not ill-gotten. It had bypassed her and it did prosper.

There was a fresh embarrassment: Jane's brother Henry had been engaged to, and jilted, a Miss Pearson before he married Eliza de Feuillide, and Frank's wife had innocently made friends with the family. 'What a contretemps! in the language of France; What an unluckiness! in that of Madame Duval.' Madame Duval is the heroine's grisly grandmother in Fanny Burney's novel *Evelina*. Miss Pearson was a pretty, wicked-looking girl with bright black eyes who gave herself airs and was a notorious flirt. After the break-up Henry had been very much upset, looking thin and ill.

Jane was growing increasingly depressed about childbearing, lamenting that the recurrently fertile Mrs Deedes, Elizabeth Knight's sister Sophia, was going to have another child. Frank's pregnant wife wanted to know via Cassandra at Godmersham how often Elizabeth nursed her baby in the course of twenty-four hours, how often it was fed and with what. This was Elizabeth's tenth, Cassandra Jane, then three months old. Frank was on half-pay waiting for a frigate, having been disappointed two or three times. He spent his time making a fringe for the drawing room curtains.

Luckily, Frank was soon at sea again. He was to command the 74-gun HMS *St Albans* for convoy duty to and from South Africa, China and the East Indies. Early in April he went aboard at Sheerness to provision his ship and was away from Southampton when his daughter Mary-Jane was born on 27 April 1807. The mother was very seriously ill but recovered. Frank came home again before sailing.

At the end of 1807 Jane noted at the back of her diary that she had started the year with £50 15s 6d (she had inherited £50 from Mrs Lillingston) and now had £6 4s 6d left. The largest item of expenditure was £13 19s 3d on clothes, followed by washing at £9 5s 11d. Presents accounted for £6 4s 4d and letters and parcels had cost her £3 17s 6d. The legacy had enabled her to treat herself to the hire of a pianoforte at £2 13s 6d.

There are no letters from Jane for the early part of 1808. She and Cassandra were paying visits together in Hampshire and Berkshire, going to Steventon, Manydown and Kintbury. Catherine and Alethea Bigg were both still single, but their sister Elizabeth was widowed and had returned home with her seven-year-old son, William Heathcote. He went to school with, and became a lifelong friend of, James and Mary Austen's son James-Edward. Years later William remembered a Twelfth Night party where Jane Austen played the part of the malicious Mrs Candour in Richard Brinsley Sheridan's *The School for Scandal* 'with great spirit'.

In May Jane and Henry spent a night at Steventon on the way to London. She stayed with him in his little house at Brompton and on 4 June saw the ladies going to court for the King's birthday celebrations. James had taken Anna to Southampton to stay with Mrs Austen and Cassandra and then brought his wife, Mary, and their children, James-Edward and Caroline, in his new chaise to stay at London's Bath Hotel in Arlington Street. On 14 June Jane met them there. James went ahead by public coach, while Mary, Jane and the children travelled to Godmersham in James's carriage. Mary and James had not been to Kent for ten years. James-Edward enjoyed playing with cousins Lizzie and Charles, but Caroline was overwhelmed by the boisterousness of her many Godmersham cousins. Caroline was then aged three. She dimly remembered this visit to Godmersham in later years. She recalled a lime tree walk and her cousins' pet rabbits, but was not really happy in a strange house.

That summer of 1808 Jane was given the Yellow Room at Godmersham and was surprised to have such a great bedroom all to herself. She found it strange to be at Godmersham with James and Mary but without Cassandra, who had stayed in Southampton. Jane was feeling lonely and sorry for herself. Elizabeth's sister Louisa Bridges was there, looking remarkably well, having recently received an inheritance: 'Legacies are wholesome diet,' commented Jane wistfully.

In June 1808 *Marmion*, a long poem by Walter Scott, had been published just four months. James was reading it aloud in the evenings to the company at Godmersham. Jane explained in a letter that she meant the late, or short, evening, between ten o'clock and supper. She wondered whether she ought to be enthusiastic about Scott's poem, which is a novel in verse, but so far was not. Its subtitle is 'A Tale of Flodden Field' and it includes the well-known ballad 'Lochinvar'.

A few months later she seems to have decided she liked the poem after all, as she sent a copy to her brother Charles in the West Indies along with a home-made rug. Charles had been blockading America's Atlantic seaboard to ensure that America, which was neutral, did no trade with France. He became engaged in Bermuda to Frances Palmer, an English rose, plump, pink-cheeked and blonde. Charles was enchanted with her fair hair. They were married on 19 May 1807. She was just seventeen. He was not able to introduce his wife to his relatives for another four years, by which time the couple had two daughters, Cassandra-Esten and Harriet-Jane. Perhaps because she had not known them from the time when they were babies, Jane never felt close to Charles's children, who were too much like their mother's family – too 'Palmery' – to please her. She also considered them badly brought up.

Getting around the country continued to be a problem for Jane. It was going to be awkward travelling back to Southampton from Godmersham.

> Edward will be going . . . to Alton, where he has business . . . and where he means his son should join him; and I shall probably be his companion to that place, and get on afterwards somehow or other. I should have preferred a rather longer stay here certainly, but there is no prospect of any later conveyance for me . . .

Edward was not going with his son back to school at Winchester, as Elizabeth was expecting their eleventh baby. Jane felt she could not impose on James and Mary, as James had no horse to ride, and she did not want to take his place or be an encumbrance. The previous day when in the carriage they had been rather squashed, and little Caroline had fidgeted. Jane was in fretful mood: 'I am sick of myself and my bad pens.'

Anna had stayed with Cassandra at Southampton and Jane was pleased with her for liking the quay. Anna had also enjoyed a visit to the Isle of Wight with Cassandra and Frank's wife, Mary. Jane tried to interest Anna's father in the girl's good taste but if James was impressed he said nothing about it. Anna seems to have been looked on as a leftover from his previous marriage and may have been understandably resentful. Jane could not resist a dig at Anna's stepmother, Mary, who was turning huffy because she suspected that Anna, now at the awkward age of fifteen, was not going to answer her letter. 'It must be for the pleasure of fancying it,' sneered Jane. In the event Mary's fears were unfounded.

Kind brother Edward later relented and promised to take Jane all the way to Southampton, with young Edward. Before leaving, Jane spent a couple of days with Mrs Knight, who had sent Jane a welcome gift of money. 'The rich are always respectable,' said Jane with characteristic bitterness. Mary went with Jane to Canterbury and Edward drove her home. Mary found Edward's ten children less troublesome than she expected. James took church services while at Godmersham, helping out the incumbent, whose wife was ill. Jane introduced him and her sister-in-law to Mrs Inman, the blind widow of a clergyman at Godmersham. Mrs Inman used to walk about the park with a gold-headed walking stick, leaning on the arm of her servant Nanny Part. She was very old and frail, but cheerful. The Godmersham children must have liked her for they used to take fruit to her after dessert. Jane wrote that they had eaten strawberries three times during the visit.

She wrote next to Cassandra that Alethea and Catherine Bigg were expected at Southampton. She was invited to stay on at Godmersham, but she thought it better to return to Southampton so that it would not look as if she were avoiding them. She explained this to Edward and Elizabeth, knowing they would understand. She did not want to forego her friendship with the Bigg sisters, whose brother she had declined to marry. He was now married to someone else. In addition, Jane was looking forward to being with Cassandra and Martha for a fortnight without her mother, who was going to Steventon.

'Elizabeth,' said Jane wryly, 'has a very sweet scheme of our accompanying Edward into Kent next Christmas.' This scheme was too expensive to be thought of. It meant travelling with young Edward when he returned home for the Christmas holidays from Winchester. 'A legacy might make it very feasible,' Jane added sadly. 'A legacy is our sovereign good.' It was maddening that while she was pinching and scraping it never occurred to relatives with surplus wealth to give her any. Frank had returned to sea and Jane dreamed of his capturing a good prize.

Edward would bring Jane home but there would be time to call neither on the Moores at Wrotham nor the Walters at Seale nor the Cookes at Bookham as Edward wanted to reach Guildford by nightfall so they could spend a couple of hours at Alton. Jane's wishes had to give way to her brother's convenience. 'Till I have a travelling purse of my own, I must submit to such things,' Jane told Cassandra wearily.

Four days later she was delighted to hear that Frank was coming home 'in the true sailor way, just after our being told not to expect him for some weeks.' The wind had been against him, but Jane hoped he was nearing Godmersham as she wrote. Fanny was in 'hourly expectation' of him there. Jane thought Frank's wife Mary, who was staying on the Isle of Wight with little Mary-Jane, would probably shorten her stay now her husband was coming back.

Jane wrote asking Cassandra if she could recommend a small present for 'Mrs FA', Mary. Perhaps a silver knife or a brooch would do? The weather had been cold and disagreeable, although it was the end of June. Jane was writing in the comfort of the library at Godmersham, where there was a fire. 'I daresay you have fires every day. My kerseymere spencer is quite the comfort of our evening walks,' wrote Jane, who had no surplus flesh. A kerseymere spencer was a short woollen jacket.

Jane had visited old Mrs Knight again and been with Elizabeth's mother, the dowager Lady Bridges, at dinner, but what with the Goodnestone and Godmersham parties and Mrs Moore there had been time for only brief chat. All Lady Bridges could do was be kind and amiable, give Jane good-humoured smiles and make friendly inquiries. One card table was formed, the rest sat and talked, and at half-past nine the party broke up. Next day James and Edward went from Godmersham to Canterbury and John Bridges left for London on his way to Cambridge, where he was to take his master's degree.

Jane grumbled that she was tired of writing long letters, but enjoyed receiving them. A relative, Miss Fanny Austen, had married Captain Holcroft of the Royal Artillery. This seems to have been a shotgun wedding as Jane was 'sorry she has behaved so ill. There is some comfort to *us* in her misconduct, that we have not a congratulatory letter to write.'

That summer Elizabeth, though more than six months pregnant with her eleventh child, was talking of taking her three girls, Fanny,

Lizzie and Marianne, to her sister Harriot Moore at Wrotham while Edward was with James and Mary in Hampshire. Elizabeth was looking well except that she'd had a cold. She was considered indeed as more than unusually active for her situation and size, Jane wrote bluntly. It may have been the frankness with which Jane discussed pregnancy that upset Elizabeth's daughter Fanny after she became Lady Knatchbull. For the mid-Victorians, pregnancy was not to be mentioned except by euphemisms such as 'in the family way' and 'in an interesting condition'. Somebody, probably Lady Knatchbull's son Lord Brabourne, has scratched out a reference to Mrs Tilson, wife of Henry's banking partner, in the same letter: ' . . . poor woman! How can she honestly be breeding again?'

James and Edward during their day out, had visited Mr and Mrs Deedes. (Mrs Deedes was Elizabeth's sister Sophia Bridges.) James, who had only three children himself, was struck by the number of children: there were eleven little Deedeses and three little Bridgeses with them. William and Sophia Deedes eventually had nineteen children. No wonder Jane lamented Sophia's frequent pregnancies and in 1817 recommended as a contraceptive measure 'the simple regimen of separate rooms'. William was Colonel of the South Kent Volunteers and Member of Parliament for Hythe from 1807 to 1812. During the peace of 1814 the Czar of Russia passed through Hythe and one of the Deedes daughters had the honour of pouring coffee for him.

Jane was not looking forward to leaving Godmersham. She had many friends in Kent and wrote feelingly that it was pleasant to be with people who knew about her connections and cared about them. Things had been very different with her Aunt Leigh-Perrot's circle in Bath. It was two years and a day since they had escaped from Bath. Kind Mrs Knight was hoping that the Austen women would benefit from their rich relations, but the Revd Thomas Leigh was still hurrying about the country and not thinking of doing anything for anybody. In a week's time, Jane wrote mournfully, her having been at Godmersham would be like a dream. Soon she would have to make orange wine. 'But in the meantime for elegance and ease and luxury: the Hattons and the Milles dine here today, and I shall eat ice and drink French wine, and be above vulgar economy.' However she assured Cassandra that when she got back to Southampton the pleasures of friendship, of unreserved conversation, of similarity of taste and opinions, would compensate for having to make do with orange wine.

Henry came down for the first week of July, and he and James went to Deal to welcome Frank, who had just arrived back on the *St Albans*. James and his family went back to Steventon on 7 July, and the next day Edward took Jane back to Southampton, spending a night at Guildford on the way. Mrs Austen went to Steventon for the second half of the month, and while she was away Catherine and Alethea Bigg stayed with Jane and Cassandra in Castle Square. Catherine had become engaged to the Revd Herbert Hill, who was formerly chaplain to the British factory [trading post] at Oporto, Portugal, but who had returned to England in 1801 because of the war. Mr Hill, quite an elderly man, was an uncle of Robert Southey. Jane hemstitched some pocket handkerchiefs as a wedding present for Catherine, adding a verse:

> Cambrick! With grateful blessings would I pay
> The pleasure given me in sweet employ.
> Long may'st thou serve my friend without decay,
> And have no tears to shed but tears of joy.

That summer the Portuguese and Spanish rose against Napoleon and England supported their fight for freedom. The conflict became known as the Peninsular War. Frank had to escort troopships to the Portuguese coast. On 21 August he watched the land battle of Vimeiro, Britain's first victory. Next day he collected the wounded and the French prisoners and early in September returned to Spithead to put the Frenchmen in the hulks. The Castle Square house was growing too small for six people and a baby plus one or two servants so Frank moved out with his wife and daughter. He went into lodgings at Yarmouth on the Isle of Wight. Perhaps Mrs FA did not get on with her mother-in-law. Possibly the arrangement did not, in today's parlance, work out.

15

Visiting

DWARD'S ACCESSION to Godmersham Park in east Kent
brought Jane Austen social opportunities beyond the reach
of most young women who lived in country parsonages, but
with them came the strain of trying to hold her own among moneyed
folk. Edward lived there after 1797, when old Mrs Knight, widowed in
1794, relinquished it to him, moving to a house called White Friars,
formerly an Augustine Friary dating back to 1325. The site of White
Friars now underlies an urban shopping centre in Canterbury.

Godmersham lay in wooded undulating country about ten miles
to the south-west of Canterbury on the River Stour. There was a deer
park with shady trees. The house was a long low building, a Palladian
mansion of white stone with two wings and a columned portico, with
one summerhouse in the form of a Doric temple and another in that of
a Gothic hermitage. In the centre of the house was a great square hall,
rich in arched carved doorways flanked by white pilasters and surmounted by pediments. The library had a white-painted wainscot em-
bellished with large and richly framed panels filled with family
portraits. There was a model of a ship in a passage.

Rich people lived in grandeur but there was little comfort by
modern standards. Carpets were scanty and there was often only one
sofa, rigid rather than squashy. There were no deep easy chairs until
Queen Victoria's reign. Before that everybody except old people and
invalids was expected to sit up straight on chairs we would consider

suitable only for dining rooms. Springs in chairs date from 1828. Knick-knacks were few and far between.

Godmersham was almost a second home to Jane but even more so to Cassandra. Jane, who went to balls at Ashford, appreciated Edward's generosity as host in doing the honours to his visitors and providing for their amusement. Both sisters were fond of their sister-in-law Elizabeth, whose eldest child Fanny, born when Jane was seventeen, was Jane's favourite niece, although she remained exceptionally fond of James's daughter Anna, too. Anna was encouraged by her aunt's example and kind critiques to attempt novel-writing herself but Fanny was the petted one. Jane kept them amused with running serial stories continued from visit to visit. Both girls were motherless, Anna from the age of two, Fanny from her mid-teens. They consulted their Aunt Jane about their private problems and relied on her absolute discretion, knowing her sense of honour was so strong that she would never pass on anything told her in confidence, not even to Cassandra.

Jane several times mentions Susannah Sackree, the Godmersham children's nurse, in her letters. Sackree lived to be ninety and saw the children of her charges. She is buried in Godmersham churchyard where she is described as 'the faithful servant and friend, for nearly sixty years, of Edward Knight, of Godmersham Park, and the beloved nurse of his children'.

One of those children, Marianne, born 1801, recalled in old age that her Aunt Jane used to bring her manuscripts with her when she came to Godmersham and shut herself up in one of the bedrooms with her nieces Fanny and Lizzie Knight to read them aloud. Marianne and the younger children, hearing peals of laughter, resented being excluded. She complained in later life that Jane, Cassandra and her sister Fanny, eight years older than herself, had all sorts of secrets together while Marianne and her younger sister Louisa were treated as mere children. But it is Marianne we have to thank for the memory of Jane sitting quietly in the library at Godmersham, her sewing on her lap, saying nothing for a long while. Suddenly Jane would burst out laughing, jump up and run across the room to find pens and paper and write something down. Then she would return to her fireside seat and go on stitching quietly as before. Marianne was only twenty months younger than her sister Lizzie, and might well have enjoyed hearing her aunt read aloud from her masterpieces. Unlike Lizzie, who had fifteen children, Marianne died unmarried. She lived to be ninety-five.

The observant Jane Austen travelled only within her native Britain and as far as is known never went further north than Staffordshire but she made the most of her limited experience and wasted nothing. She put her visits to Lyme Regis and to her relations the Leighs at Stoneleigh in Staffordshire to literary use. Her generation popularized the concept of sightseeing and holidays away from home, reviving the habit of travelling for pleasure, which had declined after the Reformation when religious pilgrimages were outlawed.

Country girl though she was, Jane often passed through London on her journeys to Kent. In 1796 she and Frank made two stops: first at Staines, then in London, where they slept at an inn in Cork Street. She gaily described London to her sister as 'this scene of dissipation and vice'. She announced facetiously that she began already to find her morals corrupted. Mrs Percival, in the early unfinished narrative *Catharine, or the Bower*, describes London as 'a hothouse of vice' but Mrs Percival is an old fool. On her way home from London Jane wrote asking her father to fetch his 'prodigal daughter'. She was hoping to find a night's lodging at Greenwich otherwise she would 'inevitably fall a sacrifice to the arts of some fat woman who would make me drunk with small beer'. 'Fat woman' is a reference to the procuress, the notorious Mother Needham, in Hogarth's series of engraved plates *The Harlot's Progress*. She entices an innocent country girl, daughter of a Yorkshire clergyman, into a life of prostitution. Mother Needham was a real person and is mentioned in Alexander Pope's satirical poem *The Dunciad*. London in the eighteenth century was a centre of vice as well as fashion, as Jane was well aware, but the reputed immorality of the city seems to have amused rather than alarmed her.

After 1801 she was able to stay in London with Henry, who had a succession of houses there. While Jane was in London as a girl she went with Henry to Astley's equestrian theatre, which she used later as setting for the renewal of Harriet Smith's relationship with Robert Martin in *Emma*.

Most of the coaches from the south and west of England set down their passengers at the White Horse Cellar in Piccadilly. This stood near to the entrance of what is now the Burlington Arcade, an elegant and expensive shopping mall. Cork Street was just nearby. Jane found in this area the locations for *Sense and Sensibility:* Sackville Street, where Elinor and Marianne Dashwood were kept waiting at the jeweller's shop while foolish Robert Ferrars was fussing over the design of a toothpick, is very near. The shop, kept by a Mr Thomas Gray, was a real one, at number 41, and appears in another novel of the period, *The Absentee* by Maria Edgeworth. Not far away is Conduit Street where the Middletons in *Sense and Sensibility* lodged and further north, beyond Oxford Street, leading out of Portman Square is Berkeley Street where Mrs Jennings had a house. The Misses Steele stayed in Holborn, a far less fashionable district. Bartlett's Buildings, their address, survived into the twentieth century, a quaint alley of dark brick houses with white window frames and doorways with pediments.

After leaving London the Austens travelled across Kent via Sevenoaks, Maidstone and Canterbury. Just short of Sevenoaks they passed through the village of Westerham. The address from which Mr Collins in *Pride and Prejudice* writes is 'Hunsford, near Westerham, Kent'. The novel was begun a few weeks after the London visit with Frank, in October 1796, though originally titled *First Impressions*.

Chevening Park, the seat of the Stanhope family, was on the route to Godmersham. Great-uncle Francis the lawyer had been employed by them and himself owned property nearby. Jane visited him occasionally and between 1792 and 1796, staying with various relatives in Bath and Kent. Chevening Park with its parsonage house (now pulled down) was like Lady Catherine de Bourgh's estate Rosings in *Pride and Prejudice* in being 'well situated on rising ground' and a 'handsome modern building'. Chevening was originally built around 1630 for the thirteenth Lord Dacre but in 1717 was sold to the first Earl Stanhope. It had been extensively renovated late in the eighteenth century. The parsonage house was later to be occupied by the Revd John Austen, a distant cousin of Jane Austen.

The fierce Dowager Lady Stanhope, wife of the second earl and mother of the third, was living in the Dower House. She was the grandmother of Lady Hester Stanhope, the noted traveller and eccentric. Hester was the same age as Jane and a distant relative on her mother's side. Old Lady Stanhope, whose Christian name was Grizel, was in her seventies, and domineering. Her bossiness provided the model for Lady Catherine de Bourgh, and her mother-in-law's name was, interestingly, Catherine Burghill. Catherine's portrait is hung in Chevening Great House.

Travelling, as has been noted previously, held perpetual difficulties for Jane. Her father only briefly kept his own carriage, her widowed mother had none at all, and Jane had to rely on lifts.

Journeys could be eventful. Jane wrote to her sister from the Bull and George at Dartford in Kent describing a near-disaster in 1798. The desk on which she wrote was nearly lost. Jane and her parents were on their way home to Steventon from Godmersham. After a night at the Bull and George it was discovered that Jane's writing and dressing boxes had accidentally been put on to the wrong post chaise, which was on its way towards Gravesend en route for the West Indies. A man on horseback was immediately dispatched and caught up with the chaise after three miles. In Jane's writing box was the sum of £7, which she said was all her worldly wealth. At the beginning of the twentieth century the manuscript of her unfinished novel *The Watsons* was kept in the narrow drawer of this desk in her house at Chawton. The desk is now in the possession of the family.

The Austens had to stop on the journey to have the coach wheels greased and their luggage nearly slipped off the vehicle. Mrs Austen suffered from the fatigue of travelling and was 'a good deal indisposed from that particular kind of evacuation which has generally preceded her illnesses'. Mrs Austen's bowels were known to give her trouble; she also had gouty swellings of the ankles. She took twelve drops of laudanum and dandelion tea.

Throughout Jane's letters to Cassandra their mother's ailments are a running theme. Jane's tone is one of dry resignation and she hints that Mrs Austen is something of a hypochondriac. When Mrs Austen claimed to have a severe head cold Jane remarked that she could feel small compassion on so-called colds without fever or sore throat. On the other hand Mrs Austen had given birth to eight children, which must have taken its toll, although she lived to be eighty-seven.

When her mother was ill and her sister away Jane took over the housekeeping, choosing things she enjoyed herself: veal stew and haricot mutton, ox-cheek with dumplings, pea soup, spare ribs. The hour for dinner, the main meal, shifted during the eighteenth century from noon until early evening and a new meal, afternoon tea, was invented to fill the gap. The Bingleys in *Pride and Prejudice* dine at six-thirty, later than their country neighbours.

In 1798 Jane wrote to Cassandra who was at Godmersham, 'We dine now at half after three, and have done dinner I suppose before you begin. We drink tea at half after six. I am afraid you will despise us. My father reads Cowper to us in the evenings, to which I listen when I can. How do you spend your evenings? – I guess that Elizabeth works, that you read to her and Edward goes to sleep.' 'Work' for ladies meant sewing. Writing from Rowling two years earlier, Jane mentioned how they were all at work making Edward's shirts and she was proud of being the neatest worker in the party. As for the dinner hour, the Austen household gradually followed the fashion, for ten years later in 1808 Jane wrote from Southampton that the dinner hour was now five.

Jane tells Cassandra in 1808 of a dinner party at White Friars with the widowed Mrs Knight, her brother, Mr Wyndham Knatchbull, and the Moores, Elizabeth Austen's sister Harriot and her husband, the Revd George Moore. The occasion and company are typical of Jane's Kent visits, which were sociable, far more so than the quiet household in Southampton. Mr Knatchbull left early and Mr Moore followed him. After their departure 'we sat quietly working and talking till ten, when he ordered his wife away and we adjourned to the dressing room to eat our tart and jelly'. Next morning Mrs Knight had a 'sad headache' (could it have been a hangover?) which kept her in bed. Jane paid a few calls and found her hostess up and recovered.

'But early as it was – only twelve o'clock – we had scarcely taken off our bonnets before company came – Lady Knatchbull and her mother; and after them succeeded Mrs White, Mrs Hughes, and her two children, Mr Moore, Harriot and Louisa, and John Bridges.' The intervals between callers were so short that Jane and Mrs Knight had little time for comfortable talk yet they had time to say a little of everything. Edward came to dinner and at eight o'clock he and Jane 'got into the chair', and the pleasures of her visit concluded with a 'delightful drive home.' A ride in a carriage was a treat.

16

Grief at Godmersham, 1808

FRANK AND MARY moved in September 1808 to Yarmouth on the Isle of Wight. By October Jane was back in Southampton and Cassandra was once more at Godmersham. Edward's sixth son, Brook-John, had been born on 28 September and the child's aunts rejoiced. Jane was relieved the birth had been over before Cassandra arrived. Mr Lyford the medical man had been with Jane and recommended cotton moistened with oil of sweet almonds for her earache, a remedy which proved successful. Jane had finished hemming a handkerchief for James's wife Mary and was expecting James to arrive and receive it on Mary's behalf. 'Mrs JA' had heard that Catherine Bigg was to be married in a fortnight. Such was Jane's life, concerned with family, friends and news.

Mrs Austen had hopes of getting away from Southampton and settling in Alton where Henry's bank had a branch. She was reconciled to the idea of buying furniture and talked of the trouble involved without considering the expense. 'Although Sunday, my mother begins it without any ailment,' wrote Jane sarcastically. Martha was away and Jane complained of being 'alone' although she had plenty of visitors. Her mother's company did not count. Jane had a mischievous running joke that there was a love affair between Martha and the Revd Dr Mant, rector of All Saints' Church. Dr Mant had been highly successful as Master of King Edward's Free Grammar School in the city from 1770 to 1795, and had ten children of his own.

A week later Jane wrote to say how pleased they were that Elizabeth was recovering so well from the birth of her latest child, and wished Edward a happy forty-first birthday. The chimney at Southampton was in a tumbledown state and being repaired by masons. The late Thomas Knight's sister had died, and Mrs Austen, unable to afford new mourning black, had picked an old silk pelisse to pieces, intending to have it made into a dress and dyed. Unfortunately their usual tailor had moved on. Jane asked Cassandra anxiously, 'How is your blue gown? Mine is all to pieces. I think there must have been something wrong in the dye, for in places it divided with a touch.' Jane seriously regretted the four shillings thrown away. It was settled that Cassandra's gown, too, was to be unpicked. Though it was the custom for very few mourners to be present at the burial, even distant connections were expected to go into black.

Jane had played Commerce with the Maitlands but she could risk only one game as the stake was three shillings and she could not afford to lose six. The Misses Maitland had been 'as civil and as silly as usual'. Jane was in a trap of poverty and boredom. Martha was about to come back, and spruce beer had been brewed to welcome her.

Life lacked excitement though not incident. There had been a fire at the local pastrycook's and a back room had been destroyed. The flames appeared as near as those at Lyme had been. Valuable china had been taken out of the house and thrown down anyhow. The house next door, a toyshop, was equally damaged and Mr Hibbs, whose house came next, was so scared out of his senses that he was giving away all his goods, including valuable laces, to anybody who would take them.

Jane was delighted to hear from Godmersham that Fanny was growing up so charming. Jane looked on this niece as almost another sister. '[I] could not have supposed that a niece could ever have been so much to me. She is quite after one's own heart; give her my best love, and tell her I always think of her with pleasure,' wrote the maiden aunt.

Martha brought back several good things for the larder and the Mr Grays of Alton had sent a pheasant and a hare. Jane suspected Henry's connivance. Martha had stopped in Winchester an hour and a half with Edward's three schoolboy sons. She admired young Edward's manners, and saw in George a likeness to his handsome Uncle Henry.

While Cassandra was at Godmersham, mourning clothes became more urgently necessary than ever. Edward's gracious wife Elizabeth died suddenly on 10 October. Although not excessively clever, she had beautiful manners and the gift of making her guests as well as her nearest and dearest happy. Her loss was a dreadful blow for her husband, her eleven children, her widowed mother and her in-laws, who were all fond of her. Her new baby lived to be seventy. Jane was shattered, but thankful that poor Edward had a religious mind to bear him up, and that Fanny had her Aunt Cassandra with her.

Fanny wrote in her diary with an unsteady hand: 'Oh! the miserable events of this day! My mother, my beloved mother torn from us! After eating a hearty dinner, she was taken *violently* ill and *expired* (may God have mercy on us) in half an hour!'

The boys at Winchester were sent away for a few days. They went to Steventon to stay with James, though Jane would have liked them to be with her. She consoled herself for what she frankly confessed to be a disappointment by thinking there would be more in the way of exercise and amusement for them there than they would have had in Southampton. Jane grieved for all the bereaved and promised to do her share of writing the necessary letters to relatives and friends. She was sure that the news would be anguish for Henry but he would exert himself to be of use and comfort. Martha was a rock, a friend and sister under every circumstance. With warmth and sincerity, Jane concluded her letter to Cassandra:

> We need not enter into a panegyric on the departed – but it is sweet to think of her great worth, of her solid principles, her true devotion, her excellence in every relation of life. It is also consolatory to reflect on the shortness of the sufferings which led her from this world to a better.

In Jane's next letter she said how terrible Edward's loss was and that it was too soon to think of getting over it. She hoped that Fanny, who was prostrated, would exert herself to comfort her beloved father. As for little Lizzie, only eight years old, Jane's heart ached for her. Jane was sending Cassandra black clothes and shoes. Jane was to wear bombazine and crepe, according to Southampton fashion. However, Jane reflected that going into mourning would not impoverish her (always a consideration) for having had her black velvet pelisse newly lined she would not need any new clothes for the winter. She had used her old cloak for the lining, and was sending Cassandra's with the like idea in mind, though she believed Cassandra's pelisse was in better repair than her own. One Miss Baker was to make Jane's mourning gown, and another her bonnet, silk covered with crepe. It was a great relief to Jane to know that the shock of Elizabeth's death had not made Mrs Knight or Elizabeth's mother, the dowager Lady Bridges, physically ill. Edward's boys were to continue to stay at Steventon. Meanwhile, the funeral had to be got through. Jane was not sure whether Edward would be able to face it. She took it for granted that Cassandra would take a last look at the corpse before the coffin lid was screwed down.

'Tomorrow will be a dreadful day for you all! Mr Whitfield's will be a severe duty! Glad shall I be to hear that it is over,' wrote Jane. 'That you are forever in our thoughts, you will not doubt. I see your mournful party in my mind's eye under every varying circumstance of the day; and in the evening especially figure to myself its sad gloom – the efforts to talk – the frequent summons to melancholy orders and cares – and poor Edward restless in misery going from one room to another – and perhaps not seldom upstairs to see all that remains of his Elizabeth . . . We are heartily rejoiced that the poor baby gives you no particular anxiety.'

Jane's cool detachment in society could not be maintained in the bosom of her family. She was grief-stricken and in this crisis offered her sister, her bereaved brother and his motherless children all the warmth of her concern and love. Her practical side came into action, enhanced by her strong sense of family loyalty.

The following week Edward's eldest sons, Edward and George, arrived at Southampton, very cold, having chosen to sit on the outside of the stage-coach without overcoats but sharing the one Mr Wise the coachman kindly gave up to them. Jane was delighted with her nephews, now in their early teens: they behaved well and spoke affectionately of their father. George, the younger boy, sobbed aloud.

One is surprised that their Aunt Mary sent the boys on a journey late in October without seeing they were well wrapped up. Jane excused her by saying she had only had time to get them one suit of clothes apiece. With no ready-mades, outfitting was a slow business. Other suits were being made locally, though Jane sighed that she did not believe Southampton to be famous for its tailoring. She hoped it would be better than what Mary had provided in Basingstoke. Edward had a black coat already but both the boys were in need of black pantaloons. 'Of course,' said their kind aunt, 'one would not have them made uncomfortable by the want of what is usual on such occasions.'

She kept the lads amused with bilbocatch (cup and ball), at which George was indefatigable, spillikins, paper ships, riddles, cards, watching the ebb and flow of the river and walks. The three of them had been to church and young Edward was deeply moved by the sermon on the text 'All that are in danger, necessity or tribulation'. After church they went to the quay where George was happily flying about from one side to the other and skipping aboard a collier. In the evening they had psalms and lessons and read a sermon at home but Jane smiled at the boys' resilience and return to conundrums as soon as the service was over. That she should have thought such a ceremony appropriate confirms her brother Henry's description of her as 'thoroughly religious and devout'.

She was afraid that her brother Edward, after the bustle of the funeral was over, might sink into depression. Fanny had written a pleasing letter. The *St Albans* had sailed the day on which the letters telling Frank that Elizabeth had died reached Yarmouth, so they could not expect to hear from him. Mary (Mrs JA) had written pleasantly to Edward's boys. Jane sniffed that this was more than she had hoped. She found it hard to give Mary credit for anything. As a treat, Jane had meant to take young Edward and George to see the celebrated ruins of Netley Abbey but it had rained.

'While I write now George is most industriously making and naming paper ships, at which he afterwards shoots with horse-chestnuts, brought over from Steventon on purpose; and Edward equally intent over *The Lake of Killarney*, twisting himself about in one of our great chairs.' This is an attractive glimpse of life with Aunt Jane. *The Lake of Killarney* was a novel by Anna Maria Porter published four years previously.

Next day they went out in a boat, rowing up the River Itchen, the boys taking the oars part of the way. Jane found their talk amusing. George's inquiries were endless, and his eagerness in everything reminded Jane of his Uncle Henry. In the evening she taught the boys a card game, Speculation, which they enjoyed so much that they could hardly be persuaded to give it up.

In the meantime, letters were flying between Southampton and Godmersham every day among various family members. A kind letter had arrived from the Fowles at Kintbury with two hampers of apples: the floor of the little garret was almost covered. At Kintbury, of the four Fowle brothers only Fulwar was still alive. He was vicar of Kintbury and Lieutenant-Colonel in the Berkshire Volunteers. Reviewing the volunteer troops near Reading in June 1805, King George III said to Fulwar, 'I knew you were a good clergyman and a good man; now I know that you are a good officer.' Fulwar and Eliza, sister to Martha and Mary Lloyd, had six children. It was their son, Fulwar-William, who described Jane Austen as 'pretty . . . like a doll . . .' and, memorably, as 'animated'.

The Stoneleigh business was concluded. Mrs Austen and her daughters got nothing. Jane writes sharply of her Aunt Leigh-Perrot's complaints and discontent. Mrs Austen was shocked, but Jane was not surprised: her aunt's was 'a sad nature'. There was news about which Jane was ambivalent: she heard via Mary at Steventon that the Leigh-Perrots were to allow James £100 a year. 'My expectations for my mother do not rise with this event,' she wrote grimly. 'We will allow a little more time, however, before we fly out.' James was expected, and Jane hoped he would take her and Martha to the theatre.

His extra £100 a year meant he planned to increase the number of his horses from one to three and Mary wanted two of them fit for women to ride. Jane suspected that Edward would be called upon to provide one of them as a present to his godson James-Edward, then ten years old. James's income would now be £1,100 a year after paying his curate £50. This was about double what his father's had been in the same living. John Bond, who had been employed by George Austen, still worked occasionally for James.

Jane was happy on Anna's account that a children's ball was planned at Manydown and Anna, now nearly sixteen, had new white shoes. In the event the Manydown ball was a smaller thing than Jane expected but it apparently made Anna very happy. Jane said it would not have satisfied her when she was Anna's age.

Jane's home, even now Frank and his family had moved out, can hardly have been anything but cramped. However, plans were now afoot for Mrs Austen and her daughters to move into a house provided by Edward.

He was able to offer his mother and sisters the choice of two houses, one at Wye in Kent near Godmersham, the other near Chawton House, his occasional residence in Hampshire. Without even looking at either they decided they preferred Hampshire. In Kent they would have been conspicuously the poor relations among Edward's friends. Edward had inherited the Chawton estate at the same time as he had inherited Godmersham but had always lived in Kent. His Hampshire properties he had rented out, merely checking on them twice a year. Now Godmersham held too many memories and he considered taking up occasional residence at Chawton House.

It was a fine large old house, built before the time of Queen Elizabeth I, with a Tudor porch, mullioned windows and a warren of corridors and passages. The older part was of flint and stone, possibly on medieval foundations, and in the middle of the seventeenth century two red brick gabled wings had been added, necessitating extra staircases. There was an immense hall and a supposedly haunted gallery. The walls were not papered but hung with tapestries and the open fireplaces still had firedogs, four-legged long metal supports for logs, instead of grates. There were portraits by the celebrated artist George Romney of Mr and Mrs Knight. This was the manor house, surrounded by a park. Edward offered his mother and sisters a much smaller house on the estate.

Henry obligingly looked the house over for them and reported there were six bedrooms and garrets for storage. Mrs Austen daydreamed of employing a manservant who could sleep in one of the garrets. Jane hoped to be settled at Chawton by the end of the next summer so that Henry could visit them in October for shooting; if they made it early in September, Edward would be able to come after taking his boys back to Winchester.

Jane determined to have as much social life as possible before leaving Southampton. Everybody in their circle seemed to be sorry they were going and everybody claimed to be acquainted with Chawton, speaking of it as a remarkably pretty village. They were all convinced they knew the house but habitually fixed on the wrong one.

Jane and Martha had enjoyed a recent public ball. They arrived at nine thirty and left before midnight. The room was fairly full, with about thirty couples.

> The melancholy part was to see so many dozen young women standing by without partners, and each of them with two ugly naked shoulders! It was the same room in which we danced fifteen years ago! I thought it all over, and in spite of the shame of being so much older, felt with thankfulness that I was quite as happy now as then.

Jane was approaching her thirty-third birthday and according to the standards of the day was on the shelf. She reported triumphantly that she had been asked to dance by a foreigner with handsome black eyes, whose name she did not know. Formal introductions no longer seemed indispensable to her. At this stage in her life such attention seemed flattering rather than insulting.

After Christmas Jane was idle and missing her sister. Frank and Mary were at Portsmouth, and Jane had to send on more clothes. Mary had an abscess on a tooth, which had been opened. An evening party with Martha's relatives had brought an unwelcome visitor, Miss Jane Murden, a relative of the Fowles who lived with them at Kintbury. She had refused to come earlier and sat ungracious and silent from seven till half-past eleven, 'for so late was it, owing to the chairmen, before we got rid of them', wrote Jane irritably. The last hour had been deadly dull, shivering and yawning round the fire. However, the supper of widgeon and preserved ginger had been delicious and all the apple butter had been eaten. Jane reflected that at Miss Murden's age one might come to be as friendless and captious as she was. The prospect of a lonely, penurious old age was never far away. James's good fortune still rankled.

Edward's wedding anniversary was 27 December, a day of sad remembrance at Godmersham. Jane talked with her fingers to a man totally deaf, and recommended a book to him. This was *Corinna*, a translation of *Corinne, ou l'Italie* by Madame de Staël, which had been published and twice translated into English in 1807. Miss Murden had found new lodgings with Martha's help and was more cheerful. Mrs Austen sold some old or useless silver and bought six teaspoons, a tablespoon and a dessertspoon. Jane was sarcastic about the 'magnificence' of the sideboard and sighed over the way she had come down in the world. Mrs Digweed was looking forward to having the Austens as neighbours again. Jane hoped Mrs Digweed would enjoy the idea at least of renewed friendship but saw little likelihood of mutual entertaining on the Austens' restricted income. The Austen women were more likely, said Jane bitterly, to become intimate with Mrs Digweed's husband's bailiff and his wife, who were said to be very good sort of people. 'Very good sort of people' was often a code phrase for 'respectable, but not our class'.

Jane was afraid of sinking into social limbo. Yet despite her clear-eyed recognition of her situation and prospects, she was happier and more optimistic than she had been for years. She looked forward to having a pianoforte again, as good a one as could be got for thirty guineas. Her old one had sold for eight. Henry was at Godmersham with his wife, Eliza, and Jane expected he would force himself to be cheerful with the children. Meanwhile Cassandra's stay at Godmersham stretched on and on. Jane was looking forward keenly to Cassandra's return, as she had been away now for several months.

Halfway through January 1809 Jane writes to defend herself against Cassandra's accusation of writing letters with little matter in them. 'We are doing nothing ourselves to write about, and I am therefore dependent upon the communications of our friends, or my own wit.'

Jane's life was quiet, but international politics, in which she took an interest, were turbulent. Britain was still fighting the Peninsular War, supporting Spain against Napoleon. Under General Sir John Moore, the Battle of Corunna was fought on 16–17 January 1809 and the British saved Spain. Moore was fatally wounded and his dying words were, 'I hope the people of England will be satisfied.' Within living memory the poem 'The Burial of Sir John Moore at Corunna' by the Revd Charles Wolfe was a standard anthology piece. Jane was shocked that the dying Sir John spoke only of public opinion in England and sent messages to friends in London with no mention of religion. She commented tartly she was sorry to hear that Sir John's mother was still alive: though a heroic son, he might not be 'very necessary to her happiness'. Whatever this may mean, it seems oddly callous, even for sharp-tongued Jane. We are reminded of Dick Musgrove in *Persuasion*, whose mother's grief at his loss is made to seem ridiculous. The death of children, whether adult or stillborn, is never less than dreadful for parents. This is another instance of Jane's deliberately distancing herself from the motherhood she feared yet perhaps secretly yearned for. The *St Albans* was at Spithead, commanded by Jane's brother Frank, having brought home the remnants of the British army.

Jane closely followed these and other public events. She knew, though most people in her social circle did not, that the Portuguese Regent, Prince John of Braganza, who had been rescued from Napoleon by the British fleet and taken to Rio de Janeiro in 1807, was about to place the Portuguese army under British training and discipline. The rumours were circulating in Southampton but not in the rest of the country. Jane wrote, 'my most political correspondents make no mention of it'. Few of the letters Jane Austen received survive. We would give a great deal to share in her political discussions.

Domestically, the departure from Southampton was fixed for 3 April, Easter Monday 1809. They were to sleep that night at Alton and stay with the Revd Samuel Cooke and his wife at Bookham for a few days, hoping to be at Godmersham on 11 April, making a detour on their way to Chawton. Should the Cookes not be at home, they would arrive earlier.

A letter had come from Paragon, rousing Jane to another burst of sarcasm. The Leigh-Perrots were complaining as usual. They found the house so dirty and damp that they had to spend a week at an inn. Their servant had let them down by finding another place. They had a new man but Mrs Leigh-Perrot did not like him: she found him and the new maidservant very, very inferior to the old. Jane might well have remembered her mother's daydreams of employing a manservant at all and fretted on the difference money made to comfort.

Jane was reading *Memoirs of an American Lady* by Mrs Anne

Grant, and *Margiana or Widdrington Tower*, a new novel in five volumes by Mrs S Sykes. She found fault with the *American Lady*, but enjoyed *Margiana*, which as usual she read aloud to share with her mother. 'We are just going to set off for Northumberland to be shut up in Widdrington Tower, where there must be two or three sets of victims already immured under a very fine villain,' she wrote gleefully.

It snowed that January, confining Jane and her mother to the house. The bad weather resulted in a sensational item being reported in the papers. Jane wrote to Cassandra:

> Has your newspaper given a sad story of a Mrs Middleton, wife of a farmer in Yorkshire, her sister and servant being almost frozen to death in the late weather – her little child quite so? I hope this sister is not our friend Miss Wood; and I rather think her brother-in-law had moved into Lincolnshire, but their name and station accord too well. Mrs M and the maid are said to be tolerably recovered, but the sister is likely to lose the use of her limbs.

With the poor weather, Jane was forced to miss church two weeks running. Jane and her mother were reading *Woman, or Ida of Athens* by Miss Sydney Owenson, Lady Morgan, which 'must be very clever, because it was written as the authoress says in three months.' They had as yet read only the preface but Lady Morgan's previous novel, *The Wild Irish Girl*, did not lead Jane to expect much. 'If the warmth of her language could affect the body, it might be worth reading in this weather. I must leave off to stir the fire and call on Miss Murden.'

Resuming her letter Jane reported on Miss Murden's lodgings, behind a chemist's shop. There was a neat parlour behind the shop itself for her to sit in, not very light as the house was built three rooms deep and the parlour was in the middle. Jane wrote ironically that it was, however, very lively from the sound of the pestle and mortar. Until halfway through the twentieth century chemists used to grind and roll their pills in their shops instead of buying them ready packed from pharmaceutical companies. Miss Murden sometimes sat with the Austens and went for walks with Jane, which could be embarrassing, as she talked too loudly.

Charles had taken a small prize, a French schooner laden with sugar, but it sank in bad weather. It was now the end of January but

Jane's September letter was the latest he had received. Charles wrote from Bermuda on Christmas Day, delighted to say that 'my beloved Fanny was safely delivered of a fine girl . . . the baby besides being the finest that ever was seen is really a good looking healthy young lady of very large dimensions and as fat as butter . . . the October and November mails have not yet reached us so that I know nothing about you of late . . .' Innocently he added a poignant postscript: 'I am very anxious to hear how dear Elizabeth has got through her late confinement.'

Jane complained of snow, wind, rain and mud, and leaks in the house, which had necessitated emptying cupboards. This turned out to be due to a blocked gutter, later cleared.

She refused to be interested in Hannah More's didactic tale *Coelebs in Search of a Wife* which she misread as 'Caleb', explaining, 'I do not like Evangelicals.' Reproved for carelessness by her sister she defended herself by saying Caleb sounded honest and unpretentious while 'Coelebs' sounded pedantic and affected.

Edward's motherless little girls, Lizzie and Marianne, aged nine and seven, were sent to a boarding school in Wanstead until their sister Fanny could engage a governess for them. This was a big responsibility for a girl of sixteen, who had in many respects to take her mother's place. Fanny was conscientious and took her duties as acting mistress of Godmersham seriously. It must have been even more traumatic for Lizzie and Marianne to be banished from their luxurious home and packed off to live with strangers after the terrible shock of their mother's sudden death. Edward was too grief-stricken to marry again. In 1811 when a Miss Allen was teaching his daughters, Jane, who so easily might have been reduced to governessing herself, spared the woman a kind thought: 'By this time I suppose she is hard at it, governing away. Poor creature! I pity her, though they *are* my nieces.' The children seem to have been too lively for Miss Allen, for she lasted less than seven months.

Jane remained in touch with a previous Godmersham governess, Anne Sharp, who had worked there for two years, leaving in January 1806. Miss Sharp's next job was as governess to one six-year-old girl but this was too much for her and after a couple of months she became companion to her employer's crippled sister. In 1811 Miss Sharp was teaching four daughters of the widowed Lady Pilkington. The baronetcy had descended to Sir William of whom Miss Sharp wrote 'highly' and Jane said, 'I do so want him to marry her! There is a dowager Lady presiding there, to make it all right.' But nothing of the kind happened. Eventually Miss Sharp set up her own boarding school.

Miss Sharp found *Mansfield Park* excellent, but preferred *Pride and Prejudice* and rated *Emma* between the two. She visited Chawton in June 1815. James-Edward Austen-Leigh met her at Chawton in 1820 after Jane was dead and told his half-sister Anna that she was horribly affected but quite amusing. If Jane had been the snob she is sometimes accused of being, she would not have formed a friendship with a governess, often regarded as merely a superior kind of servant. She wrote to her as 'My dearest Anne'. Jane respected Miss Sharp as an independent woman who earned her own bread.

The family were wanting to leave Southampton but Mrs Austen fell ill in March. They were due at Godmersham in April but were delayed once more. Frank's wife had moved to a cottage near Alton and was expecting another baby in June. Frank had gone to China and was likely to be away for two years.

The Austens left Southampton on Easter Day, 2 April 1809. They went first to the Cookes at Bookham, reached Godmersham on 15 May and stayed till the end of June. On 12 June poor Cassandra's white pelisse was covered with black mud when a gust of wind blew it against the wheels of the carriage as she was getting out. White was a fashionable colour and must have been difficult to keep clean; mud and dirt at the time included plenty of horse manure.

Eliza de Feuillide arrived at Godmersham on 22 June. She and Henry were moving from their little house at Brompton, then a village, to a smart one at 64 Sloane Street. Fanny was so impressed that she wrote in her diary that Uncle and Aunt Henry Austen had gone away 'early *ce matin. Quel horreur!*' Eliza presumably, to Fanny's dazzled eyes, exemplified the social polish Fanny was later to conclude Jane and Cassandra lacked. Fanny despised her aunts for liking the everyday names Robert and Susan, which she considered a depraved taste. Young Fanny, dear as she was to her Aunt Jane, was rather a snob.

17

Regeneration

$\mathcal{J}$ANE AUSTEN'S WRITING falls into two distinct phases, Steventon and Chawton, before and after the unhappy period at Bath. The early burlesques, *Catharine, or the Bower* and the original drafts of her early novels were written at Steventon before the move to Bath in 1800.

An early draft of *Pride and Prejudice* titled *First Impressions* was begun in October 1796 and finished in August 1797 when Jane was twenty-one, the same age as its heroine Elizabeth Bennet. Jane's niece Anna, aged four and living with her grandmother, listened to Jane reading the story aloud to her sister. Downstairs little Anna chattered of Elizabeth and Darcy, arousing anxiety in her aunts who wanted to keep the project a secret; anyway there were various real Elizabeths and Janes around, which could have been embarrassing.

Jane's proud father wrote to a publisher called Cadell three months after *First Impressions* was finished, offering 'a manuscript novel comprising three volumes about the length of Miss Burney's *Evelina*'. He asked Mr Cadell if he would be interested in looking at the work with a view to entering into some arrangement for publication 'at the author's risk or otherwise'. By this time Jane had started work on an early version of *Sense and Sensibility* called *Elinor and Marianne* of which nothing survives though it is believed to have been epistolary. The offer of *First Impressions* was rejected by return of post and after such discouragement no further effort was made to publish the novel until Jane's father was dead and she was in need of money.

Northanger Abbey, originally called *Susan*, was written in 1798–9. In some ways it reverts to the parodies Jane had been writing since she was fifteen, but was not published until 1818, the year after her death, along with her last novel, *Persuasion*.

A few months before she started *First Impressions* Jane half seriously told her sister in a letter acknowledging Cassandra's praise of her last communication that she wrote only 'for fame, and without any view to pecuniary emolument'. In fact she never did seek fame though it later crept up on her. The idea of writing for 'pecuniary emolument' on the other hand almost certainly did cross her mind.

During 1802 or early 1803 Jane made a second copy of *Susan* (a different book entirely from her epistolary novel *Lady Susan*), inserting a reference to Fanny Burney's *Belinda*, published in 1801, in the famous defence of novels and novelists at the end of the fifth chapter. Henry, through his lawyer Mr William Seymour, offered the manuscript to Richard Crosby and Son of Stationers Hall Court, Ludgate Street, London. It was accepted and Jane received £10 for the copyright. Outright sales of books with such one-off payments were customary until much later in the nineteenth century. Sometimes the author paid for the printing. Jane now had some welcome cash and the consciousness of success, but the book was not published. Crosby hung on to the manuscript for six years. He advertised *Susan* in *Flowers of Literature* in 1803, but never printed it, possibly realizing it made fun of the Gothic romances which were his own bread and butter. Jane Austen was totally unknown and he did not want to risk upsetting his established authors by her mockery. Years later, after Jane had found recognition as the author of *Pride and Prejudice*, Henry took satisfaction in telling Crosby what a mistake he had made.

During the Bath sojourn, Jane made only one creative attempt. She started another novel and completed some 17,500 words. This was *The Watsons*. She never finished it, but later recycled some of its incidents and names.

In 1809 Jane remembered the sale of *Susan* to Richard Crosby. Using the pseudonym 'Mrs Ashton Dennis' and giving her address as the Post Office at Southampton, she wrote him a sharp letter on 5 April, reminding him that early publication had been stipulated for at the time of sale. If the manuscript was lost, she told Crosby, she could supply a duplicate. If she received no reply she would seek publication elsewhere.

Crosby replied that although what she said was true up to a point, there had been no stipulation that the book should be published, nor was he bound to publish. If she or anybody else did so proceedings would be taken. He offered to sell her manuscript back to her for £10. She bought it. Discouragement could hardly be more severe.

Soon after the move to Chawton in 1809 the second fertile period began. Jane started revising her earlier novels for the press. Not all achieved publication. For example, in *Catharine, or the Bower* she substituted Hannah More's *Coelebs in Search of a Wife*, published in 1809, for the original example of pious (and dull) reading, Bishop Seckar's *Explanation of the Catechism*; but *Catharine* remained unfinished and was not published until Jane's early fragments and short pieces were collected by R W Chapman in the twentieth century.

Sense and Sensibility, the first of Jane's novels to be published, appeared in 1811. *Pride and Prejudice* was later revised and retitled, as another novel called *First Impressions* by Mrs Margaret Holford had appeared in 1801. *Pride and Prejudice* was not published till 1813. The phrase 'pride and prejudice' came from Edward Gibbon's *Decline and Fall of the Roman Empire* and was repeated in one of Jane Austen's favourite novels, Fanny Burney's *Cecilia*. The new title, contrasting alliterative abstract nouns on the model of *Sense and Sensibility*, was an improvement and provided continuity. The words 'Sense and Sensibility' appeared as a headline in a journal called *The Lady's Monthly Museum* in 1799 and may have struck Jane Austen as crisper than *Elinor and Marianne*.

Less than six years elapsed between the final revision of *Sense and Sensibility*, and the completion of her final novel, *Persuasion*. All the novels originally appeared anonymously: *Sense and Sensibility* as 'by a Lady' and *Pride and Prejudice* as 'by the author of *Sense and Sensibility*'.

After Jane's writing found acceptance, the tone of her letters to Cassandra utterly changed. The letters of her early thirties were bored, complaining, on the edge of being sour: as soon as she started to publish books, she chattered away excitedly on paper as fast as she could write. She had found a role and her self-confidence increased.

Jane Austen's career as a published author began only after she had a settled home at Chawton, comparatively small though it was. The days of wandering from lodging to lodging in Bath and confinement in cramped quarters in her brother's house at Southampton were over at last. Back in her beloved native county she could settle down to serious writing and earn money. She was much happier and her creativity blossomed. She revised *Northanger Abbey, Sense and Sensibility* and *Pride and Prejudice*, all of which had been drafted at Steventon, and composed *Mansfield Park, Emma* and *Persuasion*, all in rapid succession. *Mansfield Park* appeared in 1814, *Emma* in 1816.

Despite the celebrity of Fanny Burney and Maria Edgeworth, fiction writing was not altogether regarded as a respectable activity for a gentleman's daughter. There were many now-forgotten novels by and for women, borrowed from circulating libraries for a small subscription. Novels were expensive. At the beginning of the nineteenth century novels were bound in three volumes, often each containing 100,000 words and sold at one and a half guineas, when half a guinea was a weekly wage for many people. Life was slower and duller, and it is not surprising that people with not enough to do should find novel-reading addictive. Moralists attacked the habit. The poet Samuel Taylor Coleridge wrote, 'Where the reading of novels prevails . . . it occasions in time the entire destruction of the powers of the mind; it is such an utter loss to the reader, that it is not so much pass-time as kill-time.'

Yet despite such contumely, the novel form was well established by the time Jane Austen was writing and her earliest works were parodies. After her death her brother Henry wrote proudly that his sister's work had 'by many . . . been placed on the same shelf as a D'Arblay or an Edgeworth'. Madame D'Arblay was the married name of Fanny Burney. Maria Edgeworth hedged her bets: she asserted that novels only encouraged 'folly, error and vice' and insisted her own fictions were not novels but 'moral tales'.

The novels of Fanny Burney and Maria Edgeworth are now read only by students and scholars while Jane Austen's increase in popularity. But in her own day Jane Austen felt the need to defend her own productions in a famous passage from *Northanger Abbey* declaring that novels exhibit genius, wit, taste and knowledge of human nature.

18

Chawton, 1809

CHAWTON COTTAGE STANDS in a picturesque and traditional English village, many of its houses roofed with thatch. On 7 July 1809 Mrs Austen and her daughters moved in. For all three of them it was to be their last home. Martha Lloyd moved in with them. Five days later at Rose Cottage, Alton, a mile away, Frank's wife gave birth to a son, a brother for Mary-Jane, and Jane sent her brother a congratulatory letter in rhyming couplets including these lines:

> Cassandra's pen will give our state
> The many comforts that await
> Our Chawton home – how much we find
> Already in it to our mind,
> And how convinced that when complete,
> It will all other houses beat,
> That ever have been made or mended,
> With rooms concise or rooms distended.
> You'll find us very snug next year;
> Perhaps with Charles and Fanny near . . .

Chawton is in country even more beautiful, because hillier, than secluded Steventon. Enclosures had been carried out early in Hampshire and the farmlands had matured into a patchwork of fields and woods. Chawton parish had some sixty families, amounting to some 400 people, most of them labourers. Chawton Cottage had been the home of Mr Knight's late bailiff Bridger Seward. His widow had to move out.

Edward paid for extensions and improvements. Structural alterations cost him £45 19s 6d and plumbing £35 6s 5d. His labourers delivered firewood, chopped it up and dug the garden. He provided a donkey carriage and spent £3 4s 6d that winter on hay and corn.

Edward has been criticized for not providing earlier or more handsomely for his mother and sisters but he had eleven children, two estates to manage and consequent expenses together with a tug-of-war over his inheritance. He was amiable, kind and indulgent to all connected with him and possessed a spirit of fun and liveliness which made him popular with young people despite his perpetual ill-health.

Edward's fourth son, William, born 1798, was busy embroidering a footstool. Jane was sure his grandmamma would value it very much as a proof of his affection and industry and decided she must make a muslin cover in her favourite satin stitch to protect it from dirt. She longed to know what colours the ten-year-old boy was using.

Chawton Cottage was a real cottage which might have pleased Marianne Dashwood in *Sense and Sensibility*, for it had dormer windows and a picket fence guarding a narrow strip of front garden, so small that the door opened almost directly on to the road. According to rumour the house had once been a roadside inn. The cottage stood at a fork where the Winchester road branched off from the one to Gosport. In the fork stood a fingerpost on a grassy patch and nearby was a large shallow duckpond. The fingerpost and the duckpond have disappeared but Chawton is in a peculiarly beautiful and unspoiled part of Hampshire about five miles from Selborne, home of the naturalist Gilbert White, author of *The Natural History of Selborne*, whose life overlapped Jane Austen's.

Built of brick with a steep tiled roof and sash windows on two storeys, the house was formerly whitewashed and had a thatched lean-to at the side. Facing the road were two parlours called the dining and the drawing room. The large drawing room window was blocked up and made into a backing for a bookcase when Mrs Austen moved in, and another decorative window with the newly fashionable Gothic glazing bars opened up at the side. Edward, used to looking out on spacious parkland, assumed his mother and sisters would be distressed by their close proximity to the road though Mrs Austen's pleasure was watching the world go by. Passers-by could watch the Austens eating their meals in the dining room.

The house was modest, with low ceilings roughly finished, and none of the six bedrooms was large. At the back were the 'offices', consisting of a barn, granary, bakehouse-washhouse and a well. From the dining room all that could be seen was the busy road, with the daily spectacle of Collyer's morning coach from Winchester drawn by six horses, while the evening coach back had only four because the return journey was downhill. At noon there was the coach from Portsmouth. Boys travelling to and from school at Winchester passed with their boxes. In 1816 Jane watched countless post chaises full of 'future heroes, legislators, fools and villains'. There was a wagon for luggage or for passengers who could not afford coach fare. The house was right on the road so that, as Caroline remembered, passing carriages seemed to shake the beds.

Behind the house in Jane's time was a higgledy-piggledy sort of garden and orchard with sheds and outhouses. Three pieces of land had been put together. A thick, tall hedge divided this garden from the Winchester road, and round it was a pleasant shrubbery walk with a rough bench or two. There is a story that an oak tree, only felled in the last few years, was planted by Jane herself. And why not? We know she loved trees and mourned the fallen elms at Steventon. She could well have picked up an acorn and planted it. The tree believed to be hers has been replaced.

Within the garden were lawns, borders, fruit trees, vegetables and flowers. A turf walk, flanked by flowerbeds with a sundial at the centre, led to a yew arbour. Mrs Austen, now almost seventy, pursued needlework and gardening. She still grew her own vegetables. It was a quiet life. All the women read a great deal, and besides the housekeeping Jane and Cassandra, far from rich themselves, concerned themselves with 'the poor'. Cassandra is said after her sister's death to have taught children 'here and there' reading, writing, catechism and sewing, the obligations of their class, though Jane's letters make no mention of such charitable activity. Cassandra had a dog called Link, who always went with the servant William Littleworth for milk, and carried the milk can home in his mouth. Mrs Austen finally got her manservant.

Jane did treat herself to the pianoforte she had promised herself in Southampton. She must have been miserable over the previous years, with no means of making music until her small legacy enabled her to hire an instrument. Now, happy to have a pianoforte of her own once more, she practised chiefly before breakfast, a custom observed by other ladies at the time, and in the evenings would sing old songs to her own accompaniment. She was fond of a little French ditty about swallows: *'Que j'aime à voir les hirondelles/Volent ma fenêtre tous les jours'*. She said she would play country dances to amuse the nephews and nieces.

Several music books of hers survive; one, half-bound with mottled paper sides, contains 'twelve canzonettes for two voices, by William Jackson, of Exeter', followed by a collection of Scots songs including 'The Yellow Haired Laddie'. On the fly-leaf is written 'Jane Austen' in her own delicate writing. A manuscript book of music, bound in parchment, bears her name on the cover. Among its pieces are to be found the song called 'Ask if the Damask Rose Be Sweet', from 'Susannah, an oratorio by Mr Handel', and one of Handel's minuets. Jane was fond of songs from the shows, with titles like 'I'm Jolly Dick the Lamplighter' and 'The Tippling Philosophers'. She had 'The Wife's Farewell' from a farce called *Of Age Tomorrow* and 'The Soldier's Adieu' by Dibdin. As she copied out the words 'Remember thou'rt a soldier's wife' Jane carefully crossed out the word 'soldier's' and, loyal as always to the senior service, wrote in above the line the word 'sailor's' instead. Her niece Caroline said Jane's music was 'disgracefully easy'. But Jane enjoyed it.

Making breakfast for nine o'clock was her responsibility and she was in charge of the tea, sugar and wine stores. At the time these expensive luxuries were normally locked up. Cassandra and Martha Lloyd did the rest as Mrs Austen had given up housekeeping and no longer even sat at the head of her own table. After lunch the sisters usually went for a walk, sometimes into Alton for shopping, at others to visit the Great House, especially when their brothers were there.

Lacking money and with only a donkey cart for transport, the women led a restricted social life, mixing chiefly with relatives. Martha Lloyd's frustrations can only be guessed at, though when over sixty she married Frank, by then a widower, and ended up as Lady Austen when he was knighted. At Alton were Jane's old friend Harry Digweed and his wife, née Jane Terry. It was of her that Jane Austen said she could not bear the thought of Mrs Digweed not being 'foolishly happy after a ball'.

Jane used to climb a stile at the bottom of their garden and walk across a field to visit Miss Prowting at a neighbouring farm. The Prowtings lived in a house larger than Chawton Cottage, set back from the road. Mr William Prowting was a magistrate and Deputy Lieutenant for the county. He had two unmarried daughters, Catherine-Ann and Ann-Mary, both a little younger than Cassandra and Jane. In 1811 Ann-Mary married a sailor, Captain Benjamin Clement, and the couple lived across the road from Ann-Mary's father and sister.

Generally the Austen sisters formed few close friendships with neighbours at this time but kept up as much contact as possible with their brothers and their growing families. Edward's sons would drop by regularly on their way to and from school in Winchester. Family conversation was lively but never quarrelsome. James's daughters, Anna and Caroline, adored their Aunt Jane and her playful talk. Jane had a talent to amuse not only adults but children as well. Caroline too wrote poems and stories. Jane gently warned her that it might be wiser to write less and read more, at least until she was sixteen.

The Great House, or Chawton Manor, was only a few hundred yards away, on rising ground. The current tenant was Mr John Charles Middleton, a widower with six young children. His sister-in-law, gushing Miss Maria Beckford, kept house for him.

In the hollow lies the church where the church clerk, William Carter, played the bassoon. He and four singers sat in the front gallery, the boys and sexton in the one at the back. One of Edward's daughters helped train the male voice choir. Old Mrs Knight employed a music teacher called Mr Giffin to train the school children in hymn-singing.

One of the church singers, William Arnold, was the village postman. As well as the fee according to the weight of the letter, twopence had to be paid on delivery, one penny for the postmaster, one for the postman. Delivery services were not universal. Some letters had to be collected from the Post Office and where no post office existed, from inns. A branch of Henry's bank, Austen Gray and Vincent, was at 10 High Street Alton, so family letters could travel with bank business, saving on postage.

The Rector of Chawton was the Revd John Rawstorne Papillon. In

1803 Mr Papillon had rebuilt his rectory and lived there with his unmarried sister Elizabeth. Old Mrs Knight, who took a kindly interest in the Austen sisters' welfare, told Cassandra that he would be just the man for Jane to marry. Presumably she considered Jane at thirty-three still eligible but expected Cassandra, nearly three years older, to be dedicated to the memory of Thomas Fowle. Jane was amused and told Cassandra:

> I am very much obliged to Mrs Knight for such a proof of the interest she takes in me – and she may depend upon it, that I will marry Mr Papillon, whatever may be his reluctance or my own. I owe her much more than such a trifling sacrifice.

Their circle was full of single women, many of them genteel but poor. Men who had lost their wives, as so many did, often married not spinsters but widows, as Jane recorded in her letters. By this time Jane had probably outgrown all hopes of love and marriage for herself. She and Cassandra were better off than poor Miss Benn, sister of the Revd John Benn, rector of the neighbouring parish of Farringdon. Mr Benn had twelve children. Hard-pressed himself, he could not help his sister. She rented a cold leaky hovel from one of the villagers, old Philmore, who in 1813 ordered her out because his son wanted it. Jane mentioned old Philmore's funeral in March 1817. Miss Benn's meagre existence was a painful reminder of how far Jane and Cassandra might have sunk if Edward had not been adopted by the Knights and if other brothers had not been generous.

Jane used to write in the small living room on the right-hand side of the house where the family meals were eaten. According to family tradition she was careful that nobody, not even the servants, should know what she was about, so she wrote on small sheets of paper which could easily be put away or covered with a piece of blotting paper, relying on a creaking door to warn her when anybody was coming. This may be true, though there comes a time when scrappy jottings have to be collated and woven into coherence. A full-length novel in fair copy is a bulky object. The creaking door is still there, unoiled, as a curiosity and its noise demonstrated to visitors. It is easy for the word-processor generation to forget the sheer drudgery of writing a full-length book by hand. When it was not possible to shunt paragraphs at the touch of a button a writer had to have a clear idea of what she wanted to say and the way she wanted to say it before she started.

Edward stayed for extended periods at Chawton and lent the house to Frank and Charles when they were ashore after Middleton's lease expired. Edward arrived on 21 October 1809 with Fanny and his fifth son, little Charles, to stay at the cottage for three weeks. In November Edward went home with his children via Steventon, collecting Anna and taking her back with him.

Anna was in disgrace, having become engaged at the age of sixteen to the Revd Michael Terry, who was twice her age. Anna was unhappy at home and looking for an escape route. She had grown up starved of affection, except from her grandmother and her aunts. Michael was one of thirteen children and a graduate of St John's College, Cambridge. He would have been a good match for he was tall, good-looking and well connected; he had in prospect a good family living. But James and Mary refused to recognize the engagement and packed Anna off to Godmersham. Mary was nearing forty, and plain. She cannot have been altogether pleased to have a pretty stepdaughter flaunting evidence of her own sexual attractiveness.

In the New Year of 1810 Mr Terry's sister Charlotte pleaded on his behalf and Fanny wrote to Cassandra begging her to mediate. James reluctantly gave his consent and Mr Terry was permitted to call at Godmersham to see Anna. She returned to Hampshire and in April went to stay for three days with the Terry family. As her Aunt Jane had done seven years previously, Anna decided she had made a mistake and her father put an end to the relationship. One of Anna's daughters thought Mr Terry not clever enough for Anna, saying it would have been as bad as a match between Lizzie Bennet and Mr Collins in *Pride and Prejudice*. Fanny, having interfered from the best of motives, was disappointed. She decided Anna was as unstable as the family said she was. 'What a girl!' wrote Fanny in her diary. 'Heavens! What will she do next?' Anna's father and stepmother were exasperated and banished her to Chawton Cottage for three months. Jane, whose own equilibrium had been hard won, was worried by Anna's emotional volatility which made her fear for the girl's future happiness. She wrote a 'Mock Panegyric on a Young Friend', beginning:

In measured verse
I'll now rehearse
The charms of lovely Anna;
And first her mind is unconfined
Like any vast savannah.
Ontario's lake may fitly speak
Her fancy's ample bound;
Its circuit may, on strict survey,
Five hundred miles be found . . .

Jane's talent was not for poetry. But she was warning her niece in true eighteenth-century fashion about the dangers of emotional self-indulgence. Anna went home in mid-July with Mrs Austen.

Jane and Cassandra went to stay at Manydown and came to dinner at Steventon early in August. Young Fulwar-William Fowle, nephew to Mary and Martha, visited and heard Jane reading aloud. She was, he said, a very sweet reader. She had just finished the first canto of *Marmion* and was reading the second when William Digweed was announced. For the young boy it was like the shattering of a pleasant dream. Jane had clearly overcome her distaste for Scott's poem. Caroline said that when her Aunt Jane read aloud from Fanny Burney's novel *Evelina* it was like a play. Jane had histrionic abilities as well as a speaking voice generally agreed to be pleasant.

Edward and Fanny came to Steventon in October. Edward was also good at story-telling and the parsonage children loved him. He and Fanny went on to Chawton and stayed three weeks.

In contrast to the quiet domestic lives of their brothers and sisters the naval Austens travelled the world and pursued increasingly successful careers. Frank had returned from China earlier than expected, having managed to bring his crew safely away from Canton after friction with the Cantonese. The East India Company rewarded him with 1,000 guineas. Charles wrote from Bermuda to say he had a second daughter, Harriet-Jane, and the following May he was promoted post-captain into the 74-gun HMS *Swiftsure*.

The sisters had been together for two years without a break. In April 1811 Jane visited Henry in London, where she was correcting proofs of *Sense and Sensibility*. She had agreed to publish it at her own expense and was putting money aside to cover the expected loss.

Various commentators have assumed that Jane Austen distrusted the city and endorsed the values of rural life but in fact she seems to have found London stimulating. 'I find all these little parties very pleasant,' she told Cassandra. She might have gone to town more often if she had not been so poor, and tasted the cosmopolitan social delights enjoyed by Eliza de Feuillide, instead of making do with occasional balls in Basingstoke. Jane always took pleasure in shopping.

'I am sorry to tell you that I am getting very extravagant and spending all my money; and what is worse for *you*, I have been spending yours too,' she wrote cheerfully to Cassandra, though her writing had earned her nothing as yet. She had bought herself some checked muslin at seven shillings the yard. She had been tempted into laying out on ten yards of pretty coloured muslin with a small red spot for Cassandra at half that price. If Cassandra did not like it Jane would not be put out, she said, but would happily keep the lot. She had also bought some beaded trimming at two shillings and fourpence and three pairs of silk stockings for a little under twelve shillings though the shop had been so crowded she had been forced to wait half an hour to be served. She was having a new hat made, straw, of the riding hat shape, as well as a pretty new bonnet. 'I am really very shocking,' said Jane, taking pleasure in her own recklessness. New pelisses cost only seventeen shillings apiece, she was pleased to learn, though the buttons were expensive.

Henry would have taken her to the theatre but a cold had kept her at home. She had hoped to see Shakespeare's *King John* with the celebrated Sarah Siddons as Constance the bereaved mother, but *Hamlet* had been substituted. They settled for *Macbeth* the following Monday, but hearing that Mrs Siddons would not be acting gave up their seats. In the event they went on the Saturday to the Lyceum and saw *The Hypocrite*, based on Molière's *Tartuffe*. Jane was grieved to miss seeing Mrs Siddons. 'I could swear at her for disappointing me,' she told Cassandra.

Eliza and Henry lived in some style. A grand party, with eighty people invited, was in the offing: there was to be 'some very good music' with five professionals, three of them glee singers, as well as amateur performers. 'One of the hirelings is a capital [performer] on the harp, from which I expect great pleasure,' added Jane. Eliza went shopping with Jane, Eliza for chimney-lights for her party, thrifty Jane for darning cotton.

In the upshot everything went off well. The rooms, dressed up with flowers, looked pretty. The festivities started with a dinner of 'very fine soles' at half-past five, the musicians arrived at half-past seven in two hackney coaches and by eight o'clock 'the lordly company' began to appear. The music was as good as Jane had hoped. Glees sung included 'Strike the Harp in Praise of Bragela', 'In Peace Love Tunes', 'Rosabelle', 'The Red Cross Knight' and 'Poor Insect'. There were performances on the harp, and on harp and pianoforte together. The harp player was Wiepart, whose name Jane was told was famous though unknown to her. 'There was one female singer, a short Miss Davis all in blue, bringing up for the public line [training as a professional], whose voice was said to be very fine indeed; and all the performers gave great satisfaction by doing what they were paid for, and giving themselves no airs. No amateur could be persuaded to do anything.' The party, which did not break up till after midnight was mentioned in the *Morning Post* next day. Unfortunately Eliza's name was misspelled as 'Mrs H *Austin*'.

In addition there was news of the sailor brothers. Frank had been superseded in the *Caledonia*. Where would he live? What would he do? Frank now had a second son, born 21 April at Portsmouth. Charles was likely to be in England within the month.

The D'Antraigues and their son Comte Julien could not come to Eliza's party so the Austens went to them. 'It will be amusing to see the ways of a French circle,' said Jane.

On the way there was a near-accident in the carriage where the horses jibbed at some fresh gravel and everybody got out. Eliza caught cold. The Frenchmen took too much snuff to please Jane. Monsieur the Count was a fine-looking man with quiet manners, 'good enough for an Englishman,' said the chauvinistic Jane. He was a man of great information and taste and had some fine paintings which delighted Henry as much as his son's music had delighted Eliza. Jane, who could read French but could neither speak it fluently nor follow rapid conversation, said that if the Count would only speak English she could take to him.

Comte Emmanuel-Louis D'Antraigues and his beautiful wife,

Anne, an opera singer, were rather different from Jane's usual acquaintances. The highly educated Count was a forger and a spy. The following year, he and his wife were murdered in their house in Barnes by their servant, whose motive could have been political.

Jane was going to Catherine Bigg, now Mrs Hill, at Streatham, then still outside London, the first week in May and Eliza would kindly carry her there. By the end of the month Jane was making her usual resolutions about spending no more money and denying herself a trimming for her new pelisse.

19

Publication, 1811–12

THE EXCITING FAMILY news was that Jane had a novel coming out, but her authorship was a secret. Only Mrs Austen, Cassandra and Martha, the brothers and their wives, the Leigh-Perrots, old Mrs Knight and Fanny Knight had been let into it. Cassandra wrote to Fanny more than once, imploring her to tell nobody. Anna, though almost the same age as the responsible Fanny, was not allowed to know. Her aunts considered her less discreet.

Cassandra, who was at Godmersham, imagined that the social pleasures and attractions of the capital might distract Jane from preoccupation with her novel. The author was almost indignant. 'No, indeed, I am never too busy to think of *S and S*. I can no more forget it than a mother can forget her sucking child and I am much obliged to you for your inquiries. I have had two sheets to correct, but the last only brings us to Willoughby's first appearance.' She reported that Mrs Knight regretted, 'in the most flattering manner', that she would have to wait till May to read the book but Jane was not hopeful of its being ready before July. Henry was nagging the printer. 'I am very much gratified by Mrs K's interest in it . . . I think she will like my Elinor, but cannot build on anything else.'

As she settled into the role of professional writer Henry's house became Jane's London base and her business office. His experience in financial negotiations was invaluable to her and it was he who dealt on her behalf with publishers.

Before returning to Hampshire Jane wrote another letter to Cassandra. Among the guests at Eliza's smart musical evening had been old Mrs Knight's brother Mr Wyndham Knatchbull. His impressions of the party had been relayed to Jane, whom he had described as a pleasing-looking young woman. Jane was thirty-five. She sighed that although she could not now hope for better in the way of admiration she was thankful to have had it continue a few years longer. Women will know what she meant.

At the end of May she was back at Chawton and Cassandra still at Godmersham. Life was back to visits, gardening and gossip. Always interested in weddings, Jane noted that Colonel Orde had married their distant cousin Margaret Beckford, the Marchioness of Douglas's sister. The newspapers were saying Miss Beckford had been disinherited, but Jane opined slyly that Orde would not have married her without 'a handsome independence of her own'. Miss Beckford's father was certainly displeased. The flower seeds were coming up nicely except for the mignonette. The young peony at the foot of the fir tree had just blown and was looking handsome; the shrubbery border would soon be gay with pinks and sweet williams; the columbines were already in bloom. The syringas were coming out. A good crop of Orleans plums was expected but not many greengages.

Frank and his Mary were at Cowes and Jane and her mother thought of inviting them to Chawton on their way to Steventon. Mrs Austen offered to give up her room to them but that would leave only the best bedroom to accommodate two nursemaids and three children. Finding enough bedrooms for brothers and their growing families was as serious and recurrent a problem as transport.

Brother James was most attentive to his mother, and frequently took his daughters, Anna and Caroline, on horseback, for the lanes were too rough for a carriage, to see their grandmother and aunts. Anna was now eighteen and the seventeen years' gap between her and her Aunt Jane seemed unimportant. Anna spent her summers at Chawton and Jane tells Cassandra how on one occasion Anna had been with the Prowtings all the previous day. She had gone to learn how to make feather trimmings from their daughter Catherine-Ann and stayed to dinner. This proved convenient as the Digweeds had invited the

Austens to meet Mrs and Miss Terry. Because Anna's brief and unful-filled engagement to Michael Terry in the winter of 1809–10 had caused general embarrassment Jane was relieved that Anna was out of the way.

Anna created considerable amusement for herself and her aunt by borrowing popular novels from the circulating library at Alton. These she would scan and mockingly summarize for the ears of her aunt, who sat patiently at her needlework, nearly always for the poor. Anna and Jane found these sessions hilarious and even Cassandra was enter-tained though she teased them for being foolish and implored them not to make her laugh so much. Jane and Anna had laughed until they cried over *Lady Maclairn, the Victim of Villainy,* an eight-volume novel by Rachel Hunter, in which the heroine and numerous other charac-ters, male and female, were always in floods of tears.

Jane composed a satirical letter to Mrs Hunter who lived in Nor-wich, though of course it was never intended for the post. It ran:

> Jane Austen's tears have flowed over each sweet sketch in such a way as would have done Mrs Hunter's heart good to see: if Mrs Hunter could understand all Miss Jane Austen's interest in the sub-ject she would certainly have the kindness to publish at least four more volumes about the Flint family, and especially would give many fresh particulars on that part of it which Mrs Hunter has hitherto handled too briefly viz., the history of Mary Flint's mar-riage with Howard.
>
> Miss Jane Austen cannot close this small epitome of the minia-ture abridgment of her thanks and admiration without expressing her sincere hope that Mrs Hunter is provided at Norwich with a more safe conveyance to London than Alton can now boast; as the Car of Falkenstein, the pride of that town, was overturned within the last ten days.

Although this pretentious name for Collyer's daily coach sounds like something from a Gothic novel by Mrs Radcliffe, that is what it really was called.

A battle had been fought at Almeida in Portugal almost on the Spanish border and the *Hampshire Telegraph* had reported it. 'How horrible it is to have so many people killed!' lamented Jane; then pulling herself together with unsentimental realism she added, 'And what a blessing that one cares for none of them.' It was always a relief in wartime to find no names of relatives or friends on the casualty lists.

The garden was looking well and an apricot had been detected on one of the trees. Henry would bring Cassandra back from Godmersham to his house in Sloane Street where she would be staying about a week. Jane and Martha had unpacked some new Wedgwood ware and were about to buy currants to make wine.

In August 1811 Henry's wife Eliza arrived at Chawton, and so did Charles after seven years away. He introduced his gentle young wife, with whom he seemed very happy, and two pretty little girls. Cassandra, writing to Phila – now Mrs George Whitaker, having recently married late in life – said, 'There must always be something to wish for, and for Charles we have to wish for rather more money. So expensive as everything in England is now, even the necessaries of life, I am afraid they will find themselves very poor.' Charles was soon appointed to command HMS *Namur* and to save money his wife and children lived on board with him while the ship was in port. This was cheaper than living in lodgings, though naval wives with children had to put up with that when their husbands were at sea. The *Namur* was the flagship of Admiral Sir Thomas Williams, whose first wife had been Charles's cousin Jane Cooper.

Old King George III was expected to die, though he lived till 1820. People bought mourning black just in case. Anna and her friend Harriet walked with Jane into Alton to buy theirs and Mrs Austen had a black bombazine, a dull-surfaced twill fabric, handy.

Sense and Sensibility was published in October 1811. It was advertised in the *Star* of 30 October and the *Morning Chronicle* of 31 October and priced at fifteen shillings. The book was published at the author's expense. Cassandra wrote again to Fanny Knight to beg the Knight family not to mention that Jane had written it. The title page named her only as 'a Lady' and said, 'London: Printed for the author by C. Bosworth, Bell-yard, Temple Bar, and published by T. Egerton, Whitehall, 1811'. In its later editions the title page read, 'By the author of *Pride and Prejudice*'.

There were no early reviews but the book's reputation spread by word of mouth. Jane's immediate family knew her value. James sent her an anonymous rhyming appreciation in a disguised hand. It went:

To Miss Jane Austen the reputed author of *Sense and Sensibility*, a novel lately published:

> On such subjects no wonder that she should write well
> In whom so delighted those qualities dwell;
> Where 'dear sensibility', Sterne's darling maid,
> With sense so attempered is finely portrayed.
> Fair Elinor's self in that mind is expressed
> And the feelings of Marianne live in that breast.
> Oh then, gentle lady! continue to write
> And the sense of your readers t'amuse and delight.

This is a charming tribute from an intelligent and sympathetic reader who took a brotherly pride in his sister's success. The stress falls on the first syllable of 'Marianne', suggesting it was pronounced more like 'Marian'.

When reviews came they were favourable. The first appeared in the *Critical Review* for February 1812. The book earned:

> particular commendation . . . it is well written; the characters are in genteel life, naturally drawn and judiciously supported. The incidents are probable, and highly pleasing, and interesting; the conclusion such as the reader must wish it should be, and the whole is just long enough to interest without fatiguing. It reflects honour on the writer, who displays much knowledge of character and very happily blends a great deal of good sense with the lighter matter of the piece.

Such just appreciation is what every first novelist dreams of. The *British Critic* said it was 'a very pleasing and entertaining narrative'. The first edition sold out. Jane made a profit of £140. Had the book failed she could not have afforded to publish the rest. Although Jane had already started work on *Mansfield Park* she interrupted composition in order to revise and prune the manuscript of *First Impressions*. *Pride and Prejudice* as we now have it was altered to fit the calendars of 1811–12.

Edward arrived in Hampshire with his daughter Fanny and her cousin Fanny Cage. There were two Fanny Cages, mother and daughter. It was the daughter who was mocked by Jane Austen as being 'all superlatives and rapture'. Edward's daughter Fanny was romantically involved with a neighbouring gentleman, Mr John Pemberton Plumptre, and full of confidences about him.

In June 1812 Mrs Austen and Jane spent a couple of weeks with James at Steventon. Mary met them at Basingstoke with the carriage. Mrs Austen had decided to stay at home in future and said that she intended this, her last visit, to be to her eldest son. On 25 June, Jane and her mother went back to Chawton, taking Anna with them. Anna was prettier and quicker-witted than Fanny but Jane loved Fanny more. Anna stayed three months. Searching the circulating library at Alton for something enjoyable to read, she picked up a copy of *Sense and Sensibility*, but threw it aside with careless contempt saying, 'Oh, that must be rubbish! I'm sure of it from the title.' Jane and Cassandra, who were standing by, suppressed their mirth.

On 14 October old Mrs Knight died. It was at this time that Edward changed his name, though for convenience he and his children are generally referred to as Knight from the time of his adoption in 1783. Fanny hated changing her name from 'Miss Austen' to 'Miss Knight'. Jane decided to learn to write the letter K more elegantly. Unfortunately Edward's inheritance was disputed and he ended up paying the other claimants £30,000, most of which was swallowed up in legal costs.

In November Edward and Fanny visited with Fanny's twelve-year-old sister Lizzie and their cousin Mary Deedes. Jane referred to the party as 'Edward and his harem'. Jane was able to write to Martha who was away on a visit, '*P and P* is sold. Egerton gives £110 for it.' She added ruefully that she would rather have had £150 but she was unsurprised that her publisher was unwilling to risk more. The sale would save Henry the trouble of touting it elsewhere. The money was due in a year's time. Her publisher had spotted a bestseller.

Charles had a third daughter, another Fanny, born in December 1812. He and his wife, Fanny, left the other two with their grandmother and aunts at Chawton. The children were much improved but the maiden aunt thought method had been wanting in their upbringing. Little Cassy could be a very nice child if her parents would 'only exert themselves a little'. Jane had never tried living on shipboard with three small children.

Meanwhile Mrs Austen was busy knitting gloves and Jane was reading *An Essay on the Military Policy and Institutions of the British Empire* by Captain Sir Charles William Pasley of the Royal Engineers, which she found highly entertaining and delightfully written. She declared herself in love with the author, as much so as with Thomas Clarkson, author of *History of the Abolition of the African Slave Trade* (1808), and Claudius Buchanan, author of *Christian Researches in Asia* (1811). Yet some people are convinced that Jane Austen's interests were purely trivial.

20

A Bestseller, 1813

*P*ride and Prejudice was the hit novel of 1813. It was advertised in the *Morning Chronicle* for 28 January at eighteen shillings the three volumes. Jane wrote to Cassandra, who was at Steventon, from Chawton on 29 January, 'I want to tell you that I have got my own darling child from London.' Like other authors Jane spoke of her books as her babies, the ones she never had. 'On Wednesday I received one copy, sent down by Falknor, with three lines from Henry to say that he had given another to Charles and sent a third by the coach to Godmersham . . . The advertisement is in our paper today for the first time: eighteen shillings. He shall ask a guinea for my two next.'

Miss Benn dined with them on the very day of the book's coming out. It was read aloud to this guinea-pig listener but its authorship was kept a secret. Jane told Cassandra that Miss Benn found the story amusing and seemed to admire Elizabeth. Jane told Cassandra, 'I must confess that I think her as delightful a creature as ever appeared in print, and how I shall be able to tolerate those who do not like *her* at least, I do not know.' Mrs Austen was the reader and in Jane's opinion perfectly understood the characters but read too quickly and lacked the dramatic talent to make them speak as they ought. Jane was better able to read 'in character'. Although Miss Benn was not told why the book was of particular interest, she sensed the suppressed excitement and put two and two together. Next day Miss Benn called with Mrs Harry

Digweed, née Jane Terry, who could be relied on to spread the news among the numerous Terry clan.

The book had been 'lopped and cropped', so Jane believed it was now shorter than *Sense and Sensibility*. She was exasperated to find a misprint on page 220, where two speeches had been made into one. She wrote:

> On the whole however I am quite vain enough and well satisfied enough. The work is rather too light and bright and sparkling; it wants shade; it wants to be stretched out here and there with a long chapter – of sense if it could be had, if not of solemn specious nonsense – about something unconnected with the story; an essay on writing, a critique on Walter Scott, or the history of Bonaparte – or anything that would form a contrast and bring the reader with increased delight to the playfulness and epigrammatism of the general style.

She was not, of course, entirely serious, or she would never have 'lopped and cropped'. But this wry comment shows that she recognized how rarely comedy is accorded the respect it deserves as art. Jane had received a polite letter of congratulation from Fanny Knight but her spontaneous enthusiasm, relayed through Cassandra, was the more to be valued. Fanny's praise Jane Austen found 'very gratifying', especially as she had taken to Darcy and Elizabeth.

'Now I will try to write of something else; it shall be a complete change of subject. Ordination. I am glad to find your enquiries have ended so well. If you could discover whether Northamptonshire is a country of hedgerows, I should be glad again,' Jane told her sister. This passage has been much discussed. Until recently, readers have taken it to mean that Jane saw 'ordination' as the main theme of *Mansfield Park*. Edmund Bertram's vocation as a Church of England clergyman is certainly one strand of the plot, but hardly the most important. More recently, scholars have thought that the word 'ordination', which stands grammatically and syntactically isolated, introduces the sentence which follows it: Cassandra was staying with James at Steventon, and may have been requested to ask him about technicalities of entering the Church, for instance how long it would take for Edmund Bertram to be ordained. The interpretation of this letter is still undecided. At this time Jane was already halfway through writing *Mansfield Park*. Her sister-in-law Mary, 'Mrs JA', may have provided some of Mrs Norris's characteristics. Like Mrs Norris Mary was bossy and careful with money.

Jane herself wrote on 20 May 1813 to lay claim to a paper full of half-pence she had left on the drawing-room mantelpiece. She said lightly that though she was in no distress for money, she chose to have her due as well as the devil. She was alluding to the old saying 'Give the devil his due', meaning one must be fair to an enemy.

In February 1813 she wrote to Cassandra describing a rather dull party of whist she had attended and mentioned 'just as many for *their* round table as there were at Mrs Grant's'. Mrs Grant is a character in *Mansfield Park*. Jane had made an excuse and left, wishing the real people had been as 'agreeable a set' as her imaginary ones. She was soon complaining, 'There is nobody brilliant these days.' Four visitors had arrived, all of whom Mrs Austen was glad to see, but Jane was glad to escape by having gone out for a walk. Boring neighbours could hardly compete with the excitement of inventing a parallel society.

Enthusiastic reviews encouraged Jane in her current writing. The *British Critic* for February said *Pride and Prejudice* was far superior to others of its kind: the story was well told, the characters well drawn. The *Critical Review* for March summarized the plot and again praised the 'domestic scenes' as superior; all the characters were integrated into the tale. The *New Review* for April gave an admiring synopsis with quotations.

Everybody was guessing at the author's identity. Richard Brinsley Sheridan said at a dinner party that it was one of the cleverest things he had ever read. Another literary gentleman announced it was too clever to have been written by a woman. Annabella Milbanke, the future Lady Byron, told her mother how excellent a novel it was. She liked it because it was so probable, with none of the clichés of novel writers: 'no drownings, no conflagrations, nor runaway horses, nor lapdogs and parrots, nor chambermaids and milliners, nor rencontres and dis-guises'. Annabella, though primarily interested in mathematics, had a shrewd literary sense. Lady Davy however did not like the book. She thought the 'picture of vulgar minds and manners' should have been relieved by the agreeable contrast of 'more dignified and refined characters'. We can only wonder how she interpreted Mr Darcy. The first Earl of Dudley admired Mr Collins. The first edition sold out and a second was printed in the autumn but Jane had sold her copyright and was unable to correct misprints.

On 9 February Cassandra had left Steventon for Manydown. The Leigh-Perrots were at Scarlets. They had given up renting the house in Bath and had bought another in Pulteney Street. Mr Leigh-Perrot was confined to a chair with a broken chilblain on one foot and a violent swelling on the other. They were anxious to get to Pulteney Street, fearing the house would be broken into.

On 16 February Jane wrote to Martha. Frank and his family were at Deal again in fresh lodgings. Jane thought they must have tried lodging in every house in that town. Lodgings in Deal were cheaper than in Ramsgate, an important consideration.

As usual, and despite the excitement of the publication of *Pride and Prejudice*, Jane was keeping abreast of the national news.

On 14 January the then Princess of Wales had written to her estranged husband stating her grievances. On 8 February the letter was published in the *Morning Chronicle* and was reproduced on 15 February in the *Hampshire Telegraph*. Prince George was Regent, or King in all but name, because his father, King George III, suffered from mental illness. The poor man probably had porphyria, a rare hereditary condition, which induces irritability and delirium. In 1811 Parliament had voted the Prince as eldest son the authority to rule. He was forty-eight and his youthful good looks had dissolved in blubber. The Prince of Wales had secretly married a Roman Catholic widow, Maria Fitzherbert, whom he loved, but under family pressure set her aside to make a dynastic marriage with his cousin Princess Caroline of Brunswick. Her person and manners disgusted him: he complained her underwear was smelly, and the marriage was over before she gave birth to their only child, a daughter, nine months after the ceremony. She took advantage of her freedom and had various lovers, many of them naval officers. When the Prince died, as George IV, in 1830, he chose to have a picture of his dear Maria buried with him.

The King supported his daughter-in-law against his wayward son although it was rumoured, accurately, that she had had an illegitimate child. In 1806 a Royal Commission had been set up to investigate the Princess of Wales's morals and although nothing was proven Caroline's access to her daughter, Princess Charlotte, was restricted. Charlotte wrote to a friend, 'The print shops are full of *scurrilous caricatures* and infamous things relative to the Prince's conduct . . .'

Jane was a keen reader of newspapers, and commented to Martha Lloyd:

> I suppose all the world is sitting in judgment upon the Princess of Wales's letter. Poor woman, I shall support her as long as I can, because she is a woman, and because I hate her husband – but I can hardly forgive her for calling herself 'attached and affectionate' to a man whom she must detest . . . if I must give up the Princess, I am resolved at least always to think that she would have been respectable, if the Prince had only behaved tolerably by her at first.

Jane deplored the friendship between the Princess and Lady Oxford, a one-time mistress of Lord Byron, who flaunted her promiscuity and whose children by different fathers were known as 'the Harleian Miscellany'. She was born a Harley, and the Harleian Miscellany is an edited collection of papers in the British Museum. Lady Oxford was opposed to the Tories and the marital quarrel became political, with the Whigs supporting the disgraced Princess. Jane Austen's championship for the Princess was not infinitely elastic. She would support her only 'as long as I can'.

In March that year Mr Middleton, who rented the Great House at Chawton on a five-year lease, left when it expired, and Edward came to put everything in order. He frequently dined with his mother and sisters and saw them some time or other every day. This delighted them. Jane commented on the comfort of his company: he was now well and enjoying himself as thoroughly as any Hampshire-born Austen could wish. The beauty of Chawton was not thrown away on him.

Henry's wife, the fascinating Eliza de Feuillide, died on 24 April 1813 after a long and painful illness. Jane helped nurse her. She was buried in Hampstead parish churchyard in the same grave as her mother, Philadelphia Hancock, and her son, Hastings. Henry's words on her tombstone tell us that she was 'a woman of brilliant, generous and cultivated mind'. Soon after her death Jane stayed with Henry at the house in Sloane Street, which he gave up soon afterwards. He was still a partner in Tilson's Bank, which stood in Henrietta Street,

Covent Garden, and was planning to move into rooms over the bank. Eliza's faithful French servants, Madame Bigeon and her daughter Madame Perigord, would go with him.

In May, Henry took Jane to an exhibition of paintings in Spring Gardens. Critical opinion in general was cool but Jane was delighted to find a portrait which resembled her idea of Mrs Bingley in *Pride and Prejudice*. She was dressed in a white gown with green ornaments, 'which convinces me of what I always supposed, that green was a favourite colour with her'. A novelist, after all, rarely knows everything about the characters she has created. She could find nothing that looked like Mrs Bingley's sister Mrs Darcy, but imagined that if she did find her Mrs Darcy would be wearing yellow. Another exhibition, by Sir Joshua Reynolds, was similarly disappointing. Jane wrote playfully that this must be because of 'love, pride and delicacy' on the part of Mr Darcy who was unwilling to expose his wife's likeness to the public eye. Jane while in London visited an elegant schoolroom decorated with naked cupids. 'A fine study for girls,' was her characteristically dry observation.

Jane was able to report 'Lady Robert delighted with *P and P*.' Gratifyingly, Lady Robert Kerr had been impressed with the book before she knew who had written it. 'Of course she knows now . . . And Mr Hastings! I am quite delighted with what such a man writes about it. Let me be rational and return to my full stops.' She had been praised by the great Warren Hastings himself.

There were rumours that the character of Mr Collins was based on a certain Bishop Porteous who had towards the end of the eighteenth century held the living of Hunton in Kent and whose *Reminiscences* were pompous and verbose. It is unlikely there was any one living model though the character is convincing enough to have delighted generations of readers. Jane Austen knew plenty of pompous clergymen.

The secret of her authorship was beginning to leak out and people were asking to meet her. 'If I *am* a wild beast, I cannot help it. It is not my own fault,' she declared.

Henry had not yet moved as he was negotiating the letting of his house whence Jane was writing to Cassandra. She had been driving round in Henry's barouche. 'I liked my solitary elegance very much, and was ready to laugh all the time at my being where I was. I could not but feel that I had naturally small right to be parading about London in a barouche.' A barouche was a very grand carriage indeed. We remember Mrs Elton's boasts in *Emma* about her rich sister Selina Suckling's dislike of 'being stuck up in the barouche-landau without a companion'. In May 1813 Jane reported that 10 Henrietta Street was still all dirt and confusion but promised well.

James and Charles both came to stay at Chawton that summer. Charles had rented a house in Southend. James's children were let into their aunt's secret. They had already enjoyed reading the novels. James-Edward, though only fourteen, had the family fondness for letters in verse. He sent Jane these lines:

> No words can express, my dear Aunt, my surprise
> Or make you conceive how I opened my eyes,
> Like a pig Butcher Pile has just stuck with his knife,
> When I heard for the very first time in my life
> That I had the honour to have a relation
> Whose Works were dispersed through the whole of the nation.
> I assure you, however, I'm terribly glad;
> Oh dear! Just to think (and the thought drives me mad)
> That dear Mrs Jennings's good-natured strain
> Was really the product of your witty brain,
> That you made the Middletons, Dashwoods and all,
> And that you (not young Ferrars) found out that a ball
> May be given in cottages, never so small.
> And though Mr Collins, so grateful for all,
> Will Lady de Bourgh his dear patroness call,
> 'Tis to your ingenuity really he owed
> His living, his wife and his humble abode.
> Now if you will take your poor nephew's advice,
> Your works to Sir William pray send in a trice,
> If he'll undertake to some grandees to show it
> By whose means at last the Prince Regent might know it,
> For I'm sure if he did, in reward for your tale,
> He'd make you a countess at least, without fail,
> And indeed if the princess should lose her dear life
> You might have a good chance of becoming his wife.

James-Edward was gently teasing, as Jane thoroughly disapproved of the Prince's dissolute life. The boy did not know that Jane's work had already attracted the royal admiration.

That July Frank was captain of the *Elephant* in the Baltic. He had a fourth child, and third son, George. His wife Mary had moved to Deal so that she could be with him whenever he was in port. Jane wrote to him enthusiastically of his opportunities for seeing the world. 'Gustavus-Vasa, and Charles XII, and Christiana, and Linnaeus – do their ghosts rise up before you? I have a great respect for former Sweden. So zealous as it was for Protestantism!'

Godmersham was being redecorated and the Knight family spent the summer at Chawton to avoid 'painter's colic'. When paint was lead-based, tradesmen suffered from lead poisoning as an occupational hazard. Their customers could escape if they had two homes. Jane told Frank that Edward was at Chawton Great House planning a new garden and intending to have his children with him as soon as school broke up.

Henry was recovering from the loss of Eliza. Jane thought him 'too busy, too active, too sanguine' to grieve too long. He had been sincerely attached to her but business had taken him away so often that she was not so badly missed as other wives might be. Her illness had been long and dreadful and her death expected. It was a release.

The Revd Thomas Leigh had just died at seventy-nine. 'We are all very anxious to know who will have the living of Adlestrop, and where his excellent sister will find a home for the remainder of her days,' said Jane. For once she even pitied her Aunt Leigh-Perrot, who had lost her chance of being mistress of Stoneleigh by the 'vile compromise'. Now Stoneleigh reverted to James Henry Leigh, who owned Adlestrop Park already.

In her postscript to a letter to Frank in July 1813, Jane wrote that every copy of *Sense and Sensibility* had sold and brought her £140, besides the copyright, 'if that should ever be of any value. I have now therefore written myself into £250, which only makes me long for more.' She confided to her brother that she had another project in hand, which she hoped would sell well on the back of *Pride and Prejudice* though it was admittedly not half so entertaining.

Jane read *Pride and Prejudice* aloud to Fanny in one of the bedrooms. Fanny's sister Louisa, Edward's fourth daughter, remembered going into Jane's bedroom one evening when Jane was dressing for dinner: 'She had large dark eyes and a brilliant complexion, and long,

long black hair down to her knees.' This seems unlikely, as Jane's hair was chestnut brown and nobody else mentions such a length. Louisa was only eight or nine at the time, so her memories were possibly confused. Fifty years later, Fanny, the widowed Lady Knatchbull, read *Pride and Prejudice* again, aloud to Louisa. Louisa was by then Lady George Hill, in succession to her younger sister, Cassandra-Jane, who had married this younger son of the Marquis of Downshire and died after giving Lord George four children. Louisa bore him one.

In summer 1813 Anna, who wanted to get away from home, announced her second engagement. This was to Ben Lefroy, youngest son of the late 'Madam' Lefroy. His father had died in 1806 but his eldest brother, J H George Lefroy, had succeeded him in the living, so Ben was still in his childhood home. He was handsome, charming and intelligent, but as yet had no career. Jane was anxious because despite being sensible, very religious, well connected and not poor he had 'some queerness of temper', and Anna's showed 'much unsteadiness'. Worse, she was fond of company and he hated it. The engagement was announced on 17 August and was probably reluctantly countenanced at home, for Anna was soon taking refuge once more at Chawton Cottage.

In September Jane was with Henry in London again, accompanied by Edward and his daughters Fanny, Lizzie and Marianne. Number 10 Henrietta Street, above the bank, had been made comfortable with cleaning and painting and the Sloane Street furniture, though Henry stayed there less than a year. He employed several servants: the visitors were welcomed by the coachman, then by William the manservant and by Madame Perigord the housekeeper, while the French cook Madame Bigeon, Madame Perigord's mother, was preparing a dinner of soup, fish, bouillee (stewed meat), partridges and an apple tart. Henry was at the forefront of a new fashion. Formerly two courses had meant that a mixture of sweet and savoury dishes was spread upon the table, then all removed and replaced by another such varied selection. Now courses were sequential individual dishes, starting with soup and ending with pudding or dessert. Madame Bigeon and her daughter came to shop and cook and clean as often as he liked or as they liked. Jane told Frank that Henry had no intention of giving large parties any more. His social prominence had died with Eliza.

The family went to see *Don Juan*, a popular pantomime which delighted Lizzie and Marianne, then thirteen and twelve. They sat in a private box, 'directly on the stage', which Jane found much more pleasant than the body of the theatre. Her eyes were troublesome, plagued by London's dust and by artificial light, and she found the box less fatiguing. They left Don Juan in Hell at half-past eleven. Theatrical performances then were a mixed bag, with a play, opera, ballet and farce, the whole lasting five or six hours.

Jane writes, 'I talked to Henry at the play last night'. It seems to have been the custom to have private conversations during performances. In *Pride and Prejudice* Elizabeth and Mrs Gardiner discuss family matters and are only 'separated by the conclusion of the play'. There is no suggestion that they kept their voices down: '"Well," *cried* Elizabeth' (emphasis added).

After the theatre the party had soup and wine and water 'and then went to our holes'. Fanny and Jane shared 'poor Eliza's' bed. Edward put up at an hotel. Next night they were off to Covent Garden to see *The Clandestine Marriage* by George Colman the Elder and *Midas* by Kane O'Hara. The children enjoyed these but preferred *Don Juan*. 'I must say that I have seen nobody on the stage who has been a more interesting character than that compound of cruelty and lust,' wrote the single lady.

'Beautiful Edward' gave Jane and Fanny £5 each. With for once some 'superfluous wealth to spend', Jane went shopping for linen at four shillings the yard, and was to have a new cap in white satin and lace with a little white flower perking out of the left ear, 'like Harriet Byron's feather'. Harriet Byron is the heroine of one of Jane Austen's favourite books, *Sir Charles Grandison*. She was also having a new gown and buying one for Cassandra.

'Remember that it is a present. Do not refuse me. I am very rich.' She had heard from 'Mrs Tickars's young lady, to my high amusement, that the stays now are not made to force the bosom up at all; *that* was a very unbecoming, unnatural fashion. I was really glad to hear that they [gowns] are not to be so much off the shoulders as they were.' The bra would not be invented for more than another century. Although the ideal was a willowy, uncorseted figure, some women had obviously decided they preferred a little control.

Fanny bought stockings at Remington's, silk at twelve shillings the pair and cotton at four shillings and threepence, which she thought great bargains. When Fanny, back at Godmersham, decided that her new gown and cap were mistakes, Jane laughed tolerantly that it was one of the 'sweet taxes of youth' to choose in a hurry and make bad bargains.

Edward and Fanny ordered a Wedgwood dinner service. The pattern was a small lozenge in purple between lines of narrow gold, with the family crest. It can still be seen at Chawton Cottage.

The Austens went to Mr Spence the dentist. Fanny, whose teeth looked perfect, had gold fillings and Lizzie had her teeth filed. Poor Marianne had two teeth behind her eye teeth taken out to make room for the ones in front. With no anaesthetic, she screamed. Jane would not let the dentist inspect her mouth 'for a shilling a tooth and double it'. She thought him greedy and giving unnecessary treatment. But she did have her hair done and thought it looked hideous. With only a bit of velvet round her head, she longed for the shelter of a 'snug cap'. She did not catch cold, though she rather expected to, and recently had suffered no pain in her face. Jane's face-ache later became chronic. Perhaps her teeth were going, as her mother's had done.

There was news from Bath, where the Bridges family, Edward's in-laws, were taking the cure. The regimen was by modern standards alarming:

> Dr Parry seems to be half-starving Mr Bridges for he is restricted to . . . bread, water and meat, and is never to eat so much of that as he wishes; and he is to walk a great deal, walk till he drops, I believe, gout or no gout . . . I have not exaggerated.

Mrs Austen had been treated with leeches for headaches. Mrs Cooke later told Jane that headaches were frequent with elderly women. 'Last year I had for some time the sensation of a peck loaf resting on my head and they talked of cupping me, but I came off with a dose or two of calomel and have never heard of it since.' Cupping was a painful treatment: blisters were raised by the application of heated glasses, then burst to release blood. Blood-letting was believed to release bad humours. Calomel was a stomach medicine made of mercurious chloride, now recognized as poisonous. Henry was on his way to Chawton, with a cold and an unsettled stomach: Jane prescribed rhubarb medicine and 'plenty of port and water'.

Edward took Jane back to Godmersham with him after visiting Chawton. He had spent the previous five months there. Invitations were unwelcome to him. He had promised to take Fanny, Lizzie and Marianne to the fair at Goodnestone. He repented this rashness and hoped for a wet day, but the late September morning was bright. Jane and Fanny lived in the library except at meals and had fires in the evening. They were supposed to be getting on with *Modern Europe*, but other things got in the way. The apple crop was poor. Little Louisa, aged nine, sent her Aunt Cassandra 'a hundred thousand million kisses'.

Writing to Frank from Godmersham at the end of September 1813, Jane was sorry to hear from him that Sweden was so poverty-stricken. She mentioned the price of food, which was high because of the war, and then said, 'Let me shake off vulgar cares and conform to the happy indifference of East Kent wealth.' She expected to stay with Edward about two months. Jane had asked Frank previously if she might use the names of his old ships for *Mansfield Park* and he gave his permission. Frank warned her that this might identify the author as a member of the Austen family. The 'secret' of her authorship was spreading and she decided to make money rather than mystery out of it. Henry had blabbed, and although Jane forgave him his 'brotherly vanity and love', she was grateful to Frank and his Mary for keeping quiet. A second edition of *Sense and Sensibility* came out at the end of the month, together with a second edition of *Pride and Prejudice*. At Godmersham she was writing in the library, finishing *Mansfield Park*.

Jane told Cassandra halfway through October that Anne Lefroy's mother, Jemima Brydges, had been obliged to leave Canterbury because of her debts and nobody knew where she was. Jane was hoping to cadge a frank from Mr Lushington MP, who was chiefly young Edward's acquaintance. She considered Mr Lushington something of a waste of space. Jane was not altogether approving of Edward and George, now in their late teens, either: she thought them sports mad and extravagant. They redeemed themselves in her eyes, however, by having taken Communion the previous day.

While Jane was loved by all James's children, Edward's possibly regarded her more coolly. James's children grew up as had their Aunt Jane at Steventon Rectory; Edward's, brought up at Godmersham, had a different social position of which they cannot have been unaware. Jane seems never to have thought of this.

She was feeling neglected because she had brother Charles at the Nore and Frank's wife at Deal, both nearby, and saw nothing of them. On the other hand, she dreaded a simultaneous visit from Charles and his family, and the Moores, who had one child. 'The two parties of children is the chief evil,' wrote the aunt who considered Charles's daughters were out of hand. She was not sure whether she wanted to see the Moores or not. She would enjoy seeing 'dear Charles', but expected Cassy, the eldest girl, to be cross and disagreeable. When Charles and his wife arrived, Cassy was looking thin and poorly. Cassy suffered from seasickness and was wretched living on board with her parents, but did not want to leave them. The baby was not so pretty as formerly. Jane felt there were too many people in the house, large as it was, but the company cheered Edward up no end. Cassy got on fairly well with her cousins, but they were too many and too noisy for her. The Godmersham children were clearly not easy to manage, yet if Jane criticized their upbringing as she did that of Charles's children Cassandra must have expunged the record.

Jane was eager for news of her home. Was meat any cheaper, she asked Cassandra. Were there tomatoes at Chawton? Jane and Fanny 'regaled on them every day'. Tomatoes were still an unusual luxury. Jane advised Cassandra to get some flounces for her gowns and asked for news of the alterations at Chawton Great House. Instead of visiting her son-in-law Edward, the dowager Lady Bridges was going to remain at Bath, where the waters agreed with her. Lady Bridges' daughter Louisa, who never married, put her mother's improvement down to being out of doors, but Lady Bridges was about to try the Hot Pump, as the Cross Bath was being painted. Louisa felt better herself and thought the waters had benefited her.

Jane kept meeting people she described as very plain. She had changed her mind about Mr Lushington: now she liked him very much. 'I am sure he is clever and a man of taste. He got a volume of Milton last night and spoke of it with warmth. He is quite an MP – very smiling, with an exceeding good address, and readiness of language.

I am rather in love with him,' she confessed, consoling herself with, 'I daresay he is ambitious and insincere.' Were the grapes by any chance sour? The letter travelled free, on Mr Lushington's frank.

She was learning to like Harriot Bridges's husband, the Revd Mr Moore. He scolded a servant, but his manners to Harriot were unobjectionable and Jane was pleased to see that the couple did not spoil their boy. Either Mr Moore was making Harriot happy or she was making herself happy, concluded Jane, though she had previously thought his manners to her wanted tenderness.

At the end of October, Cassandra was in London with Henry. Jane arranged to stay with Henry on her way home that November. She loved his company. She planned to drop in on the Cookes at Bookham for a day or two. Edward was a magistrate and took his sister when he went on an inspection visit to a jail. She commented only that she went through all the feelings which everybody was likely to experience on visiting such a building: it would have been interesting to know exactly what she meant.

Jane told her sister, 'Your tidings of *S and S* give me pleasure. I have never seen it advertised.' Unknown to her, *Sense and Sensibility*, 'by a Lady', had been announced just a year previously in the *Edinburgh Review*, appearing on a list of newly published novels, along with volumes four, five and six of Maria Edgeworth's *Tales of Fashionable Life*. In the same list, among novels and novelists now largely forgotten, was *The Loyalist* by the prolific novelist and moral writer, Mrs Jane West. Jane Austen wrote to Anna the following year, 'I am quite determined not to be pleased with Mrs West's *Alicia de Lacy*, should I ever meet with it, which I hope I shall not. I think I can be stout against anything written by Mrs West. I have made up my mind to like no novels really but Miss Edgeworth's, yours and my own.' Also on the list was *Traits of Nature* by Miss S. H. Burney, not Madame D'Arblay but half-sister of the more famous Fanny. This other Miss Burney had written the novel called *Clarentine*, which Jane had dismissed as foolish, 'full of unnatural conduct and forced difficulties'. In the same list of new publications was *Tales* by the poet and clergyman George Crabbe, whom Jane declared she would have liked to marry.

Writing when she was all alone, Edward having gone to his

woods, she noted that 'I have five tables, eight and twenty chairs and two fires all to myself.' This was in the south drawing room: the second fireplace has now been closed up. She reported to Cassandra that various readers, whose opinion she valued, were delighted with *Pride and Prejudice*. She was amused by the curiosity as to who the author could be. It was gratifying to learn that she was read and admired in Ireland. There was a Mrs Fletcher, an old lady, wife to a judge, 'and very good and very clever', who was dying to know what the writer was like. Jane was flattered, of course, and may have been only half joking when she said, 'I do not despair of having my picture in the Exhibition at last – all white and red, with my head on one side.' She allowed herself the fantasy that she might marry the son of Fanny Burney, some twenty years younger than herself. Then she turned to practical matters: 'I suppose in the meantime I shall owe dear Henry a great deal of money for printing, etc.'

After a concert Jane felt so tired she wondered how she would get through the ball that was planned for the following Thursday, though she was keeping her China crepe for it. Fanny wore white sarcenet, a soft silk fabric, and silver, with silver in her hair, but despite good company there was no dancing. Officers were idle and there was a scarcity of county beaux. Jane discovered compensation for growing older: being a sort of chaperone, she found herself on the sofa near the fire and was pleased to think she could drink as much wine as she liked. Old Lady Bridges, Jane heard, 'found me handsomer than she expected, so you see I am not so bad as you think for'. Lady Bridges was to spend the winter in Bath. Dr Parry, said Jane drily, would not mind having a few more of her ladyship's guineas.

Pride and Prejudice had established Jane's reputation and she tasted the sweets of success. Sometime during the year a nobleman suggested to Henry that Jane might like to meet the French writer, Germaine de Staël. She was a dazzling celebrity, though large, coarse-featured and considered ugly. The Prince of Wales, patron of the arts, had made a point of meeting her. As a writer, Jane admired her. But Madame de Staël had been an early supporter of the French Revolution and was separated from her husband. From 1796–1806 she had been involved in a stormy affair with the writer Benjamin Constant. Jane unhesitatingly relinquished the chance to meet her. Anyway, although Jane could read French, she was far from confident about speaking it, which may have been an additional reason for avoiding embarrassment.

Jane was home for the end of the year, when a big freeze set in. London was shrouded in impenetrable fog. Heavy snowfalls made travelling almost impossible. Jane was already gestating her next book and started writing *Emma* on 21 January 1814. Visiting nephews and nieces, seeing her quietly writing at her desk in the living room, often imagined her to be merely writing letters and felt free to interrupt her. *Mansfield Park* had been accepted for publication on commission, but Egerton had not enough confidence in it to offer for the copyright.

21

A Brief Peace, 1814

*I*N MARCH OF 1814, Jane took the opportunity offered by a journey in a post chaise with Henry to London to read *Mansfield Park* aloud. Henry's approval was all that Jane had hoped for. He said, shrewdly enough, that it was different from *Sense and Sensibility* and *Pride and Prejudice*, but did not think it at all inferior to either of them. Jane only had time to read as far as Maria Bertram's ill-fated marriage to Mr James Rushworth, owner of the magnificent Sotherton estate, and feared that Henry had already gone through the most entertaining part. Henry took most kindly to Lady Bertram and her sister Mrs Norris and warmly praised the drawing of the characters. He understood them and liked Fanny. He admired the characterization of Henry Crawford in so far as Crawford was a clever, pleasant man. Jane must have been reading the proof sheets as the book was published the following May. A fragment of a letter from Jane, possibly to Frank, mentions that *Mansfield Park* was due out before the end of April. It had been due out in April, but was delayed. When Henry Austen had reached the third volume he 'defied anybody to say whether Henry Crawford would be reformed, or would forget Fanny in a fortnight.' A week later Henry had finished *Mansfield Park* and his admiration had not lessened.

Jane liked to read the latest publications. She had enjoyed reading *The Heroine, or Adventures of Cherubina*, a novel by Eaton Stannard Barrett, published the previous year. It was 'a delightful burlesque, particularly on the Radcliffe style'. She wrote, 'I have read *The Corsair,* mended my petticoat and have nothing else to do.' *The Corsair* was a new poem by Byron. She was exercised about the six weeks' official mourning for the Queen's brother, the Duke of Mecklenburg-Strelitz. Most people at parties were wearing black but Jane had felt comfortable in brown. She decided to trim her lilac sarcenet with black ribbon, since ribbon trimmings were all the fashion in Bath and she hoped would do elsewhere.

During that visit Jane had the good luck to see the actor Edmund Kean at Drury Lane Theatre in his first London part, Shylock in Shakespeare's *The Merchant of Venice.* For once she was not disappointed. She could find no fault with him anywhere and said his scene with Tubal was exquisite. She wanted to see Kean again, but, apart from him and Miss Smith, who did not quite come up to Jane's expectation, the play was badly cast and the whole dragged. The Indian jugglers, who gave daily performances in Pall Mall, seem to have been more satisfactory.

Jane's judgment that Kean was different from other actors of the day seems validated, though he was small and his voice was harsh. Lord Byron, who never met Jane Austen, saw the same production and enthused about Kean's acting: he said it was a new and natural style. William Hazlitt said Kean's was a radical reinterpretation of the part. Melesina Trench, author of *Remains,* a memoir, saw Kean as Richard III and said he was like a lion in a cage. Coleridge said watching him was like reading Shakespeare by flashes of lightning. Mary Russell Mitford, however, sneered that the 'monarch of the stage' was a little insignificant man, slightly deformed and ungraceful, unpleasing to eye and ear.

Jane's mother had asked her to buy some tea but had given her no money. Jane was regretting the rise in the price of tea: they dealt with the firm of Twinings, which is still trading at the end of the twentieth century.

There was the usual problem of transport. Jane's letter to Cassandra sounds almost farcical, but their difficulties were real and acute:

> By a little convenient listening, I now know that Henry wishes to go to Godmersham for a few days before Easter . . . there can be no time for your remaining in London after your return from Adle-

strop. You must not put off your coming therefore; and it occurs to me that instead of my coming here again from Streatham, it will be better to join me here . . . Henry finds he cannot set off for Oxfordshire before the Wednesday, which is the 23rd . . .

The Godmersham family arrived at Chawton Great House for two months, accompanied by Edward's in-laws. This made Fanny happy: she preferred her maternal grandmother the dowager Lady Bridges to Grandmama Austen.

Mansfield Park was advertised on 19 May in the *Star*, at eighteen shillings, 'by the author of *Sense and Sensibility* and *Pride and Prejudice*'. Amazingly, there seem to have been no reviews but the book was a commercial success and Jane made a profit of £350. Jane collected opinions from family and friends. Frank did not think it on the whole as good as *Pride and Prejudice* but Fanny Price delighted him and so did Aunt Norris. He admired the dialogue. 'Mrs' Augusta Bramston of Oakley Hall had thought *Sense and Sensibility* and *Pride and Prejudice* downright nonsense and hoped to like *Mansfield Park* better. Having struggled through the first volume Mrs Bramston congratulated herself on having 'got through the worst'.

Cassandra thought it quite as clever, though not as brilliant, as *Pride and Prejudice*. Louisa Knight, Edward's fourth daughter and Jane's godchild, remembered that Cassandra had tried to persuade Jane Austen to let Mr Crawford marry Fanny Price but the author stood firm. A Mrs Carrick wrote shrewdly, 'All who think deeply and feel much will give the preference to *Mansfield Park*.' Mrs Grant of Laggan, a writer herself, wrote to a friend that its picture of manners was accurate and the moral was 'rather insinuated than obtruded'. Lady Anne Romilly recognized it as true to life, with 'a good strong vein of principle running through the whole'. The Earl of Dudley preferred Austen to Edgeworth because her plots were better constructed, she had more feeling, and he was relieved that Jane never plagued the reader with 'chemistry, mechanics or political economy, which are all excellent things in their way, but vile cold-hearted trash in a novel'.

Fanny Knight was delighted with her namesake, Fanny Price, but wanted 'more love' between her and Edmund. She thought Edmund's attraction to an unprincipled woman like Mary Crawford improbable, and was not convinced that Edmund could countenance a marriage between Fanny Price and Henry Crawford. The Cookes at Bookham praised *Mansfield Park*.

Bookham was near Leatherhead, and it is believed that Jane used the little town as her model for Highbury in *Emma*. Jane went to stay with the Cookes and maybe collected local colour.

There was a brief peace in the war with France, a lull which became the setting for *Persuasion*. Napoleon had been exiled to Elba. Frank was on shore as a half-pay captain. Charles was still on the *Namur* at the Nore but his relatives hoped he and his family would soon be settled on land.

King Louis XVIII had been restored to the French throne on 2 May 1814 by England, Prussia and Russia, after France had been twenty years a republic. There was to be a grand Allied thanksgiving service in St Paul's Cathedral followed by public celebrations. Henry had collected Cassandra and she was staying with him in London. Jane wrote to her sister from Chawton on 13 June telling her to take care and not get trampled to death. In the event the Russian Emperor was so popular that crowds pressed forward to kiss his horse. The warning was no idle one: seven years previously seventeen people had been trampled to death at a public hanging. To celebrate the peace there were fireworks in Green Park where a Chinese pagoda and bridge unfortunately burst into flames and toppled into the canal. Henry the socialite was invited to a ball attended by the Czar, the King and the Prince Regent on 21 June. It cost £10,000 and was held at Burlington House. Jane was impressed: 'Oh what a Henry!'

Meanwhile Jane was kindly encouraging her niece Anna, now twenty-one, to write. Some time in the summer of 1814, Jane told Anna that one of the manuscripts Anna had sent had entertained the whole family: Jane had read it aloud to Mrs Austen ('your GM') and 'Aunt C' and they had all enjoyed it. Anna's Sir Thomas, Lady Helena and St Julian were 'very well done', and Cecilia continued to be 'interesting in spite of her being so amiable'. A few verbal corrections were all that Jane was tempted to make, she wrote, and then corrected Anna on a point of etiquette. 'As Lady H is Cecilia's superior, it would not be correct to talk of *her* being introduced; Cecilia must be the person introduced.' Then she offered a correction of Anna's style: 'And I do not like a lover's speaking in the third person . . . it is not natural.' However if Anna thought differently it did not matter. 'I am impatient for more, and only wait for a safe conveyance to return this book.'

Jane's eyes were giving out and she was in the middle of writing *Emma*. Fiction writing, when all the materials have to be self-generated, is a drain on the energies and demands intense concentration. Yet she found time to read and constructively criticize the amateur composition of her young niece. This generosity of time and effort cannot have come cheap.

A month or so later she wrote again to Anna approving of her title, *Which Is the Heroine?*, but expressing a preference for the original one, *Enthusiasm*. However, Anna may have changed the name because there was already a book called *Les Voeux Téméraires; ou, L'Enthousiasme* (*Daring Desires; or, Enthusiasm*) by Madame de Genlis. Jane responded to Anna's detailed queries with fresh encouragement. Once again she put Anna right on a question of social etiquette. 'I have . . . scratched out the introduction between Lord P and his brother and Mr Griffin. A country surgeon (don't tell Mr C Lyford) would not be introduced to men of their rank. And when Mr Portman is first brought in, he would not be introduced as "the Honourable". That distinction is never mentioned at such times; at least I believe not . . . And we think you had better not leave England. Let the Portmans go to Ireland, but as you know nothing of the manners there, you had better not go with them. You will be in danger of giving false representations. Stick to Bath . . . There you will be quite at home.' She adds that she thinks a serious conversation 'about the madness of otherwise sensible women on the subject of their daughters coming out is worth its weight in gold'. In a postscript she writes, 'Twice you have put Dorsetshire for Devonshire. I have altered it. Mr Griffin must have lived in Devonshire; Dawlish is halfway down the county.'

Anna's novels apparently were in the same mould as her aunt's. In her maturity she decided they were worthless and destroyed them. In Jane's critiques we see her usual concern for probability and social accuracy. In a letter to Cassandra written on 24 January 1813 she mentions a mistake that had crept into *Mansfield Park*. 'I learn from Sir J

Carr that there is no Government House at Gibraltar. I must alter it to the Commissioner's.' She was referring to Sir John Carr's book *Descriptive Travels in the Southern and Eastern Parts of Spain*, published 1811.

In August Jane was at 23 Hans Place in London as Henry had moved from his rooms in Henrietta Street to a house next door to his banking partner Mr Tilson. It was then nearly surrounded by fields, although behind Sloane Street. The fields were later built over to become Pont Street. Jane was agreeably surprised by the space and comfort of his rooms and the garden across which they talked to their neighbour was 'quite a love'. Jane liked to live in the downstairs room that opened on to it. There were also a balcony and a conservatory. Henry employed one maid servant only, a creditable, clean-looking young woman, and a man.

James and Edward arrived: 'their business is about teeth and wigs', for being well into their forties they did not follow the fashion, as their younger brothers did, for wearing their own hair. Henry was friendly with Miss Harriet Moore and Jane was convinced he would soon remarry. Jane liked the idea of Miss Moore better than anybody else at hand, she told Cassandra. But nothing came of it.

Henry was talking of a visit to Chawton and mentioned the possibility of calling on friends on the way. In case this came to anything, Jane asked her sister to forward by Collyer's coach her silk pelisse and a clean dressing gown which would come from the wash on Friday. On 2 September Jane was still at 'delightful' Hans Place, writing to Martha who was in Bath.

> I shall have spent my twelve days here very pleasantly, but with not much to tell . . . two or three very little dinner parties at home, some delightful drives in the curricle, and quiet tea-drinkings with the Tilsons has been the sum of my doings.

Jane was amused by the latest fashions, describing them in detail: coloured petticoats with braces over white spencers, and enormous bonnets. Long sleeves seemed universal, even for formal wear, waists were high and bosoms covered. Flounces were in. Without drawing breath or marking a paragraph, she continues she has seen 'West's famous painting . . . the first representation of our Saviour which ever at all contented me'. Benjamin West was President of the Royal Academy, painter of historical and religious subjects. The painting Jane had seen was *Christ's Rejection by the Elders*. Another intelligent woman who saw the picture, Melesina Trench, however, disliked it: for her, it was neither natural nor sufficiently noble for divinity.

Henry was convinced that the American war, declared 1812, would ruin the British. They 'cannot be conquered, and we shall only be teaching them the skill in war which they may now want'. Jane hoped that Britain, as a religious nation which she did not believe the Americans to be, would receive Heaven's protection. Her religious feeling ran deep. She read sermons for pleasure as well as for edification.

On 31 August Charles's wife, Fanny Palmer, gave birth to her fourth daughter, two weeks prematurely, on board ship. Everything went normally but a week later plump, pink-faced, blonde Fanny was dead, aged twenty-four. Her little girl lived only another fortnight. Edward set off at once to comfort his brother.

Charles resigned from the *Namur* and looked for service abroad on the 36-gun HMS *Phoenix*, which was off to the Mediterranean. He sent his three surviving daughters to their relatives in Keppel Street, where their sour-faced aunt Harriet Palmer looked after them. Mrs Austen disliked her though she admitted that Harriet was very good and very useful and that her ill-health was to be pitied. In 1820 Harriet became the children's stepmother as well as their aunt when she married Charles as his second wife.

Edward's claim to the Chawton estate was being contested by the Hintons and the Baverstocks, who had been the heirs until Thomas Knight and Thomas Knight II cut off the entail. They were looking for legal flaws in the disentailing documents. Jane's home was under threat as, if Edward had to relinquish the Great House, then Chawton Cottage would have to go too. The matter was not settled until 1818, after Jane's death, when Edward had to sell £15,000 worth of timber from Chawton to buy the Hintons off and raise another £15,000 for legal expenses.

Jane was hoping for her publisher's account while in London. She had visited Catherine Hill (née Bigg) at Streatham and was distressed that Catherine's young children should grow up with such an elderly father. He was twenty-four years older than his wife.

Back at Chawton Jane sent Anna criticisms of her latest effort, which are interesting as an indication of Jane's own practice and show her further punctilious attention to social detail:

> We are not satisfied with Mrs F's settling herself as tenant and near neighbour to such a man as Sir T H without having some induce-ment to go there; she ought to have some friend living thereabouts to tempt her. A woman, going with two girls just growing up, into a neighbourhood where she knows nobody but one man, of not very good character, is an awkwardness which so prudent a woman as Mrs F would not be likely to fall into. Remember, she is very prudent; you must not let her act inconsistently. Give her a friend, and let that friend be invited to meet her at the Priory, and we shall have no objection to her dining there as she does; but otherwise a woman in her situation would hardly go there, before she had been visited by other families . . . Sir T H you always do very well; I have only taken the liberty of expunging one phrase of his . . . 'Bless my heart'. It is too familiar and inelegant. Your GM [grandmother] is more disturbed at Mrs F's not returning the Egertons' visit sooner than anything else. They ought to have called at the parsonage be-fore Sunday.
>
> You describe a sweet place, but your descriptions are often more minute than will be liked. You give too many particulars . . .
>
> You are now collecting your people delightfully . . . Three or four families in a country village is just the thing to work on . . . I wish you could make Mrs F talk more, but she must be difficult to manage and make entertaining, because there is so much good common sense and propriety about her that nothing can be very *broad* . . .

Jane criticized Anna's clichés such as 'vortex of dissipation' and said mildly her novel lacked incident. She turned to rival authors:

> Walter Scott has no business to write novels, especially good ones. It is not fair. He has fame and profit enough as a poet, and should not be taking the bread out of other people's mouths . . .

She meant it. Scott had recently published *Waverley*, his first novel. He however wrote a favourable review of *Emma* when it came out in 1816. Scott was created a baronet in recognition of his literary work in 1820.

Anna Austen married Benjamin Langlois Lefroy on 8 November

1814. He had promised James he would go into the Church. Jane Austen approved of him as sensible, very religious and with some independence, by which she meant money. The young couple met every day that summer, taking the short cut across the meadows which reduced the distance between the Steventon and Ashe rectories to not much more than a mile. They spent a lot of time walking together in the Steventon shrubbery. Mary was irritated at being kept out of it by their devotion to each other, which she declared was foolishness, but she and James consented to the match.

Weddings were often extremely quiet by our standards: Anna's grandmother and aunts were not invited. Anna's half-sister, Caroline, was a bridesmaid and Anne Lefroy, the bridegroom's niece, was the other. They wore white frocks and had white ribbon in their straw bonnets. Between nine and ten o'clock the bride, Ben's brother's wife Sophia, Anne and Caroline were taken the half-mile to Steventon church in James Austen's carriage. All the gentlemen walked. Anna was like her Aunt Jane, with bright brown hair and hazel eyes. She wore a dress of fine white muslin with a soft silk shawl, white shot with primrose, embossed with white satin flowers, and on her head a small cap trimmed with lace to match. Mr John Henry George Lefroy, the groom's brother, performed the ceremony and James gave his daughter away.

It was a grey chilly morning and there were no heaters or flowers in the narrow-windowed church. No one was there but the wedding party, and no one else was asked to the breakfast, to which they sat down as soon as they got back. The wedding feast consisted of an ordinary good breakfast of the period: tongue, ham and eggs, bread, buttered toast, hot rolls. To mark the occasion, there was hot chocolate and there was a wedding cake. The bride and groom left soon afterwards as they had a long day's journey to Hendon in front of them. Ben's brother had a house there. Jane wondered whether the air there was polluted, as it was only twelve miles from London. Nowadays Hendon and other villages have long been swallowed up in what William Cobbett and Jane Austen called the Great Wen, or blemish on the face of the countryside.

Anna kept on writing for a while but after Jane died did not have much heart to continue. She was soon the busy mother of seven children. In one of her recurrent fits of despondency she threw her unfinished novel into the fire. Anna's third daughter Fanny-Caroline, born 1820, sat on the rug watching the papers blacken and curl and throw out sparks. However, finding herself widowed with, in Cassandra's words, 'a large family, a narrow income and indifferent health', Anna published a novella, *Mary Hamilton,* in the *Literary Souvenir* for 1833 and two small books for children, *The Winter's Tale* (1841) and *Springtide* (1842). She attempted to finish Jane's uncompleted novel *Sanditon* but only managed some 20,000 words.

Motherless Fanny Knight had written to Jane in November 1814 to ask her advice about Mr Plumptre, the boyfriend whom she had at first fancied but was now uncertain about. Consulted in confidence, Jane concealed the letter even from Cassandra. She begged Fanny to write something which could be read or told to other people. The young man was worthy but Fanny found him dull and was worried he might become Evangelical. Jane, who had previously been blunt about her dislike of Evangelicals, was more cautious now: she was not convinced that everybody ought not to be Evangelical. Fanny replied in a letter now lost, and Jane responded that she and Fanny attached different meanings to the word. It would be illuminating if we could only know what she meant here. She disliked Edward Cooper's sermons as too full of 'regeneration and conversion', which offers some clue. Fanny's young man was so strict in his views that he thought dancing and social amusements should be avoided by Christian people. Jane and Fanny were both sincere Christians but such negation seemed excessive. Wisdom was better than wit, Jane continued. But on the other hand Fanny must not think of accepting him unless she really did like him. If Fanny did not want to marry him she must behave coldly so he would conclude that he had been deceiving himself. She warned Fanny not to rely on any other person's opinions but to trust only her own feelings. Nothing could be worse than to be bound to one man and preferring another.

'I have no doubt of his suffering a good deal for a time . . . but it is no creed of mine . . . that such disappointments kill anybody,' wrote Jane with her usual robust common sense. Fanny decided to throw coldness into her manner.

Jane took a hint from Fanny's letter. 'Your trying to excite your own feelings by a visit to his room amused me excessively. The dirty shaving rag was exquisite! Such a circumstance ought to be in print. Much too good to be lost,' wrote the published novelist. She would remember Fanny and the dirty shaving rag when she made Harriet Smith in *Emma* fetishize Mr Elton's broken stub of leadless pencil and scrap of sticking plaster.

Fanny would be glad to hear that the first edition of *Mansfield Park* had sold out. Jane told Fanny, the rich man's daughter, frankly, 'I am very greedy and want to make the most of it; but as you are much above caring about money, I shall not plague you with particulars. The pleasures of vanity are more within your comprehension and you will enter into mine at receiving the *praise* which every now and then comes to me, through some channel or other.' People were readier, though, to borrow and to praise than to buy, said Jane, making the usual complaint of authors. 'Though I like praise as well as anybody, I like what Edward calls *pewter* too.'

Towards the end of November Edward and his eldest son took Jane to London to stay with Henry and negotiate a second edition of *Mansfield Park*. Egerton was unwilling to reprint and the second edition came out from John Murray in 1816 with corrected nautical details in the Portsmouth scenes thanks to help from Frank, conveniently near at hand in the Great House, which Edward had lent him. Henry was still at 23 Hans Place.

Jane went to the theatre and saw Miss Eliza O'Neal in David Garrick's *Isabella, or the Fatal Marriage*. The plot concerns a grandfather who wants to adopt a child on condition it is separated from its mother, and a husband who returns from afar to find that his wife, thinking him dead, has remarried. Mrs Siddons in the part had wrung tears from audiences but was now retired. The acting as usual disappointed Jane, because at this period it tended to be highly stylized and rhetorical, and with her sharp nose for anything false she longed for something more natural. 'I took two pocket handkerchiefs, but had very little occasion for either,' she wrote drily.

James-Edward, hearing of a possible second edition of *Mansfield Park*, sent his Aunt Jane an anonymous request for a fourth volume giving the 'useful and amiable' married life of Edmund and Fanny. The only fault of the novel, wrote the admiring nephew, was in being too short.

She visited Charles's daughters who were with their Palmer relations in Keppel Street. Three of her brothers were now widowers. She went to see Anna in Hendon and reported to Fanny that Anna's having a pianoforte was foolishness as her playing would never amount to anything and the couple would wish the twenty-four guineas had been laid out in sheets and towels. Anna had bought a purple pelisse. 'I do not mean to blame her. It looked very well and I daresay she wanted it. I suspect nothing worse than its being got in secret, and not owned to anybody. She is capable of that, you know.' Perhaps Anna had been spending her husband's money behind his back.

After Christmas Cassandra and Jane went to Winchester to stay with Mrs Heathcote and her sister Alethea Bigg, now living at No. 12 Cathedral Close. It had been Jane's most fruitful year to date.

22

Royal Favour, 1815–16

O N 2 JANUARY 1815 Cassandra and Jane left Winchester for Steventon, staying till 16 January, calling on the Bramstons at Oakley Hall, the Portals at Laverstoke and the Rector of Ashe, John Henry George Lefroy. He and his wife had six children and were to have five more. Later in the year their five-year-old son went to stay with Ben and Anna. Jane thought him terribly in want of discipline and hoped he got 'a wholesome thump or two' whenever it was necessary. Physical punishment of children was taken for granted. Jane wrote calmly in an early letter that Edward's eldest boy had been put into his first breeches and soundly whipped into the bargain.

In March Napoleon escaped from Elba and took over France again, ruling from Paris. Only the battle of Waterloo in June finished the war. Napoleon was exiled to the island of St Helena where he died some years later. Lord Byron wrote a poem as spoken by Bonaparte which began:

> Farewell to the Land where the gloom of my Glory
> Arose and o'ershadowed the earth with her name –

Jane liked it enough to copy it out and keep it.

Charles was in the Mediterranean. On 6 May he wrote to Jane from Palermo telling her that when he had praised Walter Scott's novel *Waverley* in conversation another man had told him there had been nothing for years to compare with *Sense and Sensibility* and *Pride and Prejudice*. This person, a nephew of the late Charles James Fox, was however not so fond of *Mansfield Park*. Mrs Austen too liked *Waverley* only second to her own daughter's books.

James's wife, Mary, came to stay at Chawton Cottage, bringing her observant daughter Caroline, now aged ten, with her. Caroline regarded Cassandra coolly but adored Jane. Cassy, Charles's eldest girl, lived at Chawton intermittently with her grandmother and aunts, educated by Cassandra, and Frank's Mary-Jane was often there as well. Jane supplied the children with dressing-up clothes and played house with them. She always told them that Cassandra knew more than she did and could teach them things better than she could. Caroline received this in polite silence, preferring Jane. In later life she believed that Jane genuinely looked up to her elder sister. 'The most perfect affection and confidence ever subsisted between them – and great and lasting was the sorrow of the survivor when the final separation was made,' wrote Caroline.

The Knight family did not come to Chawton the summer of 1815, as there were celebrations for young Edward's coming of age. His elder sister Fanny had to arrange his twenty-first birthday party, though there had been none for her. Jane had finished *Emma* on 29 March and began *Persuasion* on 8 August. She probably made little headway as that day Ben and Anna Lefroy arrived. They were moving from Hendon to a farmhouse called Wyards, within walking distance of Anna's grandmother and aunts. Meanwhile Ben and Anna stayed at Chawton Cottage. Anna was Mrs Austen's favourite granddaughter and the old lady was delighted to have the young couple in the house, and about to settle so near.

Jane was so disgusted with Egerton that *Emma* was not offered to him. By 29 September it had received a favourable report from John Murray's reader, though he felt it needed a little subediting. This reader, William Gifford, was also editor of the *Quarterly Review*. Murray sat on the manuscript for three weeks, thinking it would do no harm to let Jane Austen sweat a little.

That autumn she was in London again. Henry was suffering from 'a dangerous fever' of some kind. Indeed, he was expected to die and his brother James was summoned to the house. Jane nursed Henry through his illness and then his slow convalescence. He was dosed with calomel, a grey powdery medicine whose mercury and chlorine were probably poisoning him. The apothecary took twenty ounces of blood on two consecutive days and threatened to take another twenty on the third. Henry was an excellent patient, lying quietly in bed and ready to swallow anything. He lived on tea, aperient medicine and barley water. No wonder his recovery was slow. Jane sent her dirty washing home by Collyer's coach and laid plans for changing places with Cassandra when Henry next went to Oxford on business.

Murray, who had spotted a winner, offered £450 for *Emma* but wanted the copyrights of *Mansfield Park* and *Sense and Sensibility* included. Jane was angry and told Cassandra wearily that he was a rogue and she was likely to end up publishing *Emma* herself.

Before his collapse Henry dictated a letter to Murray. He found Murray's praise of the novel satisfactory but quibbled with the terms, pointing out that his sister had cleared as much as Murray was offering by the sale of the small first edition of *Mansfield Park*. Jane wrote requesting a meeting. 'A short conversation may perhaps do more than writing,' she suggested. Eventually a deal was struck: Murray would publish 2,000 copies of *Emma* on commission and would print a second edition of *Mansfield Park* with a print run of 750, also on commission.

Anna had had a baby, making her half-sister Caroline, now ten years old, an aunt. Jane wrote kindly to Caroline, 'Now that you are become an aunt, you are a person of some consequence . . . I have always maintained the importance of aunts.'

Jane corrected the proof sheets of *Emma* during this time. Writing to Cassandra, she noted that the printer had queried her spelling of 'arrowroot', which she had written as 'arraroot'. We remember that in the novel Emma sends some to Jane Fairfax, who proudly rejects it. It was until fairly recently a favoured invalid food, farinaceous, bland and easily digested.

Fanny came to stay and went with Jane to Keppel Street to see Charles's children. Henry's medical man, Mr Haden, admired Jane's work, and Fanny found him delightfully clever as well as handsome. Jane liked him as well. He was invited for the evening but to Jane's dismay Mrs Latouche and Miss East invited themselves to drink tea after dinner. She told Cassandra she was heartily sorry they were coming. She and Henry were living well on hare and rabbits from

Godmersham and pheasants from the Fowles, which cheered Jane up. 'From seven to eight the harp; at eight Mrs L and Miss E arrived.' For the rest of the evening, there seems to have been crowding to the point of discomfort: the two visitors, Henry and Jane all squeezed on to the sofa, with Fanny and Mr Haden sitting opposite. Mr Haden was invited to dinner next day. He was currently reading *Mansfield Park* and preferred it to *Pride and Prejudice*.

Mr Haden was a bright young man with a medical degree from Edinburgh and he admired Fanny. He was also musical. Jane enjoyed his clever conversation and although she considered his opinion, lifted from Shakespeare's Lorenzo in *The Merchant of Venice*, that unmusical people were fit for every kind of wickedness, an 'insanity', she liked him. Cassandra was worried that her darling niece, the eldest daughter at Godmersham, was engaging in a flirtation with a mere apothecary. Apothecaries ranked low in the social scale and their precise status was defined by the Apothecaries' Act of 1815. They were below surgeons, who ranked below physicians. Physicians alone among medical men ranked as gentlemen. Physicians prescribed. Surgeons operated. Jane told Cassandra that Mr Haden had never been an apothecary: he was a 'Haden, nothing but a Haden, a sort of wonderful nondescript creature on two legs, something between a man and an angel . . .' She refrained from establishing Mr Haden's exact status. 'We have been very little plagued with visitors this week,' added the author, preoccupied with her proof sheets. Edward took Fanny back to Kent on 8 December, after another musical evening.

One day a second and grander doctor who had been called in, Dr Matthew Baillie, who had treated Henry earlier for chest trouble, mentioned to Jane that the Prince, later to become King George IV, was a great admirer of the novels, adding that he read them often, and even kept a set in each of his residences. The Prince, though dissolute in his private life, was a man of taste and culture with an interest in languages, history, art and literature. He commissioned the Brighton Pavilion, a palace on the Indian model, with rooms in the Japanese and Chinese manner. It is a magnificent extravaganza. He died with debts of £400,000. Although Jane Austen's name had never appeared on any title page her identity was becoming known and the doctor knew that the quiet woman then approaching forty was the author of *Pride and Prejudice*.

On hearing that the author whose fictions he so much enjoyed was in London the Prince as a mark of royal favour sent his librarian the Revd James Stainier Clarke to call on her. Mr Clarke announced that he had the Prince's instructions to show her the library and to pay her every possible attention.

Jane accordingly went on 13 November 1815 to Carlton House, the Prince's London residence, and looked at the library. Carlton House was small but luxurious. A hall with green walls and Ionic columns of brown Siena marble led into ante-rooms and drawing rooms of crimson, gold, blue and rose, with flowered carpets and elaborate drapes of velvet and satin. The sombre richness of the blue velvet closet, bronze and blue and gold, contrasted with the opulent crimson drawing room with its gilded plaster, buhl and ormulu in every corner. On the south side overlooking the Mall were a conservatory that reminded her of a cathedral, an Ionic dining room, a Gothic dining room and a Gothic library.

During the visit Mr Clarke declared that if she were at work on another novel she might if she chose dedicate it to the Prince himself. Not caring at all for the Prince, Jane decided to ignore this suggestion. When Henry and Cassandra heard of this they explained that it was not so much a request as a royal command. Jane took the hint and sent the dedication of *Emma* to the printer at once.

If any reader should imagine the self-satisfied pomposity of Mr Collins in *Pride and Prejudice* a caricature, he or she has only to read the correspondence between Jane Austen and Mr Clarke. He was one of the pests authors are beset by, proffering unasked advice on how to write their books. He wanted her to write a novel about the

> habits of life and character and enthusiasm of a clergyman – who should pass his time between the metropolis and the country – who should be something like Beattie's Minstrel
>
> > Silent when glad, affectionate though shy
> > And now his look was most demurely sad
> > And now he laughed aloud yet none knew why.

Neither Goldsmith, nor La Fontaine in his Tableau de Famille
have in my mind quite delineated an English clergyman, at least of
the present day, fond of, and entirely engaged in, literature: no
man's enemy but his own. Pray dear madam think of these things.

Mr Clarke wanted not just the cosy pleasure of identifying with a
fictional character: his demand on Jane Austen was for a flattering portrait of himself. She laughed at his request and later made private fun
of it. His literary allusions were to a long poem by James Beattie
(1735–1803), *The Minstrel; or, the Progress of Genius*, and to a French
translation of a work originally written in German. Jane wrote on 11
December 1815 that she had arranged for a copy of *Emma* to be sent
to Carlton House three days in advance of publication. She hoped that
to those who preferred *Pride and Prejudice* it would not seem less witty
than its predecessor, and to those who preferred *Mansfield Park* it
would not appear at all inferior in good sense. Tactfully she added:

> I am quite honoured by your thinking me capable of drawing such
> a clergyman as you gave the sketch of in your note . . . But I assure
> you I am not. The comic part of the character I might be equal to,
> but not the good, the enthusiastic, the literary. Such a man's con-
> versation must at times be on subjects of science and philosophy of
> which I know nothing – or at least be occasionally abundant in quo-
> tations and allusions which a woman, who like me knows only her
> own mother-tongue and has read very little in that, would be to-
> tally without the power of giving. A classical education, or at any
> rate a very extensive acquaintance with English literature, ancient
> and modern, appears to me quite indispensable for the person who
> would do any justice to your clergyman. And I think I may boast
> myself to be, with all possible vanity, the most unlearned, and un-
> informed, female who ever dared to be an authoress.

The humility is mock humility and the 'boast' is a real one. Jane is
playing the game of pretending to be 'only' a woman, not clever or accomplished enough to meet Mr Clarke's requirements. Her real message lies in her subtext, the reminder to him that she is a successful
'authoress' whose talent is not at his disposal. But Clarke was as ab-
surdly egocentric as Mr Collins in *Pride and Prejudice*. Undeterred, he
persisted, digging himself into an ever deeper hole. He thanked her for
the copy of *Emma*, which despite his professed admiration he had read

only a few pages of before passing it on to the Prince Regent, and promised her a copy of a book he had written on King James II. This evidently slightly paranoid man was convinced that many Shylocks were whetting sharp knives to cut 'more than a pound of flesh from my heart' when it appeared. He assured Jane that the few pages of *Emma* which he had managed to read had 'so much nature – and excellent description of character in everything you describe'. This praise was vague enough not to offend and he soon returned to his real concern, his scheme of instructing the most talented writer of the day in her craft, though he could not be bothered to read her latest book when he held it in his hands. He took her tongue-in-cheek disclaimers literally and urged her:

> Pray continue to write, and make all your friends send sketches to help you . . . Do let us have an English clergyman after your fancy . . . show dear madam what good would be done if tithes were taken away entirely, and describe him burying his own mother – as I did – because the high priest of the parish in which she died – did not pay her remains the respect he ought to.

This implies that he wanted Jane Austen to write a novel which would be an instrument of revenge on the 'high priest'. This term is clearly sarcastic, suggesting that the parson concerned was arrogant and overbearing, as the term 'high priest' is not in use in the Church of England, and is only used in connection with pagan religions. He confides: 'I have never recovered from the shock.' Immediately he returns to the task of urging Jane Austen to write a novel according to his peculiarly personal recipe. 'Carry your clergyman to sea as the friend of some distinguished naval character about a court . . .' Mr Clarke is clearly yearning to appoint himself Jane Austen's plot consultant, as he reveals he was himself at sea and tells Jane he has arranged to send her some 'sermons which I wrote and preached on the ocean'.

Jane did not reply to this letter. Mr Clarke had not given up. Writing at the end of the following March to thank her for the Prince's presentation copies, he implored her to go on writing. Lord St Helens and many of the nobility who had been staying at the Brighton Pavilion had paid the just tribute of their praise. Mr Clarke boasted of his new appointment as chaplain and secretary to Prince Leopold of Saxe-

Coburg, who was about to marry the Prince Regent's daughter Princess Charlotte of Wales. 'Perhaps when you again appear in print you may choose to dedicate your volumes to Prince Leopold: any historical romance illustrative of the history of the august house of Coburg would just now be very interesting,' he nudged.

This was not so foolish as it sounds. The Royal Family was beset by scandal. King George III, whatever the cause of his illness, was mad; the Prince Regent was estranged from his wife, and the royal princes were living with various mistresses, refusing to marry and beget legitimate heirs. The Prince Regent's sole legitimate daughter, troubled child of a disastrous marriage, was Princess Charlotte. The newspapers were full of coarse satires on the Royal Family. These seem to have been justified. Princess Charlotte told her father that her mother had left her alone with a cavalryman, Captain Charles Hesse, in Charlotte's own bedroom and locked them in, saying in French, 'I'm going now: enjoy yourselves.' Charlotte suspected that her mother wished to compromise her and promote Charlotte's illegitimate half-brother.

The Prince Regent decided Charlotte should be married off as soon as possible but when the drunken Prince of Orange was suggested to her she fled in a hackney coach to her mother's house.

Sense and Sensibility was recommended to Charlotte by one of her 'wicked uncles', the Duke of York, who was convinced it had been written by the notorious Lady Augusta Paget. Charlotte enjoyed the novel. 'It certainly is interesting and you feel quite one of the company,' she wrote to a friend. 'I think Marianne and me [*sic*] are very alike in disposition, though certainly I am not so good. The same imprudence, etc, however remain very like.'

Headstrong Princess Charlotte had met and fallen in love with Prince Leopold when he came to London with the Russian Czar in 1814 for the celebrations of a peace which turned out to be temporary. A royal romance was going to be good, it was hoped, for the battered image of the House of Hanover. In August 1814 the Princess of Wales, Princess Charlotte's mother, had sailed to the Continent of Europe, where, lost to all dignity and decorum, she drew attention to herself and revenged herself on her husband by scandalously indiscreet behaviour. It was rumoured that in Italy she had danced naked in public. George IV finally decided to divorce his wife Caroline when he became King in 1820 and she wanted to be recognized as Queen, but she died in 1821 shortly after the coronation. George IV consoled himself with his final mistress, Lady Conyngham, known punningly as the Vice Queen. Jane Austen must once have seen her at a ball, possibly on a visit to Kent, because in 1798 she had written to Cassandra that she had changed the trimmings on her cap and was pleased to say it made her look more like Lady Conyngham than it did before, 'which is all that one lives for now'.

In 1815 it seemed to Mr Clarke that if that elegant writer, Miss Jane Austen, could be persuaded to romanticize the royal union in fiction by glamorizing the foreign bridegroom's family in order to provide the war-weary nation with a fairy-tale wedding, it would be a brilliant stroke of public relations. The young couple had been pictured at the opera by the painter George Dawe, and black and white printed copies were distributed. Jane Austen had passed their new home, Claremont Park in Surrey, on her way to London in May 1813.

The house of Saxe-Coburg was unheard of outside Prince Leopold's native Germany, where princelings were numerous. He was handsome in his cavalry uniform but so poor he lived in rented rooms above a grocer's shop. The couple married in May 1816 but Princess Charlotte was to die in childbirth in November 1817, four months after Jane Austen herself. Mr Clarke lived until 1834 and the artist J M W Turner went to his funeral.

Prince Leopold's sister married the Regent's brother the Duke of Kent, who as King William IV of England was the uncle of Queen Victoria. Victoria's husband Prince Albert was another Coburg, who brought this family into the direct line of British royal descent.

On 1 April 1816 Jane decided that the nonsensical correspondence with Mr Clarke had gone on long enough. She made polite excuses for answering two letters with one, then came to the point:

> I am fully sensible that an historical romance, founded on the house of Saxe-Coburg might be much more to the purpose of profit or popularity than such pictures of domestic life in country villages as I deal in, but I could no more write a romance than an epic poem. I could not sit seriously down to write a serious romance under any other motive than to save my life, and if it were indispensable for me to keep it up and never to relax into laughing

at myself or other people, I am sure I should be hung before I had finished the first chapter. No – I must keep to my own style and go on in my own way . . .

She knew her own value and the quality of her work. Jane could not resist incorporating some of Mr Clarke's more self-serving notions into a satirical 'plan of a novel'. This would send a clergyman hero to sea as chaplain to a distinguished naval character about the court, burying his own mother ('heroine's lamented grandmother'). The plot outlined Mr Clarke's more absurd suggestions, combined with a melodramatic story. Eventually the 'poor father, quite worn down, finding his end approaching, throws himself on the ground, and after four or five hours of tender advice and parental admonition to his miserable child, expires in a fine burst of literary enthusiasm, intermingled with invectives against holders of tithes'.

Emma was advertised as forthcoming on 2 December 1815 in the *Morning Post*, but was not in fact ready till the last week of the year, and the title page said '1816'. She wrote to Murray by messenger, 'As I find that *Emma* is advertised for publication as early as Saturday next, I think it best to lose no time in settling all that remains to be settled . . .' She agreed to leave the terms of trade to him. She wanted the edition cleared rapidly and enclosed the revised copy of *Mansfield Park*.

Until 16 December, her fortieth birthday, Jane was still in London, but looking forward to going home. She told Cassandra she positively liked the 'nice, unwholesome, unseasonable, relaxing, close muggy weather,' enjoying it 'all over me, from top to toe, from right to left, longitudinally, perpendicularly, diagonally' and selfishly hoped it would last another twenty-three days till Christmas. She ended her letter of 2 December, 'Excuse the shortness of this, but I must finish it now, that I may save you twopence.' She never went to London again.

23

Shipwreck, Bankruptcy and Other Disasters, 1816

*J*ANE RECEIVED WHAT seemed like discriminating praise from Countess Morley, thanking her for a presentation copy of *Emma*. 'I am already become intimate in the Woodhouse family, and feel that they will not amuse and interest me less than the Bennets, Bertrams, Norrises and all their admirable predecessors. I can give them no higher praise,' wrote the Countess.

Lady Morley, formerly Frances Talbot, was initially suspected by Mary Russell Mitford of having written *Pride and Prejudice*. Frances was the Earl's second wife. His first wife, Lady Augusta Paget, was believed by Princess Charlotte to have written *Sense and Sensibility*. The Earl had divorced Augusta after she ran off with another man. The Earl and Countess owned Saltram House in Devon, used when the film of *Sense and Sensibility* was made in 1995. However in private the second Lady Morley told her sister-in-law that she actually preferred *Pride and Prejudice* and *Mansfield Park* to *Emma*.

Jane said that her ladyship's approbation was gratifying. 'It encourages me to depend on the same share of general good opinion which *Emma*'s predecessors have experienced, and to believe that I have not yet – as almost every writer of fancy does sooner or later – overwritten myself.' Like every creative artist she was afraid of drying up.

Jane's brother Frank liked *Emma* enormously. He preferred it to

Pride and Prejudice, which might be considered to have more wit, and to *Mansfield Park* with its higher morality. *Emma* was like life. Cassandra liked *Emma* more than *Pride and Prejudice*, but not as much as she did *Mansfield Park*. Mrs Austen thought *Emma* more entertaining than *Mansfield Park* but not as interesting as *Pride and Prejudice*. She thought nobody in *Emma* compared with Lady Catherine and Mr Collins. Edward the farmer teased his sister about a slip in the strawberry-picking scene: 'Jane, I wish you would tell me where you get those apple trees of yours that come into bloom in June.' Edward's daughter Fanny did not like the book as well as *Pride and Prejudice* or *Mansfield Park*, because she disliked the heroine. She found Mr Knightley delightful and would have liked to see more of Jane Fairfax.

Jane had not yet met her first great-niece, Anna-Jemima Lefroy, Ben and Anna's daughter. She sent Anna a note: 'As I wish very much to see *your* Jemima, I am sure you will like to see *my Emma*, and have therefore great pleasure in sending it for your perusal. Keep it as long as you choose . . .'

Anna's comment was interesting. *Emma* was not as brilliant as *Pride and Prejudice*, nor as 'equal' as *Mansfield Park*, by which she meant 'consistent'. The characters were admirably well drawn and natural. Her favourites were Mr Knightley, Mrs Elton and Miss Bates. One or two of the conversations were 'too long'. Anna's daughter Fanny-Caroline Lefroy said many years later that in the eyes of several people the character of Emma, especially the way she looks, pointed to Anna, if only unintentionally. Indeed, the portrait combined Anna's appearance with something of her richer cousin Fanny's situation.

Dear Mrs Digweed said she could never have got through the book if she had not known the author. Maria Edgeworth also received a presentation copy which she did not acknowledge. She thought the book dull and plotless. Susan Ferrier, who had not yet finished writing her novel *Marriage*, also thought there was no story to *Emma*, but the characters were true to life and the style piquant: there was no need of mystery and adventure.

The book attracted eight printed reviews. Some people found Miss Bates a bore. John Murray privately thought the book wanted incident and romance but as publisher of the influential *Quarterly Review* he asked Walter Scott to review it. Scott praised the novel for being lifelike and wrote about Jane's other books as well but had not heard of *Mansfield Park*. He quoted, though, as an example of *Emma's* quiet though comic dialogue, the conversation between Mr Woodhouse and Isabella in Chapter Twelve. Jane was pleased, saying those were the very characters she had taken most pains with.

Jane's triumph was qualified by disasters which had struck her brothers. Henry had gone bankrupt at the end of 1815. He had not been able to attend to business while Eliza was dying or during his own protracted illness. The Alton bank of Austen Gray and Vincent, like many small country banks in the difficult postwar period, collapsed first, dragging with it the London bank of Austen Maunde and Tilson. Government contracts dried up. Henry had borrowed £20,000 from Edward, lost at a bad time as Edward was involved in his lawsuit with the Hintons of Chawton and the Baverstocks of Alton over his inheritance from Thomas Brodnax-May-Knight. Jane had only £13 7s in her Henrietta Street account, which she lost, but the £600 profit on her novels was safely invested in navy stock at five per cent.

Henry returned to his original career plan and wrote to the Bishop of Winchester about becoming a clergyman. He polished up his Greek and was disappointed when the Bishop failed to be impressed by it. However, he was approved and was ordained deacon at Salisbury the next day. He was appointed curate of Chawton at the age of forty-five on a stipend of 52 guineas a year. He became a zealous preacher of Calvinistic doctrine in the Evangelical wing of the Church, later becoming perpetual curate of Bentley, Hampshire. London had become hateful to him but his residence there had been an invaluable asset to his sister.

On 21 February 1816 Charles was shipwrecked off the coast of Smyrna, where he was chasing pirates. His captain's log reads:

> At two pm the ship struck on the rocks astern, it then blowing a gale from the north-east. Hoisted out boats and cut the masts away. Attempted to heave the ship off . . . rudder broken and washed away . . . The people immediately began to swim on shore, all the boats being stove. At four pm a Turk, with a message from the Aga, came down opposite the ship and inquired for me, when I landed, sliding down on a top-gallant mast, which reached from the wreck to the shore. Thank God, I found that no life had been lost. Walked

to the town with the marine officer and others, distant a long mile, blowing violently, with sleet and rain, and very cold. At the house of Mr Cortovitch we were received most kindly and hospitably, in supplying us with clothes, food and beds. For the crew I got a large store-house with fires, bread and wine. In spite of our misfortune I slept well.

Although Charles was cleared of all blame, this accident for a while did his career no good. Ultimately he triumphed over it, though he suffered from rheumatism and skin eruptions possibly as a result of stress. He had within a few months lost both his wife and his ship.

Jane was starting to feel ill. The catastrophes cannot have helped. Neither Henry nor Frank was able to keep up his contribution of £50 a year on which their mother depended, as Frank's money had been invested in Henry's bank, and Edward too was facing ruin.

Jane at the time was writing *Persuasion*, her last novel, with a sailor hero and several other naval men among the characters. In a letter to her niece Fanny Knight dated 13 March 1816, she said: '*Miss Catherine* is put upon the shelf for the present, and I do not know that she will ever come out; but I have a something ready for publication, which may, perhaps, appear about a twelvemonth hence. It is short – about the length of *Catherine*. This is for yourself alone.' Jane did not live to see either *Persuasion* or the other story published. She had changed its name from *Susan* to *Catherine* because another novel called *Susan* had been published in the interim. *Catherine* was retitled by Henry as *Northanger Abbey*. The two novels were published together in one volume in 1818, with a biographical notice by Henry. This account of his sister was the first whitewash operation performed by her surviving relatives.

Jane saw Fanny for the last time on 21 May 1816 when Edward took his daughter back to Kent.

Elizabeth Leigh, sister to the late Revd Thomas Leigh of Adlestrop and Stoneleigh, died. Jane wrote to her niece Caroline on 21 April, 'We all feel that we have lost a most valued old friend, but the death of a person at her advanced age, so fit to die, and by her own feelings so *ready* to die, is not to be regretted.' She invited Caroline to the fair at Alton to be held on her cousin Mary-Jane's birthday but domestic chores could not be forgotten:

We are almost ashamed to include your Mama in the invitation, or to ask *her* to be at the trouble of a long ride for so few days as we shall be having disengaged, for we *must* wash before the Godmersham party come and therefore Monday would be the last day that our house could be comfortable for her; but if she does feel disposed to pay us a little visit and you could *all* come, so much the better. We do not like to *invite* her to come on Wednesday, to be turned out of the house on Monday . . .

The wash-house at Chawton Cottage is still there. Washday was about once a month and involved backbreaking work. A blanket wash was heavy indeed. Cotton and linen had to be boiled in a copper boiler set in brick over a fire, the water having to be fetched in buckets from the pump and ladled in and out. After washing and rinsing came blueing and starching. The clothes had to be wrung out, either by hand or with an up-to-date mangle. In fine weather, the clothes were pegged out to dry. Then they had to be ironed, either with flat irons heated in the grate, or with hollow box irons filled with hot coals. Both cooled down inconveniently fast.

Washday or no washday, Jane Austen was at the peak of her career. Murray had sent her the copy of the *Quarterly Review* in which *Emma* had been favourably noticed by an anonymous critic who, unknown to Jane, was her rival Walter Scott.

In the year 1816 Jane was often surrounded by nephews and nieces. She lent them clothes for dressing up and joined in their make-believe. It is sometimes said that Jane did not like children. Like most adults she prefered them to be well-behaved. But she did her share of playing with her nephews and nieces, telling them stories and hearing them read. She encouraged them in their attempts at novel-writing, for James-Edward had acquired the family habit of scribbling. Jane wrote to Cassandra in September that his manuscript was extremely clever, written with great ease and spirit; if he could carry it on in the same way it would be a first-rate work and in a style to be popular. 'Pray tell Mary how much I admire it. And tell Caroline that I think it is hardly fair upon her and myself, to have him take up the novel line . . .' For Caroline, though only eleven, was scribbling too.

Now that Henry was a clergyman, he wrote 'very superior sermons', she told James-Edward, unlike Edward Cooper's, which were distorted by his zeal for the Bible Society. Jane teased James-Edward about some of his own writings which had disappeared and defended herself from the charge of having stolen them. She did not think such a theft would be useful to her. 'What should I do . . . with your strong, manly spirited sketches, full of variety and glow? How could I possibly join them on to the little bit (two inches wide) of ivory on which I work with so fine a brush, as produces little effect after much labour?'

Jane was here not apologising for smallness of scale, but staking her claim to be considered a finished craftsman, mistress of the art which conceals art and makes what is difficult look easy. Like his scribbling sisters, Anna and Caroline, James-Edward is noteworthy only for reminiscences of his distinguished aunt.

In May, Jane and Cassandra had been for a few weeks to Cheltenham, then a spa town, from Chawton, breaking their journey at James's house, Steventon Rectory, and leaving nine-year-old Cassandra Knight to stay with Caroline while they were in Gloucestershire. They also made a short stay with the Fowles at Kintbury, where Fulwar and Eliza were shocked by Jane's visibly failing health. Jane went about her old haunts as if she did not expect to see them again. Cassandra returned to Cheltenham with James's wife Mary and Caroline. The *Cheltenham Chronicle* of 1 August mentioned the Duke and Duchess of Orléans and Jane was entertained to think that the Duchess 'drinks at my pump'. But Jane's health was beyond the aid of spa waters.

Charles had asked to visit Chawton with his three girls. Jane wanted to see him but worried about bedrooms: he did not mention bringing a maid but if he was going to bring one there would be no bed for him, let alone one for Henry. There were other general anxieties about one family member or another. Frank's wife, Mary, seldom seemed quite well: 'Little Embryo is troublesome, I suppose,' wrote Jane, caustic as usual about mothering. Perhaps worse, 'Mrs FA' was still without a housemaid and was dreading the forthcoming visit of her parents. There was too much reason to fear that they would stay above a week. Jane's back, she wrote in reply to Cassandra's inquiry, had been almost free of pain for several days.

'Sir Thomas Miller is dead. I treat you with a dead baronet in almost every letter,' wrote Jane. Mrs Digweed was parting with both Hannah and her old cook, because Hannah refused to give up her lover, who was a man of bad character, and the cook was guilty only of being unequal to anything. Madame Perigord, formerly Henry's housekeeper, wrote to Jane after returning from her native France that the country after the Battle of Waterloo was a scene of general poverty and misery with no money and no trade. Ben Lefroy's brother Christopher-Edward had also been in France and was 'thinking of the French as one would wish, disappointed in everything'.

Jane complained that visitors left her little time for herself. She wanted a few days' quiet. 'I often wonder how *you* can find time for what you do, in addition to the care of the house,' she mused to Cassandra, amazed that fellow-writer Jane West managed to run a household, rear children and produce books. Composition seemed impossible to Jane Austen, with a head full of joints of mutton and rhubarb medicines: not garden rhubarb but an imported root from China and Tibet, used as a purgative. She enjoyed Charles's visit after all.

Edward spent three weeks at Chawton in November 1816; Henry was constantly coming and going; Charles had come home at the end of June. Mostly he stayed with the Palmer family in London to keep in close touch with the Admiralty but in November he came to Chawton, and because Edward had not succeeded in letting it, the Great House absorbed the overflow of relatives, children and servants. Something was wrong with Charles's second girl, Harriet. It seemed she had water on the brain. Jane hoped Heaven in its mercy would soon take her.

Persuasion was finished on 18 July 1816. Jane was dissatisfied with it. She was depressed, partly as a complication of her increasing illness, fearing her powers had left her. She felt the ending of the novel as it stood was tame and flat. One morning she woke feeling her gift had been restored to her, and rewrote the ending on 6 August. The title was discussed and the original plan was for it to be called *The Elliots*. It was probably given the title we have by Henry. A Mrs Barrett used to say 'Anne Elliot was [Jane] herself; her enthusiasm for the navy and her perfect unselfishness reflect her completely.'

24

Winchester, 1817

*I*N THE LAST year of her life Jane told Anna and James-Edward what happened to her characters after the novels in which they appeared ended, and other details of her plots. Miss Steele in *Sense and Sensibility* never did succeed in catching the doctor; Kitty Bennet in *Pride and Prejudice* married a clergyman near Pemberley, while Mary had to make do with one of her Uncle Phillips's clerks but was content to be a star in the society of Meryton; the 'considerable sum' Mrs Norris in *Mansfield Park* claimed to have given William Price was only £1; Mr Woodhouse in *Emma* survived and prevented his daughter and Mr Knightley from moving to Donwell for two years; the letters Frank Churchill placed in front of Jane Fairfax, which she brushed away unread, spelt out the word 'pardon'; Jane Fairfax lived for only ten years after marrying him.

She told Cassandra that in the unfinished fragment, *The Watsons*, Mr Watson was going to die, and Emma Watson would become dependent for a home on her narrow-minded brother and sister-in-law. She was to decline an offer of marriage from Lord Osborne and the interest of the story was to arise from Lady Osborne's love for Mr Howard and Mr Howard's affection for Emma, who finally was to marry him.

Jane was at work on something new when she died, the fragment to which the family gave the title *Sanditon*. The last page of the manuscript is dated 18 March 1817. Extracts were first published in

James-Edward's *Memoir*. It was first printed in full in 1925 and a facsimile was published in 1975 to mark the bicentenary of Jane's birth.

Brother James was also ailing in 1817 (he lived only till 1819, not long enough to claim his inheritance). James's handsome son James-Edward delighted his aunts when he came to stay in January 1817. He was eighteen, tall and charming. The aunts loved him for his sweet temper and warm affection. Jane wrote to Caroline saying how much better she was feeling; she was looking forward to the summer when she hoped to be stronger. Her illness was in remission. She was convinced that her debility, nausea and vomiting were due to 'bile', and that she could treat herself. She sent news of her imaginary improvement to Alethea Bigg, the sister of Harris Bigg-Wither. Jane's rejection of Alethea's brother does not seem to have affected their friendship. Jane had been reading *The Poet's Pilgrimage to Waterloo* by Robert Southey, published the previous year. She told Alethea she found the fond description of the poet's dead son Herbert in the *proem* very beautiful. Henry, newly a clergyman, was expected at Chawton, and Jane had been marking his shirts for the laundry. The postscript to this letter is revealing:

> The real object of this letter is to ask you for a receipt [recipe], but I thought it genteel not to let it appear early. We remember some excellent orange wine at Manydown, made from Seville oranges . . . and should be very much obliged to you . . .

Anna was better in health than she had been since her marriage. She already had two children, one a toddler, the other a baby in arms, and was to have five more. Ben Lefroy had not yet been ordained, and Jane fretted that she wanted to see the family settled in a comfortable parsonage house. Jane and her mother could only see Anna when she came to Chawton, as Mrs Austen was seventy-five, Jane had rheumatism in her knee and the roads were too wet and muddy for the donkey-carriage. The donkeys were having so long a run of luxurious idleness that 'I suppose we shall find that they have forgotten much of their education when we use them again,' said Jane. Ben and Anna walked over to hear her Uncle Henry preach. It had been a pleasure to see Anna, who looked so young and pretty, so blooming and innocent, that it was hard to believe she could ever have had a wicked thought in her head. Jane was remembering Anna's naughtiness during her girlish days. Soon she was lamenting that Anna was probably pregnant again: she had a bad cold and 'we fear something else; she has just weaned Julia,' Jane told Anna's cousin Fanny Knight, who was still single. 'Poor animal, she will be worn out before she is thirty.' Mrs Benn had had her thirteenth. 'I am quite tired of so many children,' grumbled Jane, making her usual complaint.

It was to Fanny whom Jane poured out her love and it was this niece who used her aunt as confidante in letter after letter. Fanny had finally chased away Mr Plumptre, who was now engaged to somebody else. Now she was wondering if young Mr Wildman, of Chilham Castle in Kent, might do. Chilham Castle was a fine Jacobean brick mansion, built by Sir Dudley Digges, Master of the Rolls to King James I, in front of an old Norman keep on a site with a pre-Roman history. The garden was the work of the famous Lancelot 'Capability' Brown, who had created a lake to fill the bottom of the valley, with planned vistas. It was at Chilham that Jane had been amused to find she had become 'a sort of chaperone'. Fanny had tested Mr Wildman by lending him Jane's novels without telling him who had written them. This was her way of checking him out for compatibility. Jane was enormously amused and the compliment doubtless pleased her. Presumably Mr Wildman failed the test, as Fanny married Sir Edward Knatchbull.

Jane called Fanny inimitable, irresistible, the delight of her life. Fanny was worth her weight in gold, or even in the new silver coinage. Jane had felt pity, concern, admiration and amusement. What a loss Fanny's intimacies would be when she married and her delicious play of mind was all settled down to conjugal and maternal affections. On the one hand, she did not want Fanny to get married, but on the other she did because she knew Fanny would never be happy until she was. She urged Fanny, in a letter of 20 February 1817, not to be unhappy over Mr Plumptre:

> Think of his principles, think of his father's objection, of want of money, of a coarse mother, of brothers and sisters like horses, of sheets sewn across, etc.

And the following month:

230

By not beginning the business of mothering quite so early in life, you will be young in constitution, spirits, figure and countenance, while Mrs William Hammond is growing old by confinements and nursing.

Jane Austen looked to marriage as productive of happiness for women, but marriage without too many children. As her sisters-in-law Anne Mathew, Elizabeth Bridges, Eliza de Feuillide and Frances Palmer were all dead, this was understandable. Jane promised Fanny that the right man would come at last, who would love her and whom she would love in return with deeper emotion than she had felt so far. Fanny looked at her spinster aunts and all their unmarried female friends and shivered. She was twenty-four and feared she was on the shelf.

Jane was revising *Persuasion:* another book was almost ready for publication, Jane told Fanny. 'You will not like it, so you need not be impatient,' she teased. 'You may *perhaps* like the heroine, as she is almost too good for me.'

Jane had been very poorly, with raised temperature and bad nights. She thought she had recovered her looks a little, which had been 'black and white and every wrong colour'. Her disease caused mottled patches on her skin.

Although retrospective diagnosis can never be certain, she is believed to have had either Hodgkin's disease or more probably Addison's disease, which in its later stages is grim. It is a wasting ailment of the adrenal glands, which are sited near the kidneys. The body produces antibodies to its own tissue. Symptoms are constant weakness and exhaustion, and a tendency to faint, combined with depression. Patients lose weight and their skin develops dark patches. People who saw Jane Austen late in her life noticed that her skin had a mottled appearance. Bowel movements become irregular and women cease to menstruate. Today the disease is treatable with steroid hormones.

Despite her weakness Jane found time to write several letters to Caroline. (The name must have been correctly pronounced 'Carolyn', for Jane mocks an acquaintance for saying 'Carol*ine*'.) In March Jane complained to Caroline of rheumatism and described herself as 'but a poor honey at present'. The donkey was pressed into service but she was too weak to ride it more than once, Cassandra walking beside her.

The animal drew the humble carriage which Jane used to get herself to Alton, where Frank was living, as Edward, now short of money himself, needed to let the Great House. Frank and his Mary now had six children aged between ten years and fifteen months.

Jane was weaker. She had needed spectacles for some time, and her eyes tired easily. Unselfish to the last, the dying Jane Austen, dizzy because of low blood pressure, hardly able to eat because of nausea, her limbs aching, chose to lie on three chairs so that her mother could have the sofa. Jane insisted that this wretched arrangement was just as comfortable as the proper couch. Even when the sofa was empty, Jane refrained from using it in case her mother might feel inhibited about relaxing on it. Mrs Austen was seventy-seven and Jane had always considered her something of a hypochondriac. But although sceptical in her letters to Cassandra about Mrs Austen's ailments Jane honoured her mother at severe cost to herself.

In March James and Mary were sorting out the affairs of the recently deceased James Leigh-Perrot on behalf of his widow, and Caroline was sent to Chawton. Jane, however, was too ill for a visitor to be convenient so Caroline went to stay with her half-sister Anna instead at their rented red brick farmhouse within walking distance of Chawton. The day after Caroline's arrival the nieces went to inquire after their Aunt Jane. She was not able to leave her bedroom but received them in her dressing gown, sitting in an armchair. She got up and greeted them affectionately. Pointing to seats by the fire, she said, 'There's a chair for the married lady, and a little stool for you, Caroline.' Caroline was shocked to see how ill Jane was looking. There was a general appearance of debility and suffering that the little girl could not mistake. Jane was very pale and her voice, normally so pleasing, was weak and low. She was not strong enough to talk for more than about ten minutes and Cassandra soon took the girls away. Anna, living so near, was able to make a few more visits, but Caroline never saw her beloved Aunt Jane again. After Caroline was grown up, she felt that she had never loved or valued Jane enough.

In April, Jane told Charles she had had a bilious attack and fever. She was now an invalid, living upstairs and being coddled. She had imagined herself to be better, but confessed that the shock of her uncle James Leigh-Perrot's will had brought on a relapse. Mr Leigh-Perrot had left everything to his wife for her lifetime, with reversion to James and his heirs. Jane had been expecting something. Mrs Austen bore up better under the disappointment. Her belief was that her brother had expected to survive his wife and to make another will after her death. The bereaved Mrs Leigh-Perrot was wretched: unpleasant and selfish though she was, she sincerely loved and was loved by her husband. She told James-Edward how generous her husband had been to her and how anxious to make up to her for 'late deprivations' in prison. 'He was the whole world to me,' she said. She added that when the Stoneleigh settlement increased their income, horses and a new carriage had been bought but ill-health spoiled their enjoyment.

That same month Jane made her own will, leaving everything to her sister, except £50 to Henry (who was still in debt after the collapse of his bank) and £50 to Madame Bigeon, who had suffered financially from Henry's misfortune. Cassandra was her executrix.

Meanwhile Edward Knight still had money worries as the lawsuit was dragging on. On 22 May Jane wrote to Anne Sharp, formerly governess to Edward's daughters, in Doncaster. Jane wrote that she could now sit up in bed; her sister and brothers had been kindness itself. She was going to Winchester for treatment, with Cassandra, her indefatigable nurse. Jane described herself, attempting humour, as a very genteel, portable sort of invalid. In two days' time she would be travelling the sixteen miles in James's carriage to comfortable lodgings which had been taken for them. 'Now that's the kind of thing which Mrs J Austen does in the kindest manner!' Jane acknowledged, but could not resist adding that her sister-in-law was not on the whole generously inclined. The fact that James was to inherit from the Leigh-Perrots after his aunt's death was not calculated to soften her judgment of Mary's character: it was too late in the day, Jane knew. The missing legacy still rankled with the dying Jane Austen. She cheered herself up with the thought that Mary might have to wait ten years before Mrs Leigh-Perrot was dead. Frank's wife had another baby, with what Jane called a much shorter confinement than Jane's own. Jane added significantly:

I have not mentioned my dear mother; she suffered much for me when I was at the worst, but is tolerably well. Miss Lloyd too has been all kindness. In short, if I live to be an old woman I must expect to wish I had died now, blessed in the tenderness of such a family, and before I had survived either them or their affection. *You* would have held the memory of your friend Jane too in tender regret I am sure. But the Providence of God has restored me . . .

Jane was hiding her head in the sand. The removal to Winchester was a doomed search for health. A relative of their own medical man had a high reputation and Jane put herself under the care of this doctor, Giles King Lyford, surgeon in ordinary at the county hospital. The case was never very hopeful. Mr Lyford told James's wife Mary that Jane's illness might be lingering, or that the end might be sudden. He was afraid there would be agony at the end.

Jane found the journey less tiring than she expected but fretted over Henry and William, who accompanied her on horseback, riding in the rain. She and her sister lodged at 8 College Street, which was a narrow picturesque lane, with small old-fashioned houses on one side, terminating in the ancient stone buildings of the famous public school. The house had a neat little drawing room with a bow window overlooking a garden with waving trees, the red roofs of the Cathedral Close and the grey cathedral towering over them. Now in private hands, and painted yellow outside, the house in College Street bears a plaque saying that Jane died there. A handwritten note in the window explains that it is not open to the public.

They were visited nearly every day by the widowed Mrs Elizabeth Heathcote and her sister Alethea Bigg of Manydown, who were living for the time in the Close. Harris Bigg-Wither had inherited Manydown in 1813. Mrs Heathcote's son was at Winchester College, and to be near him she rented a house from one of the cathedral canons. She visited Jane every day, but Alethea had soon 'frisked off, like half England, to Switzerland', as Jane wrote enviously. When Mrs Heathcote died, she owned copies of all Jane's novels.

Jane by this time lived chiefly on the sofa, able to walk no further than from one room to another. She went out once in a sedan chair and looked forward to going out in a wheelchair when the weather grew warmer but this hope was never fulfilled. Cassandra was a tireless and loving nurse, helped out by James's wife Mary. Mary had often got on

Jane's nerves but now Jane told her, 'You have always been a kind sister to me, Mary.' Jane seemed to be recovering, and Mary went home.

On 12 June, James wrote to his son James-Edward to tell him there was no hope for 'your dear valuable Aunt Jane'. Mr Lyford had candidly told them all her case was desperate. 'I need not say what a melancholy gloom this has cast over us all. Your grandmama has suffered much, but her affliction can be nothing to Cassandra's. She will indeed be to be pitied. It is some consolation to know that our poor invalid has hitherto felt no severe pain . . .'

Jane knew she was dying. One of her last letters has been mutilated by the family. A paragraph dealing with 'domestic disappointment' which did not 'concern the public' was suppressed. They allowed an expression of 'her characteristic sweetness and resignation' to stand:

> But I am getting too near complaint. It has been the appointment of God . . .

In health Jane was often tart and impatient, but now she suffered considerable pain she bore it bravely, resolutely keeping cheerful out of consideration for those around her. Henry and James, both clergymen, visited constantly to give her Holy Communion. Charles arrived on 13 June and was shocked to find Jane so ill. On 16 June he rode to Chawton on Henry's horse and found his mother poorly. Charles went back to Winchester on top of the coach on 18 June and found Jane better. Next day he saw her twice and in the evening left again, knowing he had seen his sister for the last time. Frank, whose wife had recently had a seventh baby, did not come but stayed home to comfort his mother. Edward also went to their mother.

On 27 June, Jane seemed better again and Mary, who had returned to nurse her, went home to Steventon. She told Caroline that Jane was resigned and composed, a believing Christian, though she had everything to live for. She was just learning to feel confidence in her own success. A few days later Cassandra sent for Mary again, as the paid nurse kept falling asleep. Mary, Cassandra and a maid nursed Jane in shifts.

On 9 July Jane received £15 from Hoare's bank, still trading today, where her father had had an account. This sum was interest due on her investment in navy stock.

July 15 is St Swithin's day. St Swithin was a local saint, Bishop of Winchester from AD 852. An old superstition, still current in England within living memory, says that if it rains on that day the wet weather will continue for forty days and forty nights. That year it was the date of a race-meeting, and Jane dictated a comic verse about the incongruity of horse-races on a saint's day and the saint's revenge of wet weather. It wasn't much better than her usual attempts at verse, but it showed her sense of humour was still alive although she was fading fast.

During Jane's last forty-eight hours she slept a great deal. She knew she was dying half an hour before she lost consciousness. She said she could not tell her listeners what she was suffering. When Cassandra asked her whether there was anything she wanted, she replied, 'Nothing but death.' She also said, 'God grant me patience. Pray for me, oh pray for me.' She lay gently breathing, her head almost off the bed. Cassandra sat beside her with a pillow on her lap for six hours, supporting her. Mary took over for the next two and a half hours until Cassandra came back for the last hour. There was nothing convulsed about Jane's dying look, except for a restless motion of the head. She reminded her sister of a beautiful statue. On Friday 18 July 1817 she died in Cassandra's arms and Cassandra closed her eyes. In her coffin she had an appearance of sweet serenity.

Cassandra copied out communal prayers composed by Jane, which beg forgiveness for 'every fault of temper and every evil habit in which we have indulged to the discomfort of our fellow creatures and the danger of our own souls'. She also prayed for grace to seek a 'temper of forbearance and patience . . . to be severe only in the examination of our own conduct, to consider our fellow-creatures with kindness and to judge of all they say and do with that charity which we would desire from them ourselves.' Jane's Christianity was sincere. If she was not always charitable, she was convinced she should strive to be so. She liked Bishop Sherlock's sermons, which emphasize self-knowledge. She owned a book probably given her at confirmation, *A Companion to the Altar: showing the Nature and Necessity of a Sacramental Preparation in Order to our worthy Receiving the Holy Communion, to which are added Prayers and Meditations.*

Cassandra wrote to Fanny Knight, thanking her for her tact and sensitivity in sending amusing letters when her feelings about Jane's illness would have dictated something very different. She assured Fanny that Jane had indeed enjoyed them. 'I *have* lost a treasure, such a sister, such a friend as never can have been surpassed. She was the sun of my life, the gilder of every pleasure, the soother of every sorrow. I had not a thought concealed from her, and it is as if I had lost a part of myself.'

Cassandra cut off some locks of Jane's hair, offering Fanny the choice of a brooch or a ring. Fanny had the hair set in an oval brooch, bearing simply Jane's name and the date of her death. Cassandra had hers set in a ring with pearls and wore it ever after. She sent a lock to Miss Sharp with a pair of clasps Jane sometimes wore and a small bodkin Jane had used for more than twenty years. Other locks went to other members of the family. Cassandra gave Jane's topaz cross, Charles's gift, to Martha. Henry wrote obituaries for the newspapers, listing her four published novels. It took Anna a long while to forget the habit of keeping things to tell Aunt Jane.

Jane loved Winchester's magnificent cathedral and had asked the Dean and Chapter if she could be buried inside it. She was buried there on 24 July, in the north aisle, near the black marble Norman font, and almost opposite the chantry of William of Wykeham (1323[?]–1404), Lord Chancellor of England and Bishop of Winchester, founder of Winchester College. A chantry is an endowment for the celebration of masses for the soul of the founder, and the chapel or altar set aside for them.

The funeral had to take place early, for the cathedral service began at ten o'clock. Jane's brothers Edward, Henry and Frank attended. Charles was away and James, unwell himself, was represented by James-Edward. Cassandra watched the mournful little procession down the length of the street until it turned from her sight and she had lost her only sister for ever. In some families women did not go to funerals. 'Never was human being more sincerely mourned . . . than this dear creature,' she wrote, hoping that the sorrow of those who loved her sister might be a measure of the joy with which she would be welcomed in Heaven. Cassandra always spoke of Jane with active love.

A plain black slab in the stone floor of the north aisle marks her grave. It reads:

In memory of JANE AUSTEN, youngest daughter of the late Revd GEORGE AUSTEN, formerly Rector of Steventon in this county. She departed this life on the 18th of July 1817 aged 41, after a long illness supported with the patience and the hopes of a Christian. The benevolence of her heart, the sweetness of her temper, and the extraordinary endowments of her mind obtained the regard of all who knew her, and the warmest love of her intimate connections. Their grief is in proportion to their affection, they know their loss to be irreparable, but in their deepest affliction they are consoled by a firm though humble hope that her charity, devotion, faith and purity, have rendered her soul acceptable in the sight of her REDEEMER.

By the 1850s, her grave was attracting pilgrims. Because it made no mention of her writings, a puzzled verger asked one visitor, 'Pray, sir, can you tell me whether there was anything particular about that lady; so many people want to know where she was buried?'

Early in the twentieth century a brass wall-plaque was added, funded by the profits from James-Edward's *Memoir*. It says, 'JANE AUSTEN, known to many by her writings, endeared to her family by the varied charms of her characters and ennobled by Christian faith and piety, was born at Steventon . . .', giving dates and quoting Proverbs 31: 26: 'She openeth her mouth with wisdom and in her tongue is the law of kindness.' Above is a memorial window featuring St Augustine, who used to be familiarly known as 'Austin', King David playing his harp, and St John ('In the beginning was the word . . .').

For the nephews and nieces who continued to visit Mrs Austen, Cassandra and Martha, in their own words, the chief light in the house was quenched and the loss of it cast a shade over the spirits of the survivors. In 1827 Mrs Austen died; the following year Martha Lloyd, aged sixty-four, married Frank. Cassandra lived on alone until 1845, dying at Frank's house in Portsmouth. She bequeathed Jane's gold watch and chain to their brother Henry.

Jane's will was proved on 10 September. As it was unwitnessed, Harriet Palmer and her father had to swear to the signature. Jane's funeral had cost £92. After this expense had been met and the legacies to Henry and Madame Bigeon deducted, Cassandra inherited the total wealth of England's first great and justly celebrated woman writer. It amounted to £561 2s and was taxed at three per cent.

In 1832 the publisher Bentley reprinted Jane's books in his 'Standard novels' series, buying the copyrights for a total of £250. They were reprinted occasionally, but during the nineteenth century Jane's novels remained a minority taste. The family considered them a private possession, unlikely to appeal to outsiders. In 1843 the *Foreign and Colonial Quarterly Review* mentioned her favourably. Anna copied out the article and sent it to Cassandra, who found it highly gratifying to her feelings and proof that Jane's novels possessed intrinsic merit.

In 1818 the Cambridge University Library, although a copyright library entitled to claim everything published in Britain, rejected as unimportant works by Ludwig van Beethoven and by Jane Austen. Between 1817 and 1870 there was only one complete edition of Jane's works. Since then, there have been countless editions, film and television versions, and endless commentaries and critiques. Since her death, Jane's work has made millions for other people. As early as 1930 one of her letters fetched £1,000 and by the mid-1980s a collector paid £900 for a mere scrap of her handwriting.

Sir Walter Scott wrote of Jane in his diary, 'What a pity such a gifted creature died so early!' In her lifetime the product of her hand and brain was poorly and grudgingly rewarded.

Selective Bibliography

Adams, Samuel and Sarah, *The Complete Servant* (London, 1825; repr Lewes, 1989)

Armstrong, A, *Church of England, the Methodists and Society 1700–1800* (London, 1973)

Austen, Caroline Mary Craven, *My Aunt Jane Austen* (Alton, 1952)

—— *Reminiscences of Caroline Austen* (Alton, 1986)

Austen, Jane, *Letters*, ed Deirdre Le Faye (Oxford and New York, 1995)

Austen-Leigh, Emma, *Jane Austen and Lyme Regis* (London, 1946)

—— *Jane Austen and Steventon* (London, 1937)

Austen-Leigh, J E, *Memoir of Jane Austen* (Oxford, 1926)

Austen-Leigh, Mary Augusta, *Personal Aspects of Jane Austen* (London, 1920)

Austen-Leigh, Richard Arthur, *Jane Austen and Southampton* (London, 1949)

Austen-Leigh, William, and Richard Arthur Austen-Leigh, *Austen Papers, 1704–1856* (privately printed, London, 1942)

—— revised by Deirdre Le Faye, *Jane Austen: A Family Record* (London, 1989)

Awdry, F, *A Country Gentleman of the Nineteenth Century* (Winchester, 1906)

Baring-Pemberton, W, *William Cobbett* (Harmondsworth, 1949)

Bovill, E W, *English Country Life 1770–1830* (Oxford, 1962)

Briggs, Asa, *How They Lived 1700–1815* (Oxford, 1969)

Brown, F K, *Fathers of the Victorians* (Cambridge, 1961)

Bussby, Frederick, *Jane Austen in Winchester* (Winchester, 1991)

Butler, Marilyn, *Jane Austen and the War of Ideas* (Oxford, 1975)

Byrde, Penelope, *A Frivolous Distinction* (Bath, 1979)

Castronovo, David, *The English Gentleman* (New York, 1987)

Chapman, R W, *Jane Austen Facts and Problems* (Oxford, 1949)

Collins, Irene, *Jane Austen and the Clergy* (London, 1993)

Craik, Wendy, *Jane Austen in Her Time* (London, 1969)

Devlin, D D, *Jane Austen and Education* (London, 1975)

Duckworth, A M, *The Improvement of Estate* (Baltimore, 1971)

Edwards, Anne-Marie, *In the Steps of Jane Austen* (London, 1979)

Fordyce, Revd James, *Sermons to Young Women*, 2 vols (3rd edn, London, 1766)

Freeman, J, *Jane Austen in Bath* (Alton, 1969)

Freeman, Kathleen, *T'Other Miss Austen* (London, 1956)

Gilson, David, *A Bibliography of Jane Austen* (Oxford, 1982)

Gisborne, Revd Thomas, *Inquiry into the Duties of the Female Sex* (London, 1796)

Grey, J D (ed), *The Jane Austen Handbook* (London, 1986)

Grosvenor Myer, Valerie, *Jane Austen in Her Age* (Glasgow, 1980)

Hawkridge, Audrey, *Jane Austen and Hampshire* (Portsmouth, 1995)

Heideloff, Niklaus Wilhelm von, *Gallery of Fashion* (London, 1949)

Hill, Constance, *Jane Austen: Her Homes and Her Friends* (London and New York, 1902)

Hodge, Jane Aiken, *The Double Life of Jane Austen* (New York, 1972)

Honan, Park, *Jane Austen: Her Life* (New York, 1987)

Hubback, J H and E C, *Jane Austen's Sailor Brothers* (London, 1906)

Jaeger, Muriel, *Before Victoria* (London, 1956)

Jenkins, Elizabeth, *Jane Austen: A Biography* (London, 1938)

Kirkham, Margaret, *Jane Austen, Feminism and Fiction* (Brighton and Totowa, 1983)

Lane, Maggie, *Jane Austen and Food* (London, 1995)

—— *Jane Austen's England* (London, 1986)

—— *Jane Austen's Family Through Five Generations* (London, 1984)

Laski, Marghanita, *Jane Austen and Her World* (New York, 1969)

McMaster, Juliet (ed), *Jane Austen's Achievement* (London, 1976)

Marshall, Dorothy, *English People in the Eighteenth Century* (Harlow, 1956)

Monaghan, David, *Jane Austen in a Social Context* (London and Totowa, 1981)

Parker, Rozsika, *The Subversive Stitch* (New York, 1984)

Phillipps, K C, *Jane Austen's English* (London, 1970)

Pilgrim, C, *Dear Jane: A Biographical Study of Jane Austen* (London, 1971)

Pine, Richard, *The Dandy and the Herald* (Basingstoke, 1988)

Pinion, F B, *A Jane Austen Companion* (New York, 1973)

Pool, Daniel, *What Jane Austen Ate and Charles Dickens Knew* (New York, 1993)

Porter, Roy, *English Society in the Eighteenth Century* (Harmondsworth, 1982)

Priestley, J B, *The Prince of Pleasure and His Regency 1811–20* (London, 1969)

Smithers, Sir David Waldron, *Jane Austen in Kent* (Westerham, 1981)

Southam, B C (ed), *Jane Austen: The Critical Heritage* (London, 1968)

Tindal Hart, A, *The Curate's Lot* (London, 1970)

Todd, Janet (ed), *Jane Austen: New Perspectives* (New York and London, 1983)

Trench, Melesina, *Remains* (London, 1869)

Tucker, George Holbert, *Jane Austen the Woman* (New York, 1994)

—— *A Goodly Heritage: A History of Jane Austen's Family* (Manchester, 1983)

Watson, Winifred, *Jane Austen in London* (Alton, 1960)

Weinsheimer, Joel (ed), *Jane Austen Today* (Athens, Georgia, 1975)

West, Jane, *Letters to a Young Woman* (London, 1806)

White, Gilbert, *The Natural History of Selborne* (London, 1789, repr 1887)

White, R J, *Life in Regency England* (London, 1963)

Wilson, Margaret, *Almost Another Sister* (West Malling, 1990)

Woodforde, Revd James, *The Diary of a Country Parson* (Oxford, 1935)

Young, Arthur, *Autobiography, with Selections from His Correspondence* (ed M Betham Edwards, privately printed, n d)

Young, G M, *Early Victorian England* (London, 1934)

Index

Note: Entries for wives listed by married name follow immediately after their husband's entry (e.g., 'Austen, Mrs George' follows 'Austen, Revd George'). Persons identified only by courtesy title precede those whose first name is given (e.g., 'Mathew, Mrs' precedes 'Mathew, Anne'). Entries for characters from the novels employ shortened forms of the longer titles: *P and P*, *M Park*, *N Abbey*, and *S and S*.